LED ZEPPELIN

THE ORIGIN OF THE SPECIES

LED ZEPPELIN
The Origin Of The Species: How, Why And Where It All Began

by Alan Clayson

A CHROME DREAMS PUBLICATION

First Edition 2006

Published by Chrome Dreams
PO BOX 230, New Malden , Surrey
KT3 6YY, UK

WWW.CHROMEDREAMS.CO.UK

ISBN 1 84240 345 1

Copyright © 2006 by Alan Clayson
Editorial Director   Rob Johnstone
Editor   Rebecca Candotti
Cover design   Sylwia Grzeszczuk
Interior design   Marek Krzysztof Niedziewicz

Front and Back Cover
Barry Plummer

Inside Photos
Barry Plummer
LFI
Starfile
Alan Clayson Archive

LED ZEPPELIN

THE ORIGIN OF THE SPECIES
HOW, WHY AND WHERE IT ALL BEGAN

ALAN CLAYSON

LED ZEPPELIN
The Origin Of The Species: How, Why And Where It All Began

by Alan Clayson

A CHROME DREAMS PUBLICATION

First Edition 2006

Published by Chrome Dreams
PO BOX 230, New Malden , Surrey
KT3 6YY, UK

WWW.CHROMEDREAMS.CO.UK

ISBN 1 84240 345 1

Editorial Director   Rob Johnstone
Editor   Rebecca Candotti
Cover design   Sylwia Grzeszczuk
Interior design   Marek Krzysztof Niedziewicz

Front and Back Cover
Barry Plummer

Inside Photos
Barry Plummer
LFI
Starfile
Alan Clayson Archive

A catalogue record for this book is available from the British Library.

Printed and bound in Great Britain by William Clowes Ltd, Beccles, Suffolk

To the artist otherwise known as Wreckless Eric

'The distance is nothing. It is only the first step that counts'

Mme. du Deffand

Born in Dover, England in 1951, Alan Clayson lives near Henley-on-Thames with his wife Inese. Their sons, Jack and Harry, are both at university.

A portrayal of Alan Clayson by the Western Morning News as the 'A.J.P. Taylor of the pop world' is supported by Q's 'his knowledge of the period is unparalleled and he's always unerringly accurate.' He has penned many books on music - including the best-sellers Backbeat, subject of a major film, The Yardbirds and The Beatles Box - and has written for journals as diverse as The Guardian, Record Collector, Ink, Mojo, Mediaeval World, Folk Roots, Guitar, Hello!, Drummer, The Times, The Independent, Ugly Things and, as a teenager, the notorious Schoolkids Oz. He has also been engaged to perform and lecture on both sides of the Atlantic - as well as broadcast on national TV and radio.

From 1975 to 1985 he led the legendary Clayson and the Argonauts - who reformed briefly in 2005 to launch a long-awaited CD retrospective - and was thrust to 'a premier position on rock's Lunatic Fringe' (Melody Maker). As shown by the existence of a US fan club - dating from an 1992 soiree in Chicago - Alan Clayson's following grows still as well as demand for his talents as a record producer, and the number of versions of his compositions by such diverse acts as Dave Berry (in whose backing group he played keyboards in the mid-1980s), New Age outfit, Stairway - and Joy Tobing, winner of the Indonesian version of Pop Idol. He has worked too with The Portsmouth Sinfonia, Wreckless Eric, Twinkle, The Yardbirds, The Pretty Things and the late Screaming Lord Sutch among many others. While his stage act defies succinct description, he has been labelled a 'chansonnier' in recent years for performances and record releases that may stand collectively as Alan Clayson's artistic apotheosis were it not for a promise of surprises yet to come.

Further information is obtainable from www.alanclayson.com

OTHER BOOKS BY ALAN CLAYSON

Call Up The Groups: The Golden Age Of British Beat, 1962–67
(Blandford 1985)

Back In The High Life: A Biography Of Steve Winwood
(Sidgwick and Jackson 1988)

Only The Lonely: The Life And Artistic Legacy Of Roy Orbison
(Sanctuary 1989)

The Quiet One: A Life Of George Harrison (Sanctuary 1990)

Ringo Starr: Straight Man Or Joker? (Sanctuary 1991)

Death Discs: An Account Of Fatality In The Popular Song
(Sanctuary 1992)

Backbeat: Stuart Sutcliffe, The Lost Beatle (with Pauline Sutcliffe;
Pan Macmillan 1994)

Aspects Of Elvis (ed. with Spencer Leigh; Sidgwick and Jackson 1994)

Beat Merchants (Blandford 1995)

Jacques Brel (Castle Communications 1996)

Hamburg: The Cradle Of British Rock (Sanctuary 1997)

Serge Gainsbourg: View From The Exterior (Sanctuary 1998)

The Troggs File: The Official Story Of Rock's Wild Things
(with Jacqueline Ryan; Helter Skelter 2000)

Edgard Varese (Sanctuary 2002)

The Yardbirds (Backbeat 2002)

John Lennon (Sanctuary 2003)

The Walrus Was Ringo: 101 Beatles Myths Debunked (with Spencer Leigh; Chrome Dreams 2003)

Paul McCartney (Sanctuary 2003)

Brian Jones (Sanctuary 2003)

Charlie Watts (Sanctuary 2004)

Woman: The Incredible Life Of Yoko Ono (with Barb Jungr and Robb Johnson; Chrome Dreams 2004)

Keith Richards (Sanctuary 2004)

Mick Jagger (Sanctuary 2005)

Keith Moon: Instant Party (Chrome Dreams 2005)

PROLOGUE: THE BORROWERS

'There was nothing original' - Robert Plant

Should a plumber receive a royalty every time a toilet he has installed is flushed? On the same basis, composers can make piecemeal fortunes. However, they can also risk losing vast amounts of money for - often unconscious - plagiarism. As soon as you pick out the first note after sitting down at a piano to develop some flash of musical inspiration, you have to be on your guard. Someone might own that note.

Lyrics might be a different matter, but surely every combination of even the twelve semitones in the chromatic scale have been used by now. The other day, I detected the melody of 'Street Fighting Man' in 'Lyla' by Oasis - an easy target - just as that of 'Simon Says' by The 1910 Fruitgum Company is discernable in 'Help Me Make It Through The Night'. Then there's The Lovin' Spoonful's imposition of a 1940s tune, 'Got A Date With An Angel', onto their 'Daydream' smash; that of 'While My Guitar Gently Weeps' on Roxy Music's 'Song For Europe' - and, of course, The Chiffons' 'He's So Fine' on George Harrison's million-selling 'My Sweet Lord', an affinity that sparked off the most famous civil action of the 1970s.

The resulting declaration against Harrison in 1976 led Little Richard's publisher to claim breach of copyright in a track from the twelve-year-old *Beatles For Sale* - and that rock 'n' roll penny-pincher Chuck Berry had already been compensated by court order for the few syllables quoted from his 'You Can't Catch Me' - as a tribute to him - at the start of *Abbey Road*. In 1981, the music press intimated a howl of artistic ire from Rolf Harris when Adam and the Ants' UK Number One with 'Prince Charming', appropriated the melody from one of his forgotten - though not so forgotten - singles, 'War Canoe'.

It's less trouble to plunder traditional items from time immemorial. One potent advantage is that these are public domain - which means that the artists' publishers can cream off composing income. Such rewards, however, were often deserved. In 1963, there was an imaginative rocking-up of the Cornish Floral Dance by The Eagles from Bristol, while 'Danny Boy' - from the Gaelic ballad 'Acushla Mine' - was crucified by Market Harborough's answer to Tom Jones one beer-sodden evening in the Red Lion only the other week. In the wake of Traffic's daring 'John Barleycorn' in 1970 came The Nashville Teens' spooky adaptation of 'Widecombe Fair', the West Country tale of Tom Pierce's old mare who expires, returns as a ghost 'and all the night can be heard skirling and groans.'

Whether victimless theft like this or potentially litigational, there are many hours of enjoyable time-wasting to be had in collating examples from the collected works of Led Zeppelin more than possibly any other major act that emerged from the British beat boom and its immediate aftermath. Much of it was lifted from blues, classic rock and even folk sources, but, as this saga will reveal, the group's prehistory is as steeped in the likes of Val Doonican, Herman's Hermits and the most vacuous of chart pop as with Muddy Waters, Chuck Berry and Bob Dylan - and is at least as intriguing as a fully mobilised Led Zeppelin's years of optimum impact.

Moreover, throughout chapters of uneven length and amid the loose ends and biographical cul-de-sacs, outlines dissolve and contents merge between the gradually less separate lives of the *dramatis personnae* - guitarist Jimmy Page, bass and keyboard player John Paul Jones, singer Robert Plant, drummer John Bonham - and let's not forget manager Peter Grant - prior to their coming together as Led Zeppelin in 1968.

For that Tibetan monk who's never heard of them, Led Zeppelin were, broadly, a rock group that rose from 'Brumbeat' - a blanket term for the West Midlands pop scene - and the ashes of Swinging Sixties hitmakers, The Yardbirds. Renowned session musician Jimmy Page had been approached to replace departing Yardbirds guitarist Eric Clapton in 1965, but did not join until the following autumn, initially on bass. Within weeks, however, he had reverted to a more apposite role as co-lead guitarist with Jeff Beck.

Following the latter's piqued departure in 1967, a Yardbirds in commercial decline continued as a four-piece before splitting-up in July 1968. Page and Grant - once head of The Yardbirds' road crew - began then to put together a New Yardbirds ostensibly to fulfil outstanding dates. Heard on the previous incarnation's final singles, Jones - also, like Page, the earner of anonymous credits on numerous British-made hits - was enlisted. Bonham and Plant, veterans of various unsuccessful Midlands groups, were recruited too. Guided by the formidable Grant, the four renamed themselves Led Zeppelin, and were signed to Atlantic Records. An eponymous debut album in 1969 crept into the British Top Ten, but Grant chose to focus on the more lucrative North American market.

Hot on the heels of the first effort, *Led Zeppelin II* - containing the prototypical 'Whole Lotta Love' - was a US chart-topper. Tidy-minded journalists pigeon-holed the new sensation as the ultimate 'high energy' band. With Adonis-like Plant's lung power on a par with instrumental sound-pictures of Genghis Khan carnage from the other three, Led Zeppelin soon filled the market void left by Clapton's now defunct 'supergroup', Cream. They also rivalled and then superceded The Jeff Beck Group as principal role models, then and now, for countless heavy metal outfits across the globe.

Nevertheless, by 1970's *Led Zeppelin III*, a quasi-pastoral approach had infiltrated the *modus operandi* to a noticeable degree, and its untitled follow-up up featured 'Stairway To Heaven', a slow ballad that became an in-concert finale, and the most spun track on post-Woodstock US radio. Yet any muted cleverness or restraint that might have been displayed in the studio - where they focussed almost exclusively on albums - was lost to the sweaty intensity of deafening heads-down-nononsense rock during what were now less musical recitals than uproarious tribal gatherings. To snow-blinded acclaim, often accompanied by riot, Led Zeppelin broke attendance records held previously not only by Cream, but also The Beatles and, for a while, the still-functioning Rolling Stones.

For the rest of a twelve-year existence, the ensemble continued to headline at European outdoor festivals and, especially, North American stadiums, despite - or because of - Grant severely restricting television appearances and further media exposure. His judgement proved correct, and a legend took shape. Amid eye-stretching rumours of peculiar goings-on behind closed doors in hotel suites and the privacy of their own homes, the group could afford to retire from public performance for over a year after the issue of 1973's *Houses Of The Holy*. This enabled the foundation of their own record company, Swan Song - with signings that included The Pretty Things and Bad Company as well as themselves - the recording of the *Physical Graffiti* double-album, and preparation for more barnstorming world tours that sold out automatically even as the punk storm broke and subsided.

With the means to turn their every whim into audible reality, and each member of the team from the humblest equipment-humper to the high command of Bonham, Grant, Jones, Page and Plant was firing on all cylinders. There were as yet no cracks in the image.

As wanted party guests of rock's ruling class, Led Zeppelin saw out the decade with further best-selling releases - *Presence* and 1979's *In Through The Out Door* - plus, as a holding operation during a long lay-off, a semi-documentary film, *The Song Remains The Same* and its soundtrack. However, a troubled return to the stage prompted rumours of imminent disbandmemt - and, after the sudden death of John Bonham in 1980, they did, indeed, down tools as a working band for all practical purposes, apart from rare one-off reunions with substitute drummers. However, *Coda*, a 1982 of hitherto unissued material, and, ten years later, *Remasters*, the first Led Zeppelin compilation, were among posthumous marketing triumphs that affirmed the quartet's resonance as both figureheads and grey eminences of late twentieth century pop - and, as a post script, Plant and Page renewed their creative partnership for such as 1994's *No Quarter: Unledded*, an album that mixed new material with overhauls of old favourites.

When researching this account, I listened hard to *No Quarter* and all that had preceded it - as far back as the first singles on which the individual members of Led Zeppelin appeared. I also worked through the back copies of *Midland Beat* preserved in the local studies department of Birmingham Central Library, and read many of the numerous books - ranging from scurrilous trash to well-researched, scholarly works to volumes containing just raw data - about Led Zeppelin. Investigated also were two spoken-word items - Maximum Led Zeppelin (Chrome Dreams ABCD101) and *Led Zeppelin: The Classic Interviews* (Chrome Dreams CIS2006 - with Page, Plant and Jones by *Guitar Player* magazine's Steven Rosen in 1977).

En route, I fanned out to the erudite likes of *Brum Rocked!* (TGM, 1999) and its *Brum Rocked On!* sequel (TGM, 2003), Laurie Hornsby's profusely illustrated chronicles that that likely to prove of intense fascination whether you were directly involved or have a general interest in Led Zeppelin and the evolution of British rock.

Morning became evening too and I hadn't even stopped to eat, such is the depth and breadth of John Combe's *Get Your Kicks On The A456* (John Combe Associates, 2005), which deals with Robert Plant's home town of Kidderminster's parochial heroes and many also-rans who won't mean much beyond the Black Country - The Huskies, Norman's Conquests or Custard Tree, anyone? Nevertheless, the author's commitment to his subject and a treasury of photos, clippings and further memorabilia drives a tale that, as cultural history *per se*, wouldn't have needed associations with big names to enhance it. The same applies to 2001's *'N Between Times*, Keith Farley's self-published oral history of the Wolverhampton group scene of the 1960s.

For their candour and intelligent argument, thanks are in more specific order for Dave Berry, Trevor Burton, Clem Cattini, Tony Dangerfield, Chris Dreja, Steve Gibbons, Dave Hill, Chris 'Ace' Kefford, Denny Laine, Jim McCarty, Richard MacKay,

Jacqui McShee, Dave Pegg, Brian Poole, John Renbourn, the late Tim Rose, Paul Samwell-Smith, Jim Simpson, the late Lord David Sutch, the late Carl Wayne and Bert Weedon.

Whether they were aware of providing information or not, let's have a round of applause too for Ian Ballard, Roger Barnes, Pete Cox, Don Craine, Dick Dale, Spencer Davis, Keith Grant-Evans, Eric Goulden, John Harries, Paul Hearne, Brian Hinton, Garry Jones, Graham Larkbey, Johnnie Latimer Law, Phil May, Percy Perrett, Ray Phillips, Ricky Richards, Twinkle Rogers, Lloyd Ryan, Tony Sheridan, the late Vivian Stanshall, Mike and Anja Stax, Andy Taylor, Dick Taylor, John Townshend, Paul Tucker, Ron Watts, Frank White and Pete York.

It may be obvious to the reader that I have received help from sources that prefer not to be mentioned. Nevertheless, I wish to acknowledge them - as well as Birmingham Central Library, Robert Cross of Bemish Business Machines, Sean Body (of Helter Skelter), Phil Capaldi, Kevin Delaney, Stuart and Kathryn Booth, the late Denis D'Ell, Ian Drummond, Katy Foster-Moore, Pete Frame, Michael Heatley, Dave Humphreys, Alun Huws, Mick and Sarah Jones, the late Carlo Little, Elizabeth McCrae, Russell Newmark, Reg Presley, Mike Robinson, Mark and Stuart Stokes, Anne Taylor, Warren Walters, Gina Way, Ted Woodings - and Inese, Jack and Harry Clayson.

Please put your hands together too for Rob Johnstone, Becky Candotti, Melanie Breen and all the usual suspects at Chrome Dreams for patience and understanding during the writing of a book that is meant to be as entertaining as it is academic.

Alan Clayson, January 2006

THE CRUSADER

'It was sitting around in our living room for weeks. I wasn't interested. Then I heard a couple of records that really turned me on, and I wanted to know what it was all about. This guy at school showed me a few chords, and I just went from there' - Jimmy Page[1]

On 10 October 2005, Jimmy Page received *Q* magazine's 'Icon' award, partly for being the prime mover in the formation of Led Zeppelin. Indeed, just as some English history primers start with the battle of Hastings, you could argue that the dawn of Led Zeppelin began in 1958 when fourteen-year-old schoolboy James Patrick Page from Epsom, Surrey, having proved himself in itinerant talent contests, was well-placed, had he wished, to seize the ultimate prize of a spot on ITV's *Search For Stars* talent contest, hosted by Carroll 'Mr. Starmaker' Levis, spiritual forefather of fellow Canadian Hughie Green of *Opportunity Knocks* fame.

In a clip used in those before-they-were-famous TV compilations that rear up periodically these days, interviewer Huw Weldon thrusts a stick-mike at the regionally famous Jimmy's mouth. The young man expresses an enthusiasm for angling, and, to an enquiry about his future plans, assures viewers in so many words that he doesn't think of the guitar as a key to a viable career. Attempting to make a living as a musician wasn't a sensible option for one such as him. It was a facile life, a vocational blind alley - especially if you were involved in pop. Hardly anyone lasted very long.

While making this token nod towards common sense for the sake. perhaps, of domestic harmony, Jimmy was more aware than his parents that, while once the guitar had been associated mainly with Latinate heel-clicking, it was now what Elvis Presley hung round his neck. Indeed, Scotty Moore's plain-and-simple solos in 'My Baby Left Me' and, to a greater degree, 'Baby Let's Play House', Presley tracks issued in Britain in 1956 and 1957 respectively, had persuaded Jimmy Page to teach himself the Spanish guitar he'd been given the previous year. Hand-somely endowed with a capacity to try-try again, he laboured late into the evening, to the possible detriment of even that mod-icom of homework necessary to avoid a school detention the next day.

'I always thought the good thing about guitar was that they didn't teach it at school,' smiled Jimmy, 'Teaching my-self to play was the first and most important part of my educa-tion.' [1] If he never quite grasped sight-reading at school and via a few private guitar lessons from a bloke in nearby King-ston, he'd still pore over perhaps 'Skiffle Rhythms', 'When The Saints Come Marching In' (*sic*), 'Simple Blues For Guitar' and further exercises prescribed in *Play In A Day*, devised by Bert Weedon, who, decades later, was to receive an OBE for 'serv-ices to music'.

As Baudelaire reminds us, 'No task is a long one but the task on which one dare not start'. Perhaps one subliminal ef-fect of Weedon's plebian-sounding forename was that it made the many editions of his tutor manual - first published in 1957 - seem less daunting to Jimmy, George Harrison, Eric Clapton, Pete Townshend, Brian May, Steve Hillage, you name 'em, who are reputed to have started by positioning yet uncalloused fin-gers on taut strings and furrowing brows over *Play In A Day* before advancing to pieces by the likes of Charlie Christian and Django Reinhardt in its *Play Every Day* companion.

Weedon may be seen as a role model of sorts for the teen-age Page. Bert's own adolescent self had been influenced in turn by the 'gypsy jazz' of Reinhardt, who he considered 'the great-est guitarist of all time'. Yet, during the war, a rather overawed Bert succeeded Reinhardt in the Quintet du Hot Club de France - where he was instructed by Stephane Grappelli to develop his own style rather than attempt to copy Reinhardt.

By 1956, Weedon was fronting his own outfit, and had released a maiden single, 'Stranger Than Fiction', but only his theme to television's *$64,000 Question* sold even moderately before 'Guitar Boogie Shuffle' cracked the Top Ten. Subsequent hit parade entries, however, proved less lucrative than his guesting on countless discs by bigger stars. Though he'd back visiting North Americans such as Frank Sinatra, Rosemary Clooney and Nat 'King' Cole - later, the subject of a Weedon tribute album - his bread-and-butter was accompanying domestic artistes from Dickie Valentine and Alma Cogan to the new breed of Presley-esque teen idols such as Tommy Steele, Cliff Richard and Billy Fury.

As well as having first refusal on, more or less, all London sessions until well into the next decade, Weedon solo 45s tended to hover round the middle of the Top 40. Though The Shadows were dismissive of his rival version of their chart-topping 'Apache' in 1960, they paid their respects to Bert by penning 'Mr. Guitar', his singles chart farewell. Nevertheless, he remained in the public eye through a residency on ITV's *Five O'Clock Club*, an ITV children's series - as well as a remarkable 1964 spot on *Sunday Night At The London Palladium* on which he showed that he could rock as hard as anyone.

This was noted by Jimmy Page, who'd already taken to heart the kind of advice that Weedon would still be imparting in his eighties: 'Whether you're an old professional or a raw beginner, basically, it's all about continual practice. I practice for at least an hour every day - because it's not a chore, but a pleasure. I love playing the guitar. Last night, for instance, I spent an hour and a half mastering a riff by quite a well-known pianist by applying it to the fretboard. If you're a musician - not necessarily a guitarist - you should always try something you can't do, and extend your scope by practicing until you can do it. Then find something else you can't do. Even at my age, I'm still learning. You must never stop wanting to be a better musician.

'Finally, even if you just play a scale, put everything you've got into it, get a nice tone and make it melodic. If you're not prepared to put your heart and soul into it, don't bother.'

While Jimmy did not consider himself a natural musician, his fingers hardened with similar application to the fretboard - to the degree that he forged the beginnings of both a personal style and, despite what he told Huw Weldon, an as yet unspoken fancy that he'd like to make his way in the world as an entertainer. He didn't mention it immediately as he wasn't sure how mum and dad would react.

Though he had a serviceable singing voice too, Jimmy could not see himself donning the mantle of domestic Elvis Presley. He felt more of an affinity to Scotty Moore and his successor, James Burton, the lead guitarist who Elvis shared with Ricky Nelson (whose 1961 hit, 'Hello Mary Lou', was to be one of Led Zeppelin's more light-hearted, if very occasional, repertory selections). Besides, Page and fellow teenagers had been so generally dismayed by most indigenous 'answers' that the sounds of the real thing on disc were preferable to such an act if he was booked for a local dance. Such a person rather than the gramophone was the intermission, an opportunity to go to the toilet, talk to friends, buy a soft drink.

If anyone bothered listening, it was for the wrong reasons as the too-innocuous perpetrator in struggling to scale the heights of his aspirations, afforded glimpses of unconscious comedy to his audience as he gyrated like he had a wasp in his pants, *yeah*ing and *uh-huh*ing his way through 'All Shook Up', the first UK Number One by 'this unspeakably untalented, vulgar young entertainer' - as a television guide had described Elvis after an appearance on *The Ed Sullivan Show* - the US equivalent of *Sunday Night At The London Palladium* - which would only risk screening him from the waist up. In the UK, Methodist preacher (and jazz buff) Dr. Donald Soper wondered 'how intelligent people can derive satisfaction from something which is emotionally embarrassing and intellectually ridiculous.'[2] Of 'Heartbreak Hotel', Presley's first million-seller, too, the staid *New Musical Express* - the '*NME*' - wrote, 'If you appreciate good singing, I don't suppose you'll manage to hear this disc all through.'[3] What more did Elvis need to be the rage of teenage Britain?

The exploitation of Elvis Presley - with whom Jimmy Page shared the same birthday - in the mid-1950s was the tip of an iceberg that would make more fortunes than had ever been realised since Edison invented the phonograph. All manner of variations on the blueprint were arriving by the month - because each territory in the free world seemed to put forward a challenger to Presley's throne. Off-the-cuff examples include France's Johnny Halliday, Johnny O'Keefe from Australia - and, from South Africa, Mickie Most.

Needless to say, most of these emanated from North America where innumerable talent scouts thought that all that was required was hot-potato-in-the-mouth vocals, 'common' good looks and lop-sided smirk. Some considered Jerry Lee Lewis as merely an Elvis who'd swapped piano for guitar. There were also female Presleys in Janis Martin and Wanda Jackson, and a comedy one in The Big Bopper. After Carl Perkins - an unsexy one - came bespectacled Buddy Holly, a singing guitarist whose only tour of Britain was to be so pivotal that he inflicted untold injury upon Burns, Watkins Rapier and other European manufacturers in his use of a Stratocaster.

A mute Elvis from New York, non-singing guitarist Duane Eddy was also to be highly regarded by younger fretboard icons such as George Harrison, Jeff Beck, Dave Edmunds - and Jimmy Page. He refined the 'twangy guitar' approach by booming the melodies of his instrumentals solely on the bottom strings of his Gretsch through a customised amplifier and echo chamber. Eddy's 1958 UK Top Twenty debut, 'Rebel Rouser', set the main pattern - a repeated guitar riff anchoring a sax obligato - for the next few years as hit followed contrived hit. Some were based on folk tunes but others included 'Ramrod,' Henry Mancini's 'Peter Gunn' (later overhauled by Jimi Hendrix) and self-penned 'Forty Miles of Bad Road'. Eddy scored his last big hit for many years with 1962's 'Dance With The Guitar Man', but, with or without record success, he was still guaranteed plenty of work - particularly in Britain where he'd been voted 'Pop Personality of the Year' in a 1960 readers' poll published by the *NME*.

On the same label as Eddy in Britain, a pair of pompadoured brothers called Everly could be seen by their investors as two Elvis' for the price of one, while the Capitol label thought that it too had snared one in rough-and-ready Gene Vincent - 'The

Screaming End' - who came down to earth after his breakthrough with 'Be-Bop-A-Lula'. His antithesis on Atlantic Records was Bobby Darin, smooth and, when permitted, finger-snappingly jazzy.

There were also plenty of black ones, most conspicuously in Little Richard, Bo Diddley - and, most germane to this discussion, the remarkable Chuck Berry, whose first mainstream pop hit, 'Maybelline' - which owed as much to white country-and-western as black blues - had actually predated 'Heartbreak Hotel'. Ten years older than Elvis too, this Grand Old Man of Classic Rock had absorbed the most disparate ingredients in the musical melting pot of the Americas: Cajun, calypso, vaudeville, Latin, country-and-western, showbiz evergreens, and every shade of jazz, particularly when it was transported to the borders of pop via, say, the humour of Louis Armstrong or the jump-blues of Louis Jordan.

At twenty-six, Berry turned professional as leader of his Chuck Berry Combo, working local venues with occasional side-trips further afield at the Cosmopolitan Club in Chicago. During this residency, blues grandee Muddy Waters was so sincerely loud in his praise that Berry was signed to the Windy City's legendary Chess label in 1955.

After 'Maybelline' peaked at Number Five in the US *Hot 100*, 'Roll Over Beethoven' climbed almost as high. With melodies and R&B chord patterns serving as support structures for lyrics celebrating the pleasures available to US teenage consumers, another fat commercial year generated further smashes in 'School Days', 'Rock And Roll Music', 'Sweet Little Sixteen' and Chuck's 'Johnny B Goode' signature tune.

These set-works would remain the cornerstone of Berry's stage act, first experienced by the world beyond the States when he appeared in *Jazz On A Summer's Day*, a US film documentary about a turn-of-the-decade outdoor festival. Duck-walking with his crotch-level red guitar, Chuck offended jazz pedants, but captured the imaginations of European adolescents. Certainly, Jimmy Page turned to Berry's Chess albums as regularly as a monk to the Bible. In an age when a long-playing record - LP

- cost three weeks paper round wages, such a youth made sure he got his money's worth, spinning 1958's *One Dozen Berries* or an imported *Chuck Berry Is On Top* until it was dust, savouring the tactile sensation of handling the cover, and finding no detail in the liner notes too insignificant to be less than totally fascinating.

Page was to be among those enthusiasts that soared to the loftiest plateaux of pop in the teeth of adult disapproval of the noise, gibberish and loutish excesses of the rock 'n' roll epidemic from across the Atlantic of which Berry was part. Furthermore, when, in 1959, Chuck served the first of two jail terms that would put temporary halts to his performing career, this incarceration coupled with a dearth of major European smashes only boosted his cult celebrity in Britain at a time when native rock 'n' rollers accepted a second-class and, arguably, counterfeit status to US visitors. A parallel may be drawn, maybe, between the entrancing 'over-paid, over-sexed and over-here' North American GIs during the war and the common-or-garden Aldershot-drilled squaddie with his dung-coloured uniform, peanut wages and in-built sense of defeat.

When the hunt was up for a British Presley, Tommy Steele was to the fore among those who Elvis had outfitted with vestments of artistic personality. Steele was followed by Cliff Richard and then Billy Fury - while Scotland tried briefly with Andy Stewart (!) before he donned his clan tartans to host BBC television's *White Heather Club*. See, copying Elvis and variations on the theme was how you gave yourself the best possible chance of being elevated from the dusty boards of a provincial palais to small-fry billing on round-Britain 'scream circuit' package tours and a spot on Jack Good's epoch-making pop spectacular, *Oh Boy!* on ITV, then one of but two national television channels in post-war Britain.

With this in mind, Vince Taylor from Hounslow, Middlesex, presented himself as a second Gene Vincent, and Acton's Adam Faith as a Buddy Holly sound-a-like, while two other Londoners, Duffy Power and Dickie Pride, were in a Bobby Darin bag as was - very briefly - roly-poly comedian Charlie Drake.

East End truck driver Tommy Bruce was accused of copying The Big Bopper; Gerry Dorsey from Leicester fancied himself as a Roy Orbison type, but more handsome, and Oxford's singing pianist Roy Young attempted to corner the Little Richard market - while Wee Willie Harris was bruited by his manager as Greater London's very own Jerry Lee Lewis. Sporting an enormous bow-tie and hair dyed shocking-pink, Harris wasn't above an orchestrated 'feud' with blue-rinsed Larry Page, 'the Teenage Rage' - though, banal publicity stunts aside, the two rubbed along easily enough when off-duty; Willie presenting his congratulations at Larry's twenty-first birthday party on 16 November 1957, along with guests of such magnitude as Jack Good, former boxing champion Freddie Mills and chart contenders Don Lang, Laurie London and Joe 'Mr. Piano' Henderson.

When plain Leonard Davies, Larry had packed records at an EMI factory close to his home in Hayes, Middlesex. By 1957, however, he'd been signed to the company as a singer. Yet Larry - like Wee Willie - turned out to be a British rock 'n' roll also-ran who relied chiefly on competent rehashes of US chartbusters. His go at The Del-Vikings' 'Cool Shake' attracted BBC airplay, but he came a cropper when his 'That'll Be The Day' was totally eclipsed by The Crickets' chart-topping blueprint.

While Vince Taylor and Duffy Power were OK, he supposed - Charlie Drake too as long as you didn't look at him - Jimmy Page may have watched the cavortings of Larry, Wee Willie *et al* with an arched eyebrow and crooked smile. Such observed contempt was applauded by his parents who reckoned that any idiot could caterwaul too like that Cliff Richard - even if it's difficult today to comprehend that the Bachelor Boy had once been among the most untamed of the kingdom's rock 'n rollers - but Hank B. Marvin, the lead guitarist and principal public face of Richard's backing Shadows, just about walked the line of adult acceptability then, albeit as much for his black swot horn-rims as his metallic picking and copious use of tremelo arm

More admirable for his relatively quiet dignity and achievement by effort was a guitarist local to Epsom whose name, if known to Jimmy Page, most would not recognise, even if virtually every television viewer in the country had heard his most famous composition. However, before coming up with the *Match Of The Day* theme, Rhet Stoller's second single, 'Chariot', had penetrated the Top 30 in 1960. A lazier chronicler might describe this as more Hank Marvin than Duane Eddy. Despite obvious influences, however, Stoller had already developed a sound of his own on his debut 45, a cover of 'Walk Don't Run' that swallowed dust behind that of The John Barry Seven - an *Oh Boy!* house band - and the original by The Ventures.

An intermittent release schedule since was to embrace pistol packin' 'Ricochet', buried on a 1964 B-side, and 1966's all-original *The Incredible Rhet Stoller* LP. Out of step with the post-Merseybeat chart climate, this easy-listening *magnum opus* was, nevertheless, a remarkable exercise in multi-tracking during recorded sound's mediaeval period. Moreover, the intrinsic content was solid too, if further from the twang of 'Walk Don't Run' and 'Chariot' than any buyer of these discs could have imagined.

As obscure in a less insidious way was Tony Sheridan, an awkward talent recalled mostly for 'My Bonnie', a track recorded with the pre-Ringo Beatles in Germany, where he spent most of his life after 1960. During an unhappy childhood in Norwich, 'I heard an electric guitar and any decision about my future was made for me.' He'd formed his first group, The Saints, in 1956 when copying US pop stars was still how you gave yourself the best possible chance of being elevated to small-fry billing on 'scream circuit' package tours and, if your luck held, to a slot on *Oh Boy!*, paralleling the film-cliché rise of a run-of-the-mill chorus girl to sudden Hollywood stardom. 'I did seven editions,' shrugged Sheridan, 'before I got sacked for turning up late for rehearsals, not bringing my guitar and being a general nuisance.'

He was replaced by Joe Brown, who, at moments of high drama, would turn abruptly and pick his six-string on the back of his head. Yet, despite this *kitsch*, he was to emerge as one of the most respected guitarists in the then-tiny world of British pop. With a talent deeper than mere showmanship, Brown had played Scotty Moore - or, if you prefer, James Burton - to Billy Fury's Elvis on the ten-inch LP *The Sound Of Fury* in 1959. He was soon to be much in demand too as accompanist to touring US legends such as Gene Vincent and Johnny Cash. When Joe's own well of hits ran dry by 1963, there was still session work.

Brown was, therefore, on a par with Tony Sheridan as 'the best rock guitarist in the country,' declared Ricky Richards, a Cockney rock 'n' roller, 'When Conway Twitty and people like that came over to England, they'd insist that Tony was the one hired to play for them.' You wonder how Sheridan might have fared in Britain had his momentary flowering on national television not been nipped in the bud by his own inner nature and desires. 'I've never be one to look for that acceptance that means Making It, topping the charts,' he explained, 'There had been a possibility of me joining The Shadows, but there was never any definite talk.'

Sheridan was, however, less interested in skulking beyond the main spotlight than striking out on his own as focal point of a guitar-bass-drums outfit - in which, with unusual flair, he chose not to duplicate recorded arrangements of classic rock, preferring, as he put it, 'to take a song and ravish it so that it came out in a slightly different fashion. It was how a song happened at a given moment.'

Sheridan's combo may be seen now as one of the earliest British 'power trios'. Vocalist Johnny Kidd led one too after the wife of one of two guitarists in his backing Pirates decided she wanted her man home in the evenings. Kidd did not seek a replacement, preferring the simpler expedient of continuing with just bass, drums and *one* guitar behind him. In doing so, a prototype was patented - because The Big Three, The Who, Led Zeppelin, Dr. Feelgood, Motorhead, The Sex Pistols and other diverse entities reliant on an instrumental 'power trio' were all to be traceable to the Pirates - and The Tony Sheridan Trio, who'd been permitted ten minutes on the all-British supporting cast of the legendary Gene Vincent-Eddie Cochran tour of 1960 that ended with Cochran's death in a road accident *en route* from the Bristol Hippodrome to London airport. A seat in the taxi was offered to another British guitarist on the expedition, Big Jim Sullivan, who lived in nearby Hounslow, but, luckily for him, he'd made other arrangements.

If an exciting show, the day-to-day running of this extravaganza was typical of the time in that it was characterised by excessive thrift and a geographically-illogical itinerary: 'stupid journeys from Edinburgh to the Isle of Wight by coach,' recalled drummer Clem Cattini, 'Vomit boxes, we used to call them'.

Throughout the Cochran-Vincent expedition, Tony Sheridan had displayed a wanton dedication to pleasing himself rather than the customers. Nonetheless, bound up in himself as he was, Sheridan could be mesmeric, creating true hand-biting excitement as he took on and resolved risky extemporisations in the same manner as Jimi Hendrix after him.

With Sheridan out of the way in the Fatherland, Hank Marvin became the most omnipotent of British guitarists in the early 1960s, given those like Jeff Beck, Alvin Lee, Tony Iommi - and Jimmy Page - whose professional careers began in outfits that imitated The Shadows and conjured up a back-of-beyond youth club with orange squash, ping-pong and a with-it vicar yet unaware of Merseybeat's distant thunder.

Though some local pretty boy might be hauled onstage to be Cliff for a while, he was not regarded as an integral part of the group. The concept that the Group rather than the Star could be a credible means of expression owed much to the groundwork of these grassroots craftsmen, struggling with dodgy equipment and transport, amateur dramatic acoustics and hostile audiences.

Another attraction was the implied camaraderie of a Group, reminiscent of the lately repealed National Service, minus the barracks discipline. Also you didn't have to be a Charles Atlas to be in one: look at skinny, spotty, four-eyed Godhead Hank. It was the Group's workman-like blokeism rather than any macho conviction that was admired; gruff onstage taciternity translated frequently to the uninitiated as 'professionalism'.

Jimmy Page was to remark that 'some of those Shadows things sounded like they were eating fish-and-chips while they were playing.'[4]

Furthermore, while accompanying and, later, composing songs for Cliff, their ability to function independently had them acknowledged generally as Britain's top instrumental act - so much so that The Shadows survived Merseybeat by producing material at least as good as 'Apache', 'Wonderful Land' and anything else prior to 1963.

The only serious challengers to The Shadows' supremacy were The Tornados, whose 'Telstar' was top the charts in both Britain and the USA - where no UK outfit had ever made much headway. They scored three more entries - 'Globetrotter', 'Robot' and 'The Ice Cream Man' - in 1963's domestic Top Ten before the advent of Merseybeat with its emphasis on vocals. Suddenly rendered *passe*, they soldiered on with a still-impressive workload whilst largely repeating earlier ideas on disc.

Unlike the other Tornados, lead guitarist Alan Caddy was classically-trained, having served as a boy soprano in Westminster Abbey, and studied violin before he joined a skiffle group, The Five Nutters, who were omnipresent at their own youth club in Willesden. After a transitional period as Bats Heath and the Vampires, they metamorphosed into Johnny Kidd and the Pirates in 1958.

Among few homegrown rock 'n' rollers regarded with awe, they made a television debut on ITV's *Disc Break*, plugging 1959's 'Please Don't Touch'. Much of its charm emanated from the late Caddy's galvanising riffing. However, because he was riven with self-doubt about his capabilities, another guitarist picked the staccato lead on Kidd's climactic 'Shakin' All Over'. Within a year, however, Johnny Kidd was becalmed outside the Top 50, and Caddy and his fellow Pirates - including Clem Cattini - had abandoned the apparently sinking ship, but retained their Captain Pugwash-esque stage costumes to be the Cabin Boys behind Tommy Steele's brother, Colin Hicks, a huge attraction in Italy.

Hicks proved a difficult employer, and Caddy and Cattini flew home to land on their feet as mainstays of The Tornados, assembled in the first instance to accompany Don Charles, Pamela Blue, John Leyton, Mike Berry and like proteges of console boffin Joe Meek. Following a miss with 'Popeye Twist', co-written by Caddy, the aethereal 'Telstar' was taped as a routine backing track - albeit with a poignant 'second subject' plucked by Caddy - hours before a show with Billy Fury in Great Yarmouth. Overnight, Meek transformed it into the quintessential 1960s instrumental - and a global chart-topper.

The first perceptible sign of danger occurred with 'Dragonfly', a comparative flop correlated with the exit of peroxide blond bass player Heinz Burt - and, with him, most of The Tornados' teen appeal - in autumn 1963. As injurious a departure in its way was that of Caddy after the release of 1964's *Away From It All*, an album containing four of his compositions.

By then, Caddy was well-placed to make a living as a session musician, and even become a star in his own right, but, sighed Clem Cattini, 'he never achieved his potential because he didn't believe in himself.' So it was that Alan took a job as house arranger and producer for Avenue Records, a budget label specialising in xeroxes of current hits. Next, he moved to a similar post in Canada.

Over the border in the United States, The Ventures, The Surfaris, The Routers and like combos that swam to the surface during the surfing craze all owed much to the pioneering accomplishments of Dick Dale, a Los Angeles guitarist less concerned with melodic serenity and improvisation than driving riffs *a la* Duane Eddy - and depth of sound (punctuated by trademark shuddering *glissando* descents) on the thick-gauge six-string Stratocaster he dubbed 'The Beast'.

It had been presented to him by electronics boffin Leo Fender. His previous creation, the Telecaster, was, summised the King of the Surf Guitar, 'a chicken-plucker's sound. Nobody played loud then. The loudest group around was The Champs, but the sax stood out, and they had an upright acoustic bass. Chuck Berry played through an amplifier with eight-inch speakers - nothing with any power. Dick Dale's brain wanted a sound that was fat, thick and with a punch, a knife-cutting edge. Leo took a liking to Dick Dale, who became like a son to him. Leo said "Take this guitar and Showman valve amplifier, beat them to death, and tell me what you think." The minute the first five hundred entered a venue, the sound was sucked up - so Leo built me the biggest amplifier he could, and I'd still blow up the speakers. They'd twist, tear and come right out of the cone. They'd catch on fire because of the mismatch of the ohms. Leo eventually came up with a Dual-Showman that peaked at one hundred and eighty watts, and - *voila!* - Dick Dale broke the sound barrier and became the first power-player in the world'.

Gadgetry and constant retakes, however, intruded upon the grit on *Summer Surf*, cast adrift on the vinyl oceans in July 1964. More than ever, the slick exactitudes of the studio made Dick sound uncannily like any other surf instrumental exponent. 'That's why I quit recording,' he groaned, 'Dick Dale was sick of engineers telling him they've been doing it for twenty years, and putting limiters on the guitar so that it sounded tinny.'

While Dale, Tony Sheridan, Joe Brown, Alan Caddy and even Rhet Stoller enjoyed their fifteen qualified minutes before drowning beneath the rip-tide of the British beat boom, Jimmy Page had been as a fish beneath the waves, at best a detached spectator with no stake in the developing British pop scene. Late puberty, however, had found him looking at last for an opening in a pop outfit.

The boss group in Jimmy's neck of the woods was Cliff Bennett and the Rebel Rousers, albeit based in the dreary heart of a West Drayton housing estate in outer London suburbia. They'd already released a single, recorded under the supervision of Joe Meek, and had evolved into a dependable palais draw, able to compare notes with others who had likewise broken free of provincial fetters; among them other Meek production charges such as The Outlaws and horror-rock specialists, Screaming Lord Sutch and the Savages as well as Dave Dee and the Bostons, The Rockin' Berries, Johnnie Law and the MI5, Chris Farlowe and the Thunderbirds, Jimmy Crawford and the

Ravens, The Barron-Knights - and Johnny Kidd and the Pirates, who had showed what was possible with 1960s chartbusting 'Shakin' All Over'.

Bennett too was destined for a walk-on part during British pop's subsequent conquest of the world. His combo, however, was in a state of constant flux. Among those passing through the ranks were Lord Sutch's pianist Nicky Hopkins; Chas Hodges from The Outlaws; Mick Burt, who was to join Hodges in 'Chas and Dave' a generation later, and Frank Allen, later a mainstay of The Searchers.

Among few constants was guitarist Dave Wendells, thus blocking that line of enquiry for Jimmy Page, whose first forays into public performance had included framing the declamations of *vers libre* bard Royston Ellis. What came across in a *what's-the-matter-with-kids-today?* documentary shown on British television in 1960 was that none of the girls fancied bespectacled, taper-thin Royston, dancing on his own amid the 'excitement' of a parochial hop.

It might have provided a shadowy link to 'higher' artistic expression, but the strongest motive for even the most ill-favoured youth to play a guitar was sex - about which Jimmy Page was to speak to sceptical classmates as if he had inside knowledge about it. During an intermission at a dance where your group was playing, see, a tryst afterwards could be sealed with a beatific smile, a flood of libido and an 'All right then. I'll see you later.'

Buying into what was mostly a myth then, Jimmy Page not so much dipped a toe as plunged headfirst into onstage rock 'n' roll. Immediately on leaving school in spring 1959, he had joined the Redcats, backing combo to vocalist Red-E-Lewis. Though centred in north London, the group had regular engagements at Epsom's Ebisham Hall, where it had become the pale slip of a fifteen-year-old's habit to help load their careworn equipment into the van afterwards. Finding himself near lead guitarist's Bobby Oates's instrument on its stand, Jimmy gathered the nerve to pick it up and pluck a few tentative riffs. As his notes hung in the musty air, Chris Tidmarsh, describable as the outfit's manager, thought for a moment before mentioning that, with a scholarship at some college beckoning, Oates was beset with doubts about continuing with the group.

Not long afterwards, a squeak of feedback had launched Page's audition to join the Redcats in their usual place of rehearsal. As soon as he entered this functions room above a Shoreditch pub, he'd been impressive for the splendid and newly-purchased solid-body Fender Stratocaster he lifted from a slimline case.[5] More to the point, he could more than cope with Gene Vincent's 'Rocky Road Blues', 'My Baby' by Ricky Nelson, any number of Chuck Berry and Shadows numbers and further mutually familiar rock 'n' roll they threw at him. For all his callow youth, he was casually knowledgeable about all of them.

Aware that Jimmy was on the point of beginning a 'proper job' as a laboratory assistant, Chris had laid on with a trowel spicy imagery of the fancy-free 'birds' who ringed the lip of the stage, ogling with unmaidenly eagerness the enigma of untouchable boys-next-door. Then he straightened his face and marshalled his words prior to a meeting with Mr. and Mrs. Page to quell their anxieties about the opportunities their son might be wasting in such a risky business as this pop music, and affirming his own sincerity and faith that the group would be successful.

Enough of their reservations were dissolved by Tidmarsh's persuasive manner for them to allow Jimmy to take a chance with a group that was to endure another year with Red-E-Lewis. He was superceded by 'Neil Christian', the freshly-concocted stage alias of Chris Tidmarsh, who had decided that he could better serve his clients as their new singer. Another adjustment was the Redcats rechristening themselves the Crusaders, and each member adopting a *nom de theatre*. Jimmy's was 'Nelson Storm'.

As he held the group's purse strings, Neil-Chris felt entitled to impose these changes. He also booked an exploratory two-hour recording session in a Bethnal Green studio from which the lads emerged with demonstration discs that he could hawk round record companies. The songs he selected - a Johnny

Kidd B-side, a country-and-western opus, a showbiz standard ('Red Sails in The Sunset') and morose 'Danny', remaindered from Elvis Presley's 1958 film vehicle, *King Creole* - were to demonstrate his and the Crusaders' versatility as 'all-round entertainers' rather than any individuality as a group.

One of the six discs pressed thumped onto the doormat of Joe Meek's RGM Studio, a 'bedroom' set-up above a handbag shop where traffic roared down the Holloway Road, one of north London' principal thoroughfares. Yet, while 'Telstar' was yet to come, hits had been made there already, among them John Leyton's recent chart-topping 'Johnny Remember Me'. One of British pop's most tragic figures, the mentally unstable Meek was a sound technician of extraordinary inventiveness, and, in the early 1960s at least, if an act like Neil Christian and the Crusaders attracted his interest, it stood a fair chance of Making It. The country's first true independent producer, Meek challenged the might of major companies like EMI, which, in 1962, was to release on its Columbia subsidiary, the two tracks he recorded for the Christian outfit, songs straight from Denmark Street, London's Tin Pan Alley. The A-side, 'The Road To Love' was a boy-plus-girl-equals-marriage lyric with the Crusaders less prominent than a beefy horn section - while 'The Big Beat Drum' lived in skittish female backing singers, mention of a 'crazy frog' and a lead vocal that strayed into Screaming Lord Sutch terrain.

Until all hopes of 'The Road To Love' reaching the Top Fifty had faded, Christian ensured that it was in the stage set. Though he was the principal darling of the ladies, screams reverberated sometimes when he introduced the curly-headed *wunderkind* with a precocious and dazzling dexterity. Yet while Neil was the group's Cliff Richard, 'Nelson Storm' wasn't so much a Hank B. Marvin as an Alan Caddy - because, like Johnny Kidd's Pirates, the Crusaders had chosen the cheapest expedient of dispensing with the seemingly obligatory second guitarist, which necessitated Nelson-Jimmy combining chord-slashing and lead runs with increasingly more nonchalant ease.

With that Page boy's magic fingers caressing the fret-board, Neil Christian and the Crusaders became a reliable attraction on the ballroom circuit, and you couldn't argue with a wage that was more than that of a young business executive slaving from nine to five every day. Yet 1966's 'That's Nice' was to be Neil's only UK chart entry. Long absences in Germany - where he became considerably more famous - might explain lack of further success, but it might have had more to do with a tendency for later releases to sound alike. However, like Bennett's Rebel Rousers and Lord Sutch's Savages, Christian's Crusaders served as an incubation shed for many renowned musicians - such as Ritchie Blackmore and Nicky Hopkins as well as Jimmy Page - thus justifying the citing of this merely proficient singer as 'a pivotal figure in the development of British music' on one CD retrospective.[6]

'I spent God knows how many years slopping up and down the country in a van,' scowled Christian[4]. In an era when England's only motorway terminated in Birmingham, a staggered procession of one-nighters was often truly hellish: amplifiers on laps, washing in streams, shaving in public convenience hand-basins - and trying to enjoy as comfortable a night's repose as was tenable in the front passenger seat. This was showbusiness. It was also staring fascinated across a formica table as the drummer makes short work of a greasy but obviously satisfying fry-up in a transport cafe in Perth that, calculated chips-with-everything connoisseur Johnnie Law, 'served the worst food in the world'.

After days of inactivity at home, a telephone call would banish the individual Crusaders' recreational sloth and, within the hour, they'd be driving, driving, driving to strange towns, strange venues and strange beds, shoulder-to-shoulder in a van on which forebodings of calamity might be focussed. In a sufficiently doubtful condition to have require a check-up that morning, it might lose impetus somewhere near Carlisle to give up the ghost on the Scottish border. Optimistic that all it'd take would be a little tweaking about with the engine for them to be on our way, the Crusaders and Neil might repair to a convenient wayside cafe where a light-hearted mood would persist until a surly mechanic came, shook his head under the bonnet, and disappeared to fetch a replacement part.

As the desultory repartee of the coffee circle stretched into the late afternoon, 'The Road To Love', might have dribbled from the jukebox, none of the Crusaders recognising immediately either the song, its singer or its irony.

Endless centuries later, powdery snowflakes would thicken, and a breakdown truck might arrive to cart the group and its wretched vehicle twenty miles to the nearest garage where the diagnosis would be depressing... thirty quid before I even start... lucky you didn't have an accident... should have left it down south...

At journey's end after a frightening two-hour dash in a twilight blizzard, the Crusaders would lug the equipment up four punishing staircases to the auditorium, one or two of them tempted to flick V-signs at Christian's back as he strode off to find the promoter. Tired, alert with hunger and devoid of will, they might have soundchecked forever in front of the arriving customers, but too soon advanced the hour for the peacocks to show their feathers. Hastily fed and superficially rested, from the crises of the past twelve-odd hours came a merging of the customers' surging gaiety and the group's shell-shocked frenzy. At one point the crowd almost take over - almost but not quite - as Neil, guarding his qualified stardom with the venom of a six-year-old with a new bike, pulled out every trick in his book, but, always a generous show-off, he didn't forget to direct the adulation of the mob towards the backing players.

Nevertheless, just the ticket for the morning after was hauling the hated gear down to the dodgy van for the whole process to begin again - including worrying about whether they'll even reach the next fire-exit entrance to the dusty half-light of an empty venue. Jimmy, the 'baby' of the group, had taken a challenging book for idle hours, but it struck him then that he'd barely glanced at it the entire trip.

That evening, he stood on the boards in his usual way but with glassy eyes, a hostage to the beat. By the third number, he was his old self again, but that flash while it lasted was disturbing. Maybe it was the trials of the past two days getting to him, but there's a Judy Garland in all of us, especially when singing or playing an instrument is your only saleable trade, and you're in much the same dilemna as the olde tyme rockers and black bluesmen of that ghostly pre-Beatles era.

THE ART STUDENT

*'I was doing a lot of painting and drawing in what free time
I had, so I thought I'd go to art college - but, of course, I
couldn't stop tinkering around with my guitar'* - Jimmy Page[1]

A bout of glandular fever was the final incentive for Jimmy Page to give notice to Neil Christian. This was unfortunate but by no means disasterous, and, with hardly a break in the booking schedule, Christian found a replacement in an Albert Lee, who'd backed Duffy Power and Dickie Pride when both were protégés of 1950s pop svengali Larry Parnes.

Mr. and Mrs. Page, meanwhile, had lost no time in reminding their son that it wasn't too late for him to start an apprenticeship, snare some cushy office job or go to college. As it had been during his chat with Huw Weldon, he felt obliged to support an attitude that, deep down, wasn't his own - that unless you'd been born into the entertainment business, it was considered unwise to regard it as a tenable career. This, admittedly, was in an age when television as a domestic fixture was still novel enough to be regarded by censorious great-aunts as meddling with dark forces - and that anything to do with music was not a man's trade somehow.

For a start, it had no practical value. Put crudely, music was all right as a hobby, but could you rely on it for a weekly wage? Moreover, should you shine at art in class - as Jimmy had - this was also treated as a regrettable, if lesser, eccentricity. Some of his former teachers and fellow ex-pupils, therefore, were to shake their heads - almost as if viewing a funeral cortege - when they saw Jimmy Page entering the portals of Sutton Art College, where he commenced a painting course in 1962. To compound his folly, he continued to hone his fretboard skills in its atmosphere of coloured dust, palette-knives, hammer-and-chisel and lumpy impasto.

He became ever-present at extra-mural sessions in cloakroom, common room and empty life class, either strumming guitar or listening to records that were taken seriously by few arty bohemians. For most, the only interest that any type of pop held seemed to be when it was a nod to Dada or integrated into installations, mixed media events and grainy experimental films that at best were vaguely if mostly head-scratchingly entertaining. Pop Art too was predicted as a coming trend at those demimonde parties Page attended where table lamps were dimmed with headscarves; Man Ray hung on the walls, and LPs of the coolest modern jazz were scattered artlessly around the record player. Sometimes, there was in-person entertainment too - scat-singing, bongo-pattering or a saxophone honking inanely - while the eyes of cross-legged beatniks were closed in ecstasy at the sheer joy of being anarchistic, free-loving and pacifist - or at least being seen to sound and look as if they were.

Pop Art's British pioneers included Peter Blake, Richard Hamilton and Edinburgh-born Eduardo Paolozzi, all interpreting signals from New Yorker Andy Warhol's mannered revelling in junk aesthetics. Scorned then by the cultural establishment, its aim, see, was to bring humour and topicality back into art via a sort of earnest superficiality. Hence Warhol's well-known fascination with soup-cans, Brillo pads and comic-strip philosophy. 'There's nothing to explain or understand' was his explanation of his fascination with the brashest of junk-culture: advertising hoardings, magazines such as *True Confessions, Tit-Bits* and *Everybody's Weekly*; escapist horror flicks about outer space 'Things' - and, of course, turn-of-the-decade pop music. constipated as it was with one-shot gimmicks, dance crazes and - just arrived this minute - the all-American piffle of insipidly handsome boys-next-door like Bobby Vee, Bobby Vinton and Bobby Rydell, all hair-spray and bashful half-smiles.

Unlike many other students, Jimmy Page was not snooty about a non-ironic love and knowledge of lowbrow pop. Living in the shadow of the bomb, nearly everyone else at college seemed to be 'sent' by Lewis, Meade Lux, rather than Lewis, Jerry Lee. As a 'sign of maturity' too was an 'appreciation' of either modern or, more often, traditional - 'trad' - jazz. At students union shindigs, enthusiasts would don boaters or top hats, and a variety of hacked-about formal wear, drink heavily of cider, and launch into vigorous steps that blended a type of skip-jiving with the Charleston in a curious galumphing motion to the puffing and plinking of a trad band during an post-skiffle craze bracketed roughly by international best-seller 'Petite Fleur' in 1959 - attributed to Welwyn Garden City trombonist Chris Barber's New Orleans Jazz Band, but, essentially, a clarinet solo - and the same unit framing the ebullient soprano of Barber's then-wife Ottilie Patterson over the closing credits of 1962's *It's Trad Dad!* movie.

Nobody was interested in Chuck Berry or Bo Diddley,' grimaced Jimmy Page[1]. Nonetheless, while he painted, Jimmy was likely, given the choice, to have, perhaps, a Berry B-side on instant replay. Strewn around his monophonic Dansette too were discs by Diddley, Jerry Lee, Gene Vincent, Ricky Nelson and all the rest of them. It may be seen now as inevitable that 'a conflict between music and art arose,'[1] and that, one evening at home, he finally came out with it: he wasn't intending to be either a second Picasso or a designer of Christmas cards, he was going to be a professional guitarist. All the same, he listened hard enough to his parents' appeals to him to stay on at college for the time being, and agree to explore the most sensible options within the limits of pop.

The extent to which they were prepared to let him make a go of it went as far as his mother buying Jimmy a tape recorder, and permitting him to commandeer the front room as a workshop, and thus fill it with all manner of further electronic paraphanalia. Eventually, he turned it into a recording studio of sorts, an Aladdin's cave of editing blocks and jack-to-jack leads linking his mum's gift to further tape recorders. One day he produced a drum kit, which hastened the construction of more effective sound-proofing than, say, egg-boxes and mattresses.

Jimmy was also seeking to invest in additional guitars whose sounds suited specific purposes such as a Gretsch Chet Atkins Country Gentleman which dwalfed him, and a Les Paul custom - and he had envied Frank White of Jimmy Crawford and the Ravens, the first British owner of a twin-necked

Gibson, a magnificent, gleaming-white object like one Elvis had pretended to play in one of his awful movies. Page's own one would be a long time arriving.

White was a pupil at a Sheffield grammar school when he became to Crawford and the Ravens as Jimmy Page had been to Neil Christian and the Crusaders. Frank, however, did not choose to immediately return to formal education, electing instead to lead his own trio, earning the wildest applause for the blues items that he'd be slipping in with increasing frequency.

Yet, while Page, White's southern compeer, was, ostensibly, still studying at Sutton Art College, he was being sounded out about 'sitting in' with not so much a group as a loose 'collective' called Blues Incorporated, who, as the name implied, played the stuff to the exclusion of everything else. Thus far it was the most conspicuous manifestation of the British blues movement, which is usually dated from Mississippi songster Big Bill Broonzy's London concert debut - with his then-novel twelve-string guitar - in September 1951. Born when Queen Victoria was still alive, the influential Broonzy passed away in 1958, leaving younger men to define what are now clichés of the idiom.

Still cult celebrities then, Broonzy and later visitors to Europe - among them Sonny Boy Williamson, Muddy Waters, Victoria Spivey, Otis Rush and John Lee Hooker - were to obtain a sharper profile via bohemian scorn for the Top Ten toot-tooting of traditional jazz, even if many famous pop musicians either gained their first toehold on showbusiness by falling meekly into line in a semi-professional trad band or were inspired by the form. Best-remembered as a mainstay of Cream and lesser rock 'supergroups', Jack Bruce, for instance, toured Italy in 1960 with The Murray Campbell Band - whose stage attire embraced kilts, sporrans and gorgets - before room was found for him in The Scottsville Jazzmen. Moreover, a rendition of 'The Old Rugged Cross' by Ottilie Patterson motivated future 1970s hitmaker Steve Gibbons to blow a month's wages as a plumber on a banjo, and endure long weekly bus journeys for six months of expensive tutorials.

From Chris Barber's outfit, two sacked sidemen, mouth-organist Cyril Davies and guitarist Alexis Korner, formed Blues Incorporated in 1961. A home was found for the ensemble in a downstairs room between a jeweller's and the ABC teashop on Ealing Broadway. From its inaugural evening on St. Patrick's Day 1962, the club was patronised immediately by blues enthusiasts from other West London suburbs as well as Surrey, Middlesex, Kent and beyond. At later meetings, customers would learn of other blues strongholds such as the Crawdaddy and L'Auberge - both in Richmond - Eel Pie Island hotel, Blues Incorporated's Tuesday night residency at the Marquee and, also in central London, Ken Colyer's Studio 51.

As a hangover from trad, Blues Incorporated was primarily an instrumental unit with a few semi-permanent members, but otherwise loose enough for a rapid turnover of personnel, frequently drawn from the throng of art students and weekend dropouts who queued to thrash guitars and holler the blues. These amateurs were responsible for many well-intentioned musical assassinations but among the frayed jeans, CND badges and beatnik beards were future Kinks, Yardbirds, Manfred Mann, Rolling Stones and Pretty Things - all poised to breach the Top Twenty within three years without much compromising their hirsute images, and by sticking to their erudite guns musically. Nevertheless, it wasn't an easy road to travel back in 1962. With a scholarship at the Central School of Art beckoning, Dick Taylor, a founder member of the Stones, had baulked when the group suggested going professional. Yet mixed feelings at their unforeseen clamber into the Top Thirty the following year caused Dick to reflect that the rewards of being in a group might now extend beyond beer money and a laugh.

If never a blues purist, Jimmy Page's commitment to this 'starvation music' had him pitching in during the Marquee's blues nights in an interval group with Cyril Davies, who had left Blues Incorporated after mithering about his preference for a narrower, Chicago-style interpretation of the music rather than Alexis Korner's 'everything from Louis Jordan to Martha and the Vandellas'.[7]

Like Korner, however, Davies was also part of the London studio crowd. Brian Poole, nominal leader of The Tremeloes, remembered, 'Cyril was late for a session. He turned up in a full-length raincoat with holes in the pockets, and about ten harmonicas fell out of the hem of it. He asked what key the number was in, and then did a perfect take.'

Davies was, therefore, a useful referee when, during one of those Marquee evenings, Jimmy Page impressed members of Mitcham's Brian Howard and the Silhouettes, who were looking for a guitarist to help out on a session for their two EMI singles, 'Somebody Help Me' and, issued in 1963, 'The Worryin' Kind' (and their respective B-sides). Cyril told them that he was sure that Jimmy could deliver the goods as competently in the studio as he did on the boards.

'LITTLE JIM'

*'Before I knew where I was, I was doing all these studio
dates at night, while still going to art college in the
daytime. There was a crossroads, and you know which one I
took'* - Jimmy Page[8]

Further session work followed. That with the most pronounced bearing on Page's future was a hand in Mickie Most
and the Gear's 1964 revival of 'Money Honey', and, early the
previous year, Jet Harris and Tony Meehan's chart-topping 'Diamonds' on the recommendation of tape operator Glyn Johns, a
friend from Epsom, who moonlighted as vocalist with The Presidents, a combo that enjoyed parochial renown.

To Jimmy, sessions represented a more comfortable vocational option - and a sensible resolution of his Huw Weldon
caution - than once more spending too many moonlight miles on
the trunk roads of Britain in the company of Christian and his
Crusaders and their sort when there were still few, if any, motorways to sidestep stop-start shunts through each and every city
centre all the way to Rhyl, Exeter, Middlesborough, Inverness...
places he'd been, apparently, though he was damned if he could
even find them on a map.

In the retractable sphere of the studio. you didn't have
to like what you did, but if you were sufficiently versatile, you
could work near home in the employ of whoever called the shots,
with no extra time or favours done - or, indeed, any interest in
the music you were being paid on a regulated scale to play.

Subsequent years of such employment were to have a
lasting and beneficial effect - particularly as Page understood
straightaway that it entailed a different discipline to being on
the road where you had to adapt to the mood and musical incon-
sistencies of the hour. Paradoxically, while errors were retractable in the studio, you couldn't get away with so much.

In the beginning, a typical studio date was fretting subordinate rhythm chords to the riffs and solos of Big Jim Sullivan, four years Jimmy's senior and the former leader of The

Big Jim Sullivan Combo, who covered Ral Donner's Presley-esque 'You Don't Know What You've Got' in 1961. He'd also been Alan Caddy's immediate replacement in Johnny Kidd and the Pirates. Overlooking the likes of Caddy, Bert Weedon, Rhet Stoller, Joe Brown and The John Barry Seven's Vic Flick, Jimmy would maintain that 'without Big Jim, producers were desperate. When I came on the scene, work quickly escalated. Big Jim had been carrying the whole weight on his shoulders, and I was the only other new face.'[9]

Sullivan and Page's interaction may be illustrated by their ghosted presence on releases by Dave Berry and the Cruisers. From Sheffield - like Jimmy Crawford and the Ravens - this outfit were fully mobilised by 1961 with recurring dates within an area roughly outlined from Hull to Skegness to Mansfield to Barnsley - and trading in a predominantly black US repertoire, covering a waterfront from the disparate pre-war output of such as Lead Belly, Ma Rainey and Cab Calloway to contemporary rhythm-and-blues - and its rock 'n' roll derivation - whether Bo Diddley, The Drifters, Rosco Gordon, Arthur Alexander and, particularly, Chuck Berry - who had provided the man born David Holgate Grundy with his very stage surname.

If he didn't pander to assumed audience desires for Top Twenty preferences, the first screams were reverberating already for Dave Berry from girls in fishnet, suede and leather clustered round the central microphone, their evening made if they locked eyes with one who was by mid-1963 as much a star in south Yorkshire as The Beatles were becoming nationally.

Looking for if not *the* New Beatles then *a* New Beatles, Decca signed Dave and his group that summer, and assigned them a producer, Mike Smith.[10] They proved a sound investment, initially with a maiden single, 'Memphis Tennessee', in the British and Australasian Top Twenties. However, as it had taken EMI's accursed Liverpudlians fourteen hours to tape their first LP, Smith was aghast at the eight it took the anxious Yorkshire boys to make 'Memphis' and its B-side. In future, he told them, they'd be replaced - with the exception of X-factor Dave

- with hired hands quicker off the mark. The Cruisers could then learn the song off the record. Apart from hurt pride, it wouldn't matter. No-one would be any the wiser. OK, lads?

So it was that Sullivan and Page were among those gathered by Smith for the follow-up. B-sided by a xerox of Muddy Waters' 'Hoochie Coochie Man', it was - of all things - a gripping revival of Elvis Presley's 'My Baby Left Me'. Presley himself had unearthed the number from the repertoire of black bluesman Arthur Crudup, who was to die in poverty in 1974, still awaiting a fat cheque for his services to the King.

Dave, Jimmy and, to a lesser degree, Big Jim had been long and pragmatically steeped in the blues by the time they assembled in Decca's West Hampstead complex for the 'My Baby Left Me' session. Berry had been furthering the cause back in the jive hives of his native Sheffield in days when pop stardom was only a far-fetched afterthought - while, as well as his Marquee stints with Cyril Davies, Jimmy found the self-confidence to contribute to an album by Sonny Boy Williamson, taped in London in January 1965, four months before the latter's mojo stopped working. 'Sonny Boy was very old and very drunk,' remembered drummer Mickey Waller, 'but he didn't moan and complain like some of the bluesmen. We started at 10am, and it was all done by 1pm. Also, there were no overdubs. We all sat in a circle and played. Jimmy had already been around a bit, and knew the blues backwards'[11] - and you may say he did: on the revival of Otis Rush's 'I Can't Quit You Baby' on the first Led Zeppelin LP he copied religiously the guitar solo note-for-note.

'The Brits took it much more seriously,' grinned Ahmet Ertegun[12] founder in the 1950s of Atlantic, a US record label that, while buoyed financially to a large degree by the likes of mainstream white Bobby Darin and imported one-hit-wonder Acker Bilk, preferred to specialise in the blues end of jazz, rhythm-and-blues and, during the next decade, soul music. 'American blues meant one thing to a group of black guys from Long Beach,' added Eric Burdon of The Animals, a former Newcastle art student who had ritually inked the word 'BLUES' in his own blood across the cover of an exercise book into which lyrics of the same had been copied, 'and quite another to people like me, Eric Clapton, Jimmy Page and Keith Richards.'[13]

It had been a genre that none of them had been able to touch at first. Their purpose once was just to absorb the messages as they came. Blues appeared to be peculiar then to black American experience,[14] though much of it was purchasable in the Home Counties only after wending across the ocean to outlets like Dobell's in the West End and Carey's Swing Shop in suburban Streatham.

Jimmy Page had also been receiving mailed lists and order forms from untold US independent labels like Excello, Aladdin, Atlantic and Imperial, and those British labels that began issuing R&B singles such as James Brown's 'Think' - on Parlophone in 1961 - and - via Pye International's R&B series - material in all vinyl formats by Bo Diddley, Howlin' Wolf, Muddy Waters and other executants of the sacred sounds.

In Britain, blues in each of its sub-divisions remained, to all intents and purposes, the exclusive property of a knotted-brow fringe who patronised venues like the Ealing club. It was a comparatively unknown quantity even in the USA, lurking in the shadows at most in mainstream pop. Indeed, releases by such as Jimmy Reed, Slim Harpo, Muddy Waters and Howlin' Wolf were big hits in Uncle Sam's 'race' or 'sepia' market without figuring at all in the music trade periodical, *Billboard*'s pop *Hot 100*. Yet blues wasn't particularly popular amongst citified young blacks, being music their migrant parents still liked.

Back in the rural Deep South, Buddy Knox, a rock 'n' roller from the same region as Buddy Holly, couldn't recall hearing a single disc by a black singer until he visited New York - though, through radio static, others his age might have tuned in by accident to muffled bursts of what white segregationalists heard as 'the screaming idiotic words and savage music' of faraway Streveport's rhythm-and-blues station KWKH where 'Stan The Man And His No-Name Record Jive' span The Midnighters' 'Sexy Ways', 'Sixty Minute Man' by The Dominoes and 'Too Many Drivers' by Smiley Lewis - all about sex and all banned from white radio. 'If you don't want to serve negroes in your place of business,' ran one racist handbill, 'then do not have negro records on your jukebox.'[15]

For Britons less aware of ingrained racial tension, such discs - when they got round to hearing them - were 'something new and exciting,' deduced Ahmet Ertegun, 'In a sense, they were appreciating something the Americans did not value.'[12]

'As far as white people were concerned, especially suburban kids,' continued Mick Jagger, 'It was interesting because it was underclass music that they'd had no experience of or, in fact, that didn't exist by the time they had got to it anyway, almost. It was disappearing. That culture was on its way out.'[16]

Seeing what was coming, Duffy Power, no longer a Larry Parnes cipher, was to release consecutive 1964 A-sides of Mose Allison's 'Parchman Farm' and, also with Jimmy Page on guitar, 'I Don't Care', a virtual rewrite of 'Hoochie Coochie Man' just as 'I'm The Face' by the High Numbers - soon to become more renowned as The Who - was Slim Harpo's 'Got Love If You Want It' grafted to Mod-speak lyrics. The Spencer Davis Group's first single, a ginger-up arrangement of John Lee Hooker's 'Dimples', was bound for deletion too. The same fate befell Tommy Bruce and the Bruisers' leeringly credible lurch through Hooker's 'Boom Boom'.

Attention to the *Muddy Waters At Newport* LP had resulted in sound readings of 'Hoochie Coochie Man' by Manfred Mann and Long John Baldry as well as Dave Berry. Then there was to be The Pretty Things' riveting dash through Bo Diddley's 'Road Runner', and The Primitives - a Pye 'answer' to the Things - and their passable go in 1964 at Sonny Boy Williamson's 'Help Me' with the original as a helpful demo, and assistance from a now more ubiquitous Jimmy Page.

However, lending credence to trad jazz trumpeter Kenny Ball's jaded opinion that British R&B was just 'rock and roll with a mouth-organ' were legion executions of items that might have gone down a storm onstage, but sounded thuggish on vinyl in their blunt lyrics and stylised chord cycles. All Hohner Bluesvampers and 'I Got My Mojo Working' were outfits with names like The Howling Wolves, The T-Bones, The Boll Wee-vils, The King Bees, The Dimples and, gawd help us, The Little Boy Blues. With the best of intentions, they'd try to emulate the Jimmy Reeds, Slim Harpos and Howlin' Wolves from the juke joints and speakeasies of black America, but the outcome - especially vocal - was generally nothing like.

Certainly, it didn't always reconcile easily on disc, and most groups were lost amongst the lesser lights scrimmaging for work in such as the Cubik in Rochdale, Warrington's Heav-en-and-Hell, the Golden Torch in Stoke-on-Trent and any other new venues that had sprung up along with the Swinging Lon-don-type boutiques now operational in provincial town centres. Booking fees were often a minus amount following deductions, and 'Do you know anywhere we can sleep tonight?' became a frequent enquiry of hangers-on in frowsy dressing rooms.

Yet 1964 was a fierce time for R&B and no mistake. *Melody Maker*'s 'Pop Fifty' for January had showed the Stones withdrawing from the top with an unrevised 'Little Red Roost-er', whose blues pedigree was traceable through Sam Cooke to the first recording by Howlin' Wolf with its writer Willie Dixon on double bass. At their most rugged, the Four Pennies were making a Top Twenty killing with Lead Belly's 'Black Girl'. Almost despite themselves, the Things, Them and others in the fresh harvest of R&B hitmakers were becoming celebrities.

From Birmingham, The Spencer Davis Group had been slower in gaining ground in the charts, though, long before the opening of the Ealing club, all four of its members had been listening hard to the blues, even in the late 1950s when it was possible for someone like B.B. ('Blues Boy') King or John Lee Hooker to sell records by the ton without a minute's airplay on white radio.

Just as a hypnotic boogie undercurrent was the stylistic trademark linking Hooker's 'Boom Boom' and 'Dimples', so a bottleneck approach was the common thread between Elmore James - whose 'Rollin' And Tumblin' was to be a blues 'standard'

- and his mentor Robert Johnson, who'd recorded virtually all of his output in 1937, a few months before his purported death by poison at the age of twenty-four.

Another of post-war blues' major voices was Aaron 'T-Bone' Walker whose full-throated singing and terse guitar passagework was echoed by Albert King. In turn, Albert's influence was felt by Jimmy Page, Jeff Beck and, moreso, Eric Clapton - notably in Cream's revival of King's 'Born Under A Bad Sign' in 1968 - and others who'd paid heed during the early 1960s wave of British blues.

Perhaps the most respected of all present day black blues guitarists, B.B. King left his mark principally in a clean, jazz-tinged fretboard style with its note-bending trademark. Indeed, when Page, Clapton, Mike Bloomfield and other well-known white guitarists were sincerely loud in praising him, it made commercial sense for King to gear his music for a wider market - which was to spawn 1970's Grammy-winning 'The Thrill Is Gone', his only Top Twenty hit. Renowned guest artists on later projects included Carole King, Steve Marriott, Ringo Starr and Alexis Korner. One of the few surviving links between cotton pickin' rural blues and contemporary rock, King has been awarded an honorary university doctorate and, in tuxedo and bow-tie, has long been capable of filling both Caesar's Palace in Las Vegas and the Royal Albert Hall.

This, however, was as far-fetched as Mick Jagger's knighthood when, in 1963, the Dave Berry version of 'My Baby Left Me' had stalled at Number Thirty-Seven in the domestic chart, even after Radio Luxembourg gave his 'Hoochie Coochie Man' a few spins too. A change of strategy had been in order - and the Don Valley bluesman found another voice for 'Baby It's You', a Burt Bacharach morosity that The Beatles had covered on their first album.

Even more lachrymose than this Top Thirty restorative were 1964's 'The Crying Game' and its twin, 'One Heart Between Two', heartbreak *lieds* by jobbing songwriter Geoff Stephens. The first came within an ace of a domestic chart-topper, while the second battled to Number Forty-One three months later -

but they were so similar in arrangement, that it could have gone either way. With Dave's wounded baritone anticipating Bryan Ferry's more mannered crooning by a decade, 'The Crying Game' had been scored initially for orchestra but this was ditched in favour of a starker focus on fragile zither *glissandos*, and an aptly tearful guitar *obligato*. His runs cemented by the plain strumming of Jimmy Page - nicknamed 'Little Jim' - his young sidekick, Big Jim Sullivan achieved this with a volume pedal at his feet, creating a novel 'cello-like effect.

This device - also foot-operated - may be regarded now as a precursor of the wah-wah, an effect devised orginally to make a guitar sound like a brass mute via an uncomplicated set-up involving output jacks and, usually, a by-pass switch. However, with the commercial manufacture of the Cry-Baby in the mid-1960s, the wah-wah was to become connotational with 1960s 'progressive' music.[17]

Bert Weedon claimed to be 'the first in Britain to use the wah-wah pedal, but I'm not keen on effects pedals. I've always performed standing up, and I like to move around on stage - because otherwise it looks boring. Rather than pedals, the sound hinges on how you place your fingers, and hit the strings.'

Contrary to myth, Jimmy Page was never to be a major advocate of effects pedals either, believing like Bert that tone lay in the hands of the guitarist - as instanced by the restrained wah-wah effect, he produced without particularly noticeable artifice in the opening bars of a ghosted solo on The First Gear's otherwise routine 1964 single, 'Leave My Kitten Alone'.

Yet he - and Big Jim Sullivan - purchased not only a Cry-Baby as soon as it came out, but also a fuzzbox after Keith Richards brought one back from his Rolling Stones' first US trip in 1964. When designed by Gibson two years earlier, the Maestro Fuzztone had been intended to approximate the rasp of a saxophone, but, partly through Keith blasting out the riff on 1965's '(I Can't Get No) Satisfaction' on his, it - like the wah-wah - was to swiftly assume a personality of its own. Further endorsements would come from The Beatles, who fed a bass guitar through one when preparing their winter album, *Rubber*

Soul, in 1965, and it was also to electroplate 'Keep On Running' and 'Somebody Help Me'[18], consecutive British chart-toppers for The Spencer Davis Group, as well as late 1965's 'You Make It Move' and its 'Hold Tight!' follow-up by Dave Dee, Dozy, Beaky, Mick and Tich.[19]

With both this latest hardware and hard-won fretboard dexterity at his command, Little Jim, not such a kid now, was by then on a par with Big Jim as one of the brightest stars in the London studio firmament, even if he hadn't been 'the only other new face' for long. Another had been his replacement in the Crusaders, Hertford's gifted if under-valued Albert Lee, who had next joined Chris Farlowe and the Thunderbirds and endured frequently harsh Crusader-like conditions in Germany before the privacy of the studio became more agreeable to contemplate than the cruel winter of 1962 when 'we almost froze to death - and almost wrote ourselves off when the van turned over on the ice. I was glad to come back after that one - but I flew straight back out there to play with this German band, Mike Warner and the Echolettes, for three months. Warner dumped us, and it took me ages to scrape up the fare home.'[20]

On the way in too was Chris Spedding, a Sheffield contemporary of Frank White[21], whose heart was in jazz, even as he marked time with a London country-and-western outfit as well as tenures in blue-blazered, tuxedoed uniform, churning out light orchestral and upbeat muzak under the batons of middle-aged bandleaders on luxury liners and at debutante balls before graduating to session work.

Spedding and Albert Lee were to be, however, nowhere as prolific as the more versatile Jimmy Page, with and without Big Jim Sullivan, on a diversity of singles, famous and obscure, recorded during a schedule of maybe a dozen sessions a week for almost six years. Off-the-cuff - and chronologically illogical - examples on which Page was audible are Val Doonican's 'Walk Tall'; 'The Pied Piper' from Crispian St. Peters; 'It Hurts When I Cry' by Sean Buckley and his Breadcrumbs; 'Hold Me' from P.J. Proby; Cliff Richard's 'Time Drags By'; 'That's Nice' by old boss Neil Christian; a xerox of The Yardbirds' 'Turn Into Earth' by Al Stewart[22]; The Nashville Teens' 'Tobacco Road'; 'You Don't Believe Me', opening track on The Pretty Things' second LP, *Get The Picture*; 'I Pity The Fool' with a group fronted by the fellow destined to be David Bowie; 'Sittin' On a Fence' from Twice As Much; 'Young Love' by Bo and Peep; 'The Last Waltz' by Gerry Dorsey - after his 1966 rebirth as 'Engelbert Humperdinck' - and, pedalling his wah-wah, on Leapy Lee's maddeningly catchy 'Little Arrows'.

Jimmy also earned his tea break by ministering to acts ranging from the jogalong country-pop of The Lancastrians (from Cheshire!) to the lowdown blues of John Mayall. In between, Page delved into folk rock with such as a Nico yet to join The Velvet Underground, just as Joey Molland was yet to form Badfinger when one of The Masterminds - on whose 'She Belongs To Me', a Bob Dylan cover, Page is loud and clear.

He was there too during Dave Berry's restless farewell to the domestic charts with 'Little Things' and overtly sentimental 'Mama'. However, after 1965's 'This Strange Effect' entered myth as Holland's biggest-selling disc, a winning streak *sur le continent* continued until Berry finally hit serious trouble with such as 'Picture Me Gone', waltz-time 'Forever' and 1968's 'Do I Still Figure In Your Life', as inexplicable a miss for Berry as it had been for composer Pete Dello's own outfit, Honeybus - but not for 1965's 'She Just Satisfies', the one and only solo single by Jimmy Page.

Featuring him on vocals and all instruments apart from Bobby Graham's drums, it layered lyrics by Barry Mason onto 'Revenge', an instrumental composed by Larry Page, now one of about half-a-dozen pop managers in Britain that really counted for anything. 'Revenge' was musical ballast for his Kinks' first LP (and covered by Ray MacVay as a short-lived opening theme for ITV's *Ready Steady Go* pop series). As 'She Just Satisfies', it was neither a profound insight into the human condition nor a masterpiece of melody, this pot-shot at the charts by a London studio insider, leaning on his contacts, just as 'Mary Anne' by now-established console engineer Glyn Johns was that same year.

Johns had been a sporadic recording artiste in his own right since 1962 when he was fronting The Presidents. With an ear also cocked to the far-off roar of the crowd too, Ritchie Blackmore, then resident guitarist at Joe Meek's RGM studio, tore it up on both anachronistic sides of 'Getaway' and 'Little Brown Jug', coming across like Duane Eddy with attitude. In 1965 too - and in the wake of Barry McGuire's 'Eve Of Destruction' - session singer Barry St. John irritated the lower reaches of the British charts with his only entry, a less bombastic 'protest' item in Tim Rose's 'Come Away Melinda'. Likewise employed mainly to back other acts, The Mike Sammes Singers were to score a Top Twenty hit of their own in 1967 with 'Somewhere My Love'.

While 'She Just Satisfies' was a resounding flop, it was something Jimmy could bequeath to his grandchildren if he had any. His standing in the industry also put him in a position to impose unsolicited ideas upon those too much in awe of the situation to splutter, 'We'd rather not, sir'. Hence, the appearance of 'Just Like Anyone Would Do', 'The Last Mile' (with Andrew Loog Oldham) and 'Wait For Me', respective Page-penned B-sides by The Fifth Avenue, Gregory Phillips and The Fleurs De Lys. Dave Hill of Wolverhampton's 'N Betweens was to remember when Bobbie Graham, the session drummer, who was also a talent scout for Disc-Barclay, a French label, came to the Midlands: 'he discovered the 'N Betweens and recorded us in Pye studios in Marble Arch. Jimmy Page turned up during the session, and got us to do 'Little Nightingale', a number he'd written - which was included on a rare French EP.'

Through Graham's French connection too, Page appeared on *British Percussion* an LP by Le London All-Stars (*sic*), co-writing three of its tracks, and ministered to releases by Gallic luminaries such as Françoise Hardy[23] and Eddy Mitchell.

Yet, more than any other renowned British sessionman, Page is remembered too for what he did not do. The autobiographies of both Ray Davies of The Kinks and Dave, his lead guitarist brother, do not mention Page, who myth maintains played lead - or was it rhythm? - guitar on 1964's chart-topping 'You

Really Got Me' - which later ages would cite as primal heavy metal. This story may have been a music business equivalent of a fisherman's tall tale, evolving perhaps from Page's presence on self-explanatory *Kinky Music*, an easy-listening instrumental album by the group's manager's own Larry Page Orchestra, just as George Martin had done the year before for his studio charges on 1964's *Off The Beatles Track*.

Naturally, *Kinky Music* included a lushly-arranged 'Revenge', but of more import on this *ultima thule* for Kinks collectors is 'One Fine Day', a opus by their Dave Davies, otherwise unheard, bar a 1964 cover by Shel Naylor, one of Larry's lesser luminaries - and also featuring Jimmy Page.

Jimmy was present and correct too on both sides of the following winter's 'I Can't Explain', the smash that made The Who the toast of would-be Mods. It also contained help from a vocal trio, John Carter, Perry Ford and Ken Lewis, who, together and apart, had decided that it would do no harm to try some records in their own right. Carter-Lewis and the Southerners' 'Your Momma's Out Of Town' - an opus by Mitch Murray, another professional tunesmith - had had no physical existence outside the studio apart from press photographs of Ken, John and three of the better-looking members of the session team responsible - which included a grinning Jimmy Page.[24]

He had played too on both the previous single, 'Sweet And Tender Romance', and its syndication by two Scottish sisters, The McKinleys, who shared the same Denmark Street production company. This Carter-Lewis opus was to be exhumed as a B-side by P.J. Proby, who was startled by Jimmy Page's quick study of the guitar part, unaware as he was of the fellow's hand in the two previous versions.

Arguing that no-one within the spectrum of the beat boom had capitalised on the Four Freshman-Hi Los close harmony sound as The Four Seasons and Beach Boys had done in the States, Carter and Lewis - with Perry Ford - as The Ivy League, proved this judgement correct with 1965's 'Funny How Love Can Be' high in the charts. Two more entries followed before the three signed off with 'Willow Tree', a well-crafted melancholia that appealed to bedsit girls, grannies and those too tough to admit they liked it. While he played on the records, Jimmy Page could not be tempted to pitch in when the League took the product on the road. Indeed, Carter and Lewis themselves also threw in the towel to resume a songwriting partnership that had started when both were Birmingham schoolboys.

With the inevitable commercialisation of flower-power, they cashed in quick with 'Let's Go To San Francisco Parts 1 & 2', spread over two sides of a single by The Flowerpot Men - who, initially, were even more insubstantial than Carter-Lewis and the Southerners, though, more or less, the same musicians were hired to provide the accompaniment. While theirs were the voices heard on the disc, Lewis and Carter's unwillingness to be more than *eminences grises* necessitated the assembly of a quartet to mime it on *Top Of The Pops* and go on the road. Consisting of session singers and latter-day Ivy Leaguers, the touring Flowerpot Men were to make their debut supporting Traffic and The Vanilla Fudge at Finsbury Park Astoria in October 1967. In beads, chiffon robes and like regalia, they delivered four-part harmonies whilst tossing dying chrysanthemums into the audience.

By then, all the flowers were already wilting, but the organisation was to struggle on with a follow-up, 'A Walk In The Sky' that was too aswarm with jarring musical fragments to be clasped to the public bosom. Two further flops were so dispiriting that the next intended 45, the desperate 'Let's Go Back To San Francisco', was postponed indefinitely.

The long term failure of the project was infinitely less hurtful to battle-hardened metropolitan studio denizens like Carter, Lewis, Page *et al* than that of Them was to the personnel of this Belfast R&B group. They'd migrated to an uncertain London future in the middle of 1964, having signed to Decca a few months earlier. At their very first date at the label's West Hampstead complex, they'd been disconcerted to find session players on clock-watching stand-by - as they would be on all subsequent Them releases too - to complete the prescribed four tracks in three hours.

Among those favoured by producer Tommy Scott would be Jimmy Page, Andy White - renowned today for drumming on The Beatles' 'Love Me Do' - Perry Ford and Ulster expatriate Phil Coulter, also a rising songwriter, on keyboards. Coulter was also put in charge of the day-to-day organisation of Them, whose vocalist, Van Morrison, unhappy with the results, was to recall that 'Page played rhythm guitar on one thing, and doubled a bass riff on another. That's all he did.'[25]

As lead vocalist, Morrison was the only one who wasn't dispensable behind the scenes. He was to cite that first Decca taping as the moment that Them was over, its potential crushed before it was ever revealed to a national public. His hackles may have risen a little, but he kept his peace, waiting to do his guide vocal in front of a skull-like chrome microphone while his comrades puffed apprehensive cigarettes, gnawed chewing gum and tuned up.

The session with its Musicians Union-regulated tea breaks got underway. The Rolling Stones had challenged this regime by running over into the graveyard hours only recently, and newcomers like Them were expected to finish within the alloted time during conventional London office times or an evening period with a jobsworth locking-up well before midnight.

For first-timers, Them - albeit with helpmates - acquitted themselves well enough, banging out Bo Diddley's 'You Can't Judge A Book By The Cover', three minutes-worth of 'Turn On Your Love Light' from Bobby Bland, some Morrison originals and Slim Harpo's 'Don't Start Crying Now' which Dick Rowe chose to have issued as an A-side in September 1964.

'Don't Start Crying Now' shifted plenty in loyal Ulster, but there was little else to indicate that Them were superior to legion other British acts plundering those Chicago and Mississippi motherlodes. Nevertheless, a few months later, Them rose above the common herd with a second single, 'Baby Please Don't Go'. Its composition was attributed to Big Joe Williams, a Mississippi songster of the 1920s. It had since been recorded by, amongst others, Muddy Waters, John Lee Hooker,

Chris Barber's band - and most recently, by Georgie Fame and the Blue Flames on an in-concert LP. 'Baby Please Don't Go' was also in the air in similar R&B venues throughout the country. Decca's design was to get out the Them arrangement - now regarded justly as definitive - on a single before anyone else did.

Much of its appeal emanated from the tingling lead guitar section. Friction about the continued use of session players may have contributed to drummer Ronnie Millings' resolution to pursue a calling as a milkman back in Belfast rather than face another dispiriting week with Them before the new disc appeared in the shops early in November with a severely-edited 'Gloria' on the B-side.

Them's 'Gloria' might have been sturdy enough to rate as an A-side had it not been coupled with an opus as stunning as 'Baby Please Don't Go' - which reached a UK apogee of sorts when it supplanted Manfred Mann's '54321' as *Ready Steady Go*'s theme tune. Over seven weeks, Them progressed to a tantalising peak as ballast in a Top Ten with Twinkle, The Kinks, The Moody Blues and Manfred Mann all vying to topple Georgie Fame, suddenly at Number One with 'Yeah Yeah' by 'jazz sage' Jon Hendricks, a singer who touched on the blues extremities of pop.

It was mostly on the strength of the song recorded rather than Them's looks and personalities that ensured that they were not destined to be one-hit-wonders. 'Here Comes The Night', a Latin-slanted ballad of lustful envy by Bert Berns, a music business jack-of-all-trades from New York, had been put forward as a contrast to the R&B intensity of 'Baby Please Don't Go'. There had almost been an upset in this plan because perfidious Decca had hedged its bets by rushing out a cover by Glasgow's Lulu and the Luvvers - with Jimmy Page helping out on this too - months before Them's already-taped 'Here Comes The Night' appeared in March.

Unfortunate though this was, the Scottish group faltered after a week at Number Fifty before sinking without trace. Such a poor performance might not have been a good advertisement for the song *per se*, but it guaranteed a clear run for Them, whose 'Here Comes The Night' crashed straight in at Number Six. Could anyone not empathise with the young Irish group's mortification when, before the disc began slipping in April, only the Beatles' 'Ticket To Ride' blocked its passage to Number One?

As well as Them recordings, Jimmy Page also assisted on two flop singles by another star-in-waiting of similar stylistic akin to Van Morrison. Steve Marriott was a former child actor who'd appeared in *The Famous Five* television series in the late 1950s and made a West End theatre debut in Lionel Bart's *Oliver!* in 1962. Not liking to see this public exposure going to waste, Decca engaged him as an Adam Faith sound-a-like. Then, as singing guitarist with a backing group, he had another miss with a sly cover of 'You Really Got Me' for the US market - which may have involved Jimmy Page, hence further confusing affinity to The Kinks.

This was far less lucrative than his emergence as the knock-kneed and diminutive front man of The Small Faces, a Mod act as pre-eminent as The Who, attacking their early releases with a choked anguish revealing an absorption of R&B, and an exciting if sometimes slipshod fretboard style that belied the saccharine quality of such as 'Sha-La-La-La-Lee' and 'My Mind's Eye'.

Only a telephone call away if his services were needed, Jimmy Page logged The Small Faces output for a purpose that was then non-specific. He had to laugh at Marriott and Ronnie Lane, the group's second-string vocalist, granting themselves composing credits for 'You Need Loving', an LP track that was, effectively, a Booker T and the MGs-ish refashioning of 1962's 'You Need Love' from the portfolio of Willie 'Little Red Rooster' Dixon, 'which we stole,' confessed organist Ian McLagan, 'or, at least, the chorus was a steal. It was a nick Steve used to do. He would use Muddy Waters/Willie Dixon vocal lines in songs, because that's what was influencing him. He was a sampler - well, he was more than a sampler because he was actually doing it.'[26]

In Led Zeppelin's hands, it was to be retitled 'Whole Lotta Love' and attributed to Page and Robert Plant - with the latter leaning heavily on Marriott's phrasing.[27] It was also to be the subject of a 1987 civil action for plagiarism that was settled out of court with a pay-off to the aggrieved Dixon. No-one said much, if anything, about 'You Need Loving'.

THE NIGHT-TIMER

'John Paul always displayed good taste and good ideas. He wasn't the usual run-of-the-mill player' - Tony Meehan (obit)[9]

While he will be best-remembered as the most unobtrusive mainstay of Led Zeppelin, bass guitarist John Paul Jones is on a par with Jack Bruce and the late John Entwistle for the respect he has earned from other artists for inventiveness, instrumental dexterity, exacting musical standards and acrobatic flair for inprovisation.

Rather than the treadmill of the road, however, sessions were initially a better financial bet for Jones, born John Baldwin on 3 January 1946 in Sidcup where the postal districts of London bleed into Kent. North-west of the divisional Medway River, and as far from the White Cliffs of Dover as it was feasible to be without leaving the shire, John was, therefore, a 'Kentish Man' as opposed to a 'Man of Kent'.

He was also an only child, embodying many of the common characteristics, notably a self-contained adeptness at entertaining himself. This was also a family trait as John's parents were a showbusiness couple. They were principally a musical comedy duo, but father Joe was also a pianist suffiently gifted to have been heard on BBC radio's Light Programme with Ambrose and his Orchestra - from whom oozed musak arrangements of Handel, Offenbach, Ravel and Rossini as well as selections of similar ilk from the newly-established *New Musical Express* record sales and sheet music charts.[28] In 1952, Mario Lanza, a Pavarotti of his day, came close to Number One with a light opera aria, while Ronnie Hilton, a former apprentice engineer from Leeds with a sub-Lanza tenor, was cited by the *NME* as Britain's most popular vocalist. Among his rivals were the similarly neo-operatic Lee Laurence, 'Forces Sweetheart' Vera Lynn and Donald Peers, 'the Cavalier of Song'.

Such 'pop' music was commensurate with a comfy, pre-rock 'n' roll Britain epitomised by hello-hello-hello policemen, monocled cads, kilted Scotsmen - and straight-backed old maids free-wheeling sit-up-and-beg bicycles with basketwork carrier-bags down rolling lanes to evensong in the mellow sunshine of parting day in the county referred to as 'the Garden of England'. Nonetheless, though quite well-to-do, John Baldwin's family did not freight household vocabulary with PG Woodhouse phrases like 'right-ho!' and 'jolly good', or look out from their break-fast room on story-book meadows and woodland. Nevertheless, sooty foxgloves might have sprung up beneath sepia skies on the bomb-sites that remained after the Luftwaffe's contribution to the urban renewal programme from London's East End to the quickly over-populated 'Medway Towns' that fanned out from Gillingham and Chatham towards the capital.

One consequence of victory in the Second World War was that London and north-west Kent's docks, naval depots and quayside garrisons ceased to spoonfeed bloodshed in the English Channel and North Sea. More insidious was an accelerated growth of the county's estuarian conurbations that had been swallowing up the Garden of England since the Industrial Revolution. Nonetheless, when John Baldwin was an infant, tap water was still a council election promise in certain far-flung hamlets, while in the poorer urban districts, gas rather than electricity lit kitchens where margarine was spread instead of butter, and noisy copper geysers hung above sinks in which a mother would both bathe babies and wash dishes from a Sunday lunch on a newspaper tablecloth. But, with her sense of hearing not yet dulled by the ever-increasing volume of traffic, it was easy to differentiate between individual sounds of local vehicles belonging to, say, the vicar, the publican, the district nurse - or the milkman, if his crates weren't being transported by a plodding pony instead.

Passing a junior school on the way to the shops mid-morning, she'd catch multiplication tables chanted mechanically and *en masse*, perhaps to the rap of a bamboo cane on a teacher's inkwelled desk. While he may have endured the unimaginative and often frightening regime prevalent in most state primaries in the early 1950s, John Baldwin was packed off to boarding school in Dorset where he discovered a dislike of organised games - and for keyboard lessons freighted with carping discipline enforced perhaps with a ruler on errant digits. He was, however, so able to disassociate the music from the painful drudgery that the hymns, canticles and psalms during divine service at this seat of learning - and in the Church local to his Sidcup home - came to be accompanied sometimes by Baldwin, whose inherited musical interests had been formalised further by extra-curricular tutorials on the school's chapel pipe organ. From wheezy Magnificats, he was to move on to emulating as far as he could the fluid electric keyboards beneath the jazzy hands of such as Fats Waller and, later, Jimmy Smith, 'Brother' Jack MacDuff, and Richard 'Groove' Holmes.

To please his father, John took up the saxophone briefly, but was put off by the unpredictable harmonics that set his teeth on edge. The learning process was infinitely more logical on a choice of instrument that was to determine his working life. He expressed his longing for it via an experiment on a ukelele gathering dust on top of the family's upright piano. He attempted to string it like one of these futuristic electric bass guitars that had infinitely more volume and depth of sound than upright 'bullfiddles' and, certainly, the makeshift broomstick-and-tea chest efforts thrummed in most skiffle outfits. Perhaps the most singular road-to-Damascus moment was when the fifteen-year-old heard 'You Can't Sit Down' by Chicago's Phil Upchurch Combo. It was a dance instrumental spread over both sides of a 1961 single that teetered on the edge of the domestic Top Forty. It also featured a bass guitar solo.

Less specifically, Baldwin was excited too by the first UK releases by Tamla-Motown, a promising black label from Detroit. Though the vocal arrangements of, say, 'Money' by Barrett Strong and The Marvelettes' 'Please Mr. Postman' were distinctive, John felt that it was the bass guitar part - an actual sound rather than the mere presence it was on most British-made discs - that made the truest difference, giving a song its outward shape and direction, and lifting a band off the runway to glide on the strongest musical winds.

He decided to put action over daydreaming. After his father was cajoled into acting as hire purchase guarantor for a solid-body bass, John Baldwin fed it through the amplifier of a doctored television, and, as there was no-one to instruct him or even a worthwhile tutor manual available, tried thrumming whatever bass lines were annotated in sheet music, beginning with 'Freight Train', a skiffle hit by Chas McDevitt. More thought-provoking was playing along with music broadcast on the Light Programme.

Soon, he had the confidence to play regularly with other amateur musicians of like persuasion at a Church youth club that convened after Sunday evensong. Somehow or other, a group smouldered into form, albeit one without a drummer, obliging John to develop an unusually percussive style concentrated on the lower frets. His first cash-in-hand engagement was with a band in which his father fingered piano. Further parochial bookings at wedding receptions, street parties and fêtes were to extend to better-paid work in US air bases - such as one just beyond Dartford where a youth named Mick Jagger had obtained a holiday job as a PE instructor. Like the Rolling Stone-in-waiting, Baldwin was introduced to the more specialist aspects of blues, country-and-western and further transfixing North American pop via the jukeboxes and record players at these encampments.

At seventeen, Baldwin broke loose from this regional orbit when he was invited to attend an audition in an upstairs function room of a central London pub for a group to be assembled to accompany drummer Tony Meehan and Jet Harris, who plucked a given instrumental number's melody on a guitar tuned just an octave higher than John's four-string bass, now a Burns powered by a Truvoice bass amplifier with speakers almost as tall as himself. Though they were fresh from three weeks at Number One with 'Diamonds', their debut single, Jet and Tony had been hot property for quite a while, having served time in what many regard as the 'classic' line-up of The Shadows.

On stage at many a back-of-beyond town hall dance, *circa* 1961, you'd witness a quartet happily presenting a set consisting entirely of deadpan Shadows imitations. The fellow with the Stratocaster might be sporting Hank B. Marvin-via-Buddy Holly black horn-rims, while the peroxide blond bass player was a Jet Harris *doppleganger*, transfixing the girls with his brooding intensity. As a member of such combos himself, while John Baldwin didn't attempt to turn himself into a biological duplicate of Harris, he succumbed to the uniform suits and the intricately synchronised footwork just like those of the front-line Shadows.[29]

That Marvin and Harris were the principal public faces of The Shadows is exemplified by the title of 1975's *Specs Appeal*, and more blatantly by Jet's immediate solo success with 'Besame Mucho' and 'Man With The Golden Arm'. Both these were hits just prior to Harris dismissing his accompanying Jet Blacks, and teaming up, with Tony Meehan, after he left The Shadows too, for 'Diamonds' - which ended the brief reign of their old group's 'Dance On!' at the top of the charts in January 1963 - and another brace of smashes that year, 'Scarlet O'Hara' and 'Applejack'.

While he conducted himself both personally and musically with cautious politeness at the audition, John Baldwin was taken on by Jet and the late Tony with whom he remained for the next year, along with guitarist John McLaughlin, a twenty-year-old Yorkshireman - later, a jazz-rock colossus - and, prior to a spell with Georgie Fame's Blue Flames, saxophonist Glen Hugues. Smart new amplifiers were provided by the publicity-conscious Vox firm, but Baldwin himself had to purchase a bass congruent with the Fender instruments that McLaughlin and Harris played.

On the road with these older boys, it wasn't all smiles, particularly after the gifted but self-destructive Harris was badly injured later in 1963 when his chauffeur-driven Humber collided with a bus. As a consequence, the group fell apart, and Jet's boozing - and intake of amphetamines - increased, and were central to a resumption of his solo career and his subsequent emergence as a booker's risk. He was so far out of it that, on one occasion, he introduced his latest backing combo, The Innocents, four times before stopping during the introductory bars of a latest single, and stumbling into the wings.

It had been at the suggestion of Harris's manager that John Baldwin had adopted the stage alias 'John Paul Jones' after the 1959 movie of the same name about the War Of Independence naval hero. He was introduced thus on the boards after he offered his services to the steadier half of the now-sundered duo. The Tony Meehan Combo had been launched in 1964 after its leader made the Top Forty - just - with 'Song Of Mexico'. That, as far as the record-buying public was concerned, was that for the Combo, whose stage act tended to bring out the hostilities within certain sections of the audience. Anticipating jazz-rock by at least five years, 'We were doing the sort of thing that Chicago and Blood-Sweat-and-Tears came up with later,' averred Meehan, 'but we were booed off.'[30]

Nevertheless, room had been found for Meehan at Decca, one of Britain's four major record labels, as a producer. He was answerable to middle-aged Dick Rowe, who, after overseeing The Stargazers's 1953 Number One, 'Broken Wings', had became the company's head of artists-and-repertoire - A and R - and was recognised as a key talent spotter of the UK record industry. Later 1950s singers who also thrived under his aegis included Lita Roza, Dickie Valentine and Billy Fury. For a while, he left Decca to work for Top Rank for whom he procured a chart entrant, via Joe Meek, in John Leyton. When the label folded, he returned to Decca to minister to further hits such as 'Diamonds'. However, for all his Top Ten triumphs, Rowe has earned a historical footnote as 'The Man Who Turned Down The Beatles' - after a recording test on New Year's Day 1962 - on the grounds that 'four-piece groups with guitars are finished'.

In fairness, executives with other companies were just as blinkered. Provoked by the quartet's infuriating success with EMI, a chastised but cynical Rowe began saturating Decca with peas from the same Merseyside pod. In January 1963 alone he made off from Liverpool with The Big Three, Beryl Marsden,

Billy Butler and, because their drummer was ex-Beatle Pete Best, Lee Curtis and the All-Stars. On George Harrison's recommendation he looked southwards and signed The Rolling Stones in May. Dave Berry and the Cruisers, The Nashville Teens, John Mayall's Bluesbreakers, Them, Unit 4 + 2, The Moody Blues, The Applejacks and The Zombies were among further acquisitions, but for each such hitmaking unit, there was also a Beat Six, a Bobby Cristo and the Rebels, a Brumbeats, a Sandra Barry and her Boyfriends, a Gonks, a Barry and the Tamberlanes, a Bunnies, a Tommy Bishop's Ricochets, a Falling Leaves...

Rowe's yardstick of professionalism was a 1962 signing, Brian Poole and the Tremeloes: dependable in the studio as both session players and in their own right; neatly coiffeured; garbed in not-too-way-out suits, and given to stage patter that didn't include swearing or overt attempts to pull front-row girls - everything a decent pop group ought to be. Before being allowed to record under their own name, Poole and two Tremeloes were used as a vocal trio on such masterpieces of song as Jimmy Savile's 'Ahab The Arab' and, recalls Brian, 'If you listen to the Vernons Girls' cover of 'The Locomotion', it sounds more like blokes apart from the lead vocal. That was us too. We also backed auditionees that came in - either us or The Kestrels with Roger Greenaway, Roger Cook and Tony Burrows. Even when we were famous, we were helping out on sessions - because it paid really well.'

Sons of Bristol, The Kestrels were a close harmony outfit whose easy professionalism guaranteed if not Brian Poole-sized hit parade placings, then regular employment on mid-1960s package tours and variety seasons. Setting themselves up in London as songwriters too, Cook and Greenaway's tenacity paid off when their 'You've Got Your Troubles' for The Fortunes in 1965 established them as a middle-of-the-road hit machine with a knack for hummable melodies and lyrics more impressive for sound than meaning. As 'David and Jonathan', the two Rogers themselves were to make 1966's UK Top Twenty twice with a cover of The Beatles' 'Michelle' and their own 'Lovers of The World Unite' but, with the failure of subsequent discs, they ceased public appearances as a duo. If now functioning separately as occasional recording artists, this was incidental to the team's composition and production work for others acts for which Cookaway Music was formed.

With no existence beyond recording and television studios, some Cook-Greenaway acts (e.g. Congregation, Harley Quinne) were to be created simply to front specific projects. The most enduring of these would be Blue Mink, assembled in 1969 with Cook and Madeleine Bell as lead vocalists for a four year chart run. During this period, Greenaway and Cook also illuminated commercial breaks on ITV with jingles extolling the virtues of Typhoo tea, Woodpecker cider and other products.

Studio servitude at Decca, therefore, could be a springboard to renown or at least better-paid work. Such was the pervading mood when John Paul Jones commenced a transition from the live circuit to full-time session work during an era when it's not too much of a exaggeration to say that the order of the day then was sticking a microphone in front of a group and hoping for the best.

Today, lead vocals float effortlessly over layers of treated sound - and making a living in pop is also a much more acceptable vocational option to parents. In middle-class homes in the provinces - even as close to Swinging London as Sidcup - the 1950s didn't really end until about 1966. For a boy to go on the road with a beat group - almost always all male - was almost the equivalent of a girl becoming a burlesque dancer. To Mr. and Mrs. Baldwin, therefore, their John had made a well-judged choice for self-advancement while remaining true - after a shadowy fashion - to his family background: showbusiness without the show.

There were, however, the fulfilling of existing engagements with the fading Tony Meehan Combo - and, in 1964 too, a similar single by none other than John Paul Jones himself. An overhaul for six-string Fender bass of a traditional ditty, 'Baja' was an attempt to fill what was perceived - wrongly - to be a market void for a Jet Harris of the mid-1960s. It had been taped during a session at London's Regent Sound complex with

The Andrew Oldham Orchestra, assembled from London session shellbacks - including Jimmy Page and Big Jim Sullivan - by The Rolling Stones' manager for easy-listening *mélanges* of mostly current hits and acclamatory originals such as 'There Are But Five Rolling Stones' and '365 Rolling Stones (One For Every Day Of The Year)'.

These were shoehorned onto a 1964 LP, *16 Hip Hits* - and the production of 'Baja' by Oldham - who also brokered the deal withn Pye for its release - may have been John Paul's reward for his stepping in after arranger Mike Leander accepted a post as staff producer at Decca. 'I wanted to arrange, Andrew wanted to produce, and neither of us was very choosy,' smiled Jones, 'I was grateful because he trusted me with these sessions and all these musicians. I was allowed to write them nice, interesting little things, especially for woodwinds. We'd always have a couple of oboes or French horns. He gave me a chance to do all these weird things. He kind of let me get on with it, but he had a very clear idea of what he wanted. The records we made were more the underground really. The very fact that they didn't sell actually gives you a certain freedom; you can do what you like, having a good time and getting paid for it. His sessions were always fun. So many others were banal, mundane, very boring. You couldn't wait to get out of them.'[31]

A possible escape from this often dull orbit presented itself that same year when, apparently, Jones was shortlisted when a vacancy occurred in The Shadows, despite the levelling blow of the beat boom and its emphasis on vocals rendering their stock-in-trade instrumentals old hat. However, with the late John Rostill rather than John Paul Jones on bass, The Shadows rode the storm.

Jones was also in a sound position to make more conspicuous hay during this nicotine-clouded high summer of British pop. To let off steam after studio hours of take after take of the the same song, he sat when time permitted at the electric organ for Herbie Goins and the Night-Timers, led by a black ex-US servicemen who, when awaiting imminent demobilisation, had sung on 1964's *Red Hot From Alex*, the second LP by Alexis

Korner's Blues Incorporated. Encouraged by both Alexis and customer reaction to their onstage efforts with the group at the Ealing club and elsewhere, Herbie and fellow GI Ronnie Jones decided to seek their fortunes as entertainers in Britain.

Their stamping ground, however, was not concentrated on the Blues Incorporated circuit but Soho watering holes like The Crazy Elephant, The Scene, The Roaring Twenties, the less fashionable Marquee and, crucially, The Flamingo, self-proclaimed 'Swinging Club of Swinging London', albeit 'extremely seedy, hot and sweaty,' reckoned Jones, 'but a brilliant vibe. Everyone was into black R&B and some jazz.'[31]

The Flamingo, Crazy Elephant and so forth were patronised by hip West Indians, GIs on a pass and prototype Mods. This sharply-dressed, principally male clientele were often of a lower social caste than the middle class bohemians who were still still heading for darkest Ealing - 'because they weren't jazzers,' opined John Paul, 'There was this little white R&B movement, which grew up quite separately, and would evolve into the Stones and The Yardbirds. I wasn't really involved in the white group scene. We were into Otis Redding and they were all into Chuck Berry and the Chess people, blues twits really. As a musical scene, they just didn't rate. It was more punk than R&B.'[31]

Yet the Flamingo's most popular outfits were led by white vocalists like Georgie Fame, Graham Bond, Chris Farlowe and Zoot Money, though the likes of Herbie Goins were welcome to 'sit in'. The next step for Goins was the formation of a backing group for himself - and Ronnie Jones who was very much the junior partner in the enterprise, taking on only those items thought unsuitable for front man Herbie.

In common with Zoot, Georgie *et al*, Herbie Goins and The Night-Timers' repertoire was founded on the latest developments in R&B which often ventured into what was becoming known as 'soul music' as it stretched from smooth Motown to James Brown call-and-response panic, all infused with Goins' trademark accompaniment of horns and female chorale.

Within months, word of his outfit's atmospheric sets and let-me-hear-you-say-'yeah' routines in prestigious West End showcases - and provincial watering holes like Basildon's Locarno and The Twisted Wheel in Manchester - reached the ears of Parlophone, the EMI subsidiary then anxious to stake a claim in the growing Mod market epitomised by huge attendance figures at a rash of new clubs like Blaises, The Pontiac, Tiles and Woolwich's Location that had suddenly pocked London. Identifying Goins as the main man, the contract would cover only him, leaving the nebulous Night-Timers to fend for themselves. In parenthesis, the most famous members would be guitarists John McLaughlin and Dave Mason, who served Herbie briefly between leaving Worcester's Hellions and joining Traffic in 1967 - and John Paul Jones.

While records were destined to be adjuncts to Goins' earnings on the road, October 1965 brought the subsequent issue of his debut 45, 'The Music Played On', a ballad perhaps better suited for cabaret than a mob baying for 'Midnight Hour' in the Flamingo. Underpinned by John Paul's growling organ, 'The Music Played On' was coupled with the more characteristic 'Yield Not To Temptation'. Next up was 'Number One In Your Heart', subject of saturation plugging on pirate radio, and selected as the title track of Herbie Goins only non-compilation album, released after 1966's 'Incredible Miss Brown', a made-to-measure offering by *Song For Europe* tunesmiths Phil Coulter and Bill Martin, had edged him nearer the national hit parade.

Though this bouncy concession to mainsteam pop with its *accelerando* coda was a flop, the B-side, 'Comin' On Home To You' - a group composition - was a more vivid streamlining of Herbie and his Night-Timers' in-concert power. Another version was also heard on vinyl on *Sounds Of London* album, a mid-1960s collection of tracks by some of the most popular acts in metropolitan clubland.

Despite packed houses wherever he appeared, it's conceivable that highbrow soul connoisseur Goins was one of these artists who are 'too good for the charts'. Pop is an unfair, erratic business, and it must have been galling for him when the likes of Geno Washington and the Ram Jam Band, and Jimmy James and The Vagabonds each crept into the lower rungs of the Top Fifty, and even the album list in the mid-1960s. Perhaps Herbie should have taken a leaf from Washington's book with a completely 'live' album of tried-and-tested crowd-pleasers and sweaty intensity.

Many middle-aged ravers might pontificate that you had to have been there - but, perfected over hundreds of hours on the boards, Goins' polished vocal attack lent him the self-confidence to record material that less assured British-based soul shouters would shun. Off-the-cuff examples included 'I Don't Mind', blueprinted by James Brown in 1960, and a 'Knock On Wood', taped within weeks of the release of Eddie Floyd's Stax original, and taken at a defiantly slower tempo to invest it with stronger definition and increased tension. Conversely, a race through the Bobby Bland warhorse, 'Turn On Your Love Light' proved just as effective. Moreover, who else attempted The Rolling Stones' '(I Can't Get No) Satisfaction' while a similar Otis Redding treatment was still thundering in the dark of London discotheques? I will risk a howl of derision from aged Mods by suggesting that the Goins version exudes more period charm than that of the late Otis.

It was Goins and his band's most convincing interpretations of US soul smashes that guaranteed them work if not chart placings - and it was this that necessitated their disbandment as the 1970s dawned. Yet, though an anachronism by then, they were still buoyed by a loyal following that paid to see them regardless of passing fashion.[32]

By then, John Paul Jones had been long departed from the Night-Timers. He hadn't been that dismayed by its lack of chart success. There were so many other options beyond session work that needed only his commitment. Even if he hadn't been in the innermost in-crowd of the London studio scene, Sidcup and its environs had been bursting with beat groups that might have welcomed him with open arms. In 1964, Peter Frampton, a prodigious fourteen-year-old from Beckenham joined

The Preachers who recorded a 45 for Columbia prior to renaming themselves Moon's Train for another one-shot single - for MGM - produced by Bill Wyman of The Rolling Stones. Indeed, a bartering tool when the fellows were looking for a record deal was Wyman's tenure with The Cliftons, the group that had mutated into The Preachers in 1963.

John Paul also knew a namesake, David Robert Jones, a school acquaintance of Frampton, and maker of several flop 45s as front man of The King Bees, The Manish Boys and then The Lower Third. He'd reached this impasse despite assuming the permanent *nom de théâtre* 'David Bowie' and, later, much of the persona of singing actor Anthony Newley.

Bowie was to claim that, when he was seventeen, John Paul, almost exactly one year his senior to the day, cajoled him into sampling 'grass'. It was packed into a large cigarette called a 'reefer' and smoked communally. Jones had used it, so he'd said, to unwind tense coils within after shows with Jet and Tony. Through hanging around with the likes of fast-mouthed Pete Meadon, who served as The Pretty Things' press officer and then manager of both The Who and Jimmy James and the Vagabonds, John Paul had also become aware of Preludin, a brand of appetite suppressant for dieters, that contained amphetamine sulphate - 'speed' - the dazzling effects of which could be counterbalanced by barbiturates. Jones also observed the older Meadon dipping into a surruptitious pocket every now and then for a blue or purple capsule.

'Pop music was all pills in those days,' admitted Jones. Indeed, ultra-Mod Meadon and other of John Paul's acquaintances seemed to know the ways and means of obtaining with ease 'Purple Hearts', 'Black Bombers', 'Mandies', 'French Blues' and other controlled drugs whose active constituents helped you stay awake, fall asleep, calm nerves and lift a blue mood.

That the so-called 'straight' member of Led Zeppelin may have been a bit of a raver was instanced further by he and Pete Meadon gatecrashing a coming-of-age party at 11 Downing Street for Caroline Maudling, the Chancellor of The Exchequer's daughter. Such stories filtered back to David Bowie,

Peter Frampton and luminaries of further north-west Kent pop groups like Group X, The Quiet Five, The Trojans and so many other outfits battling with hire-purchase payments, unreliable vans and rough nights at the Bromel in Bromley Court Hotel, Bexleyheath's Black Prince and the Gun Tavern down Church Street, Croydon.

Most roads led nowhere for these groups, but there was always a chance that one might. From Sidcup's very Art College, students Phil May and ex-Rolling Stone Dick Taylor had been forming The Pretty Things in 1963, and the job of bass player could have been John Paul Jones'for the asking. Certainly, he revised his perspective about 'this little white R&B movement' that was 'more punk than R&B', and followed the Things' later activities with interest, though he hadn't been a conspicuous afficianado - unlike Van Morrison, Sex Pistols svengali-in-waiting Malcolm McLaren and punk methuselah Charlie Harper (of The UK Subs) - when the Things fermented briefly in underground security.

Because Jones and Led Zeppelin came to much admire the Things, and have appeared to have used their vocational shipwrecks as their seamarks, the group's career is worth chronicling at length. Their take on black rhythm-and-blues had once been 'starvation music', though it was of more appeal to John Paul Jones than the pseudo-intellectual complacency he'd perceived in British jazz. While the blues wasn't the Word made vinyl to John, he was to be sufficiently erudite a consumer to suggest the superimposition of a riff from 1969's *Electric Mud*, an album aimed directly at the white market by Muddy Waters, on *Led Zeppelin IV*'s 'Black Dog'. More pertinent to this present debate, he recognised that, for example, The Pretty Things' self-penned 'Judgement Day' owed much to 'Hoochie Coochie Man' just as their '13 Chester Street' did moreso to 'Got Love If You Want It.'

This was forgivable. Everyone was doing it, albeit not with the same abandoned drive as the Things, whose long-haired, reprobate image also held instant allure for record company talent scouts looking for an act to combat the hit-making Stones in mid-1964. After testing the chart water with maiden single 'Rosalyn', the Things notched up their biggest smash with 'Don't Bring Me Down' in that autumn's Top Ten. Climbing almost as high, the 'Honey I Need' follow-up lived in a careering chord cycle thrashed behind a ranted vocal: punk or what?

Projected as wilder, fouler and more peculiar than the Stones - kind of Terry-Thomas to their David Niven - the Things flashed into respectable homes via *Top Of The Pops* cameras; May's cascading tresses - the longest male hair in the country - flickering across a complexion on which no hit record could prevent adolescent spots erupting. While the most liberal parents fought for control of their features, the effect was most keenly felt by their short-back-and-sides sons, transfixed guiltily by the Things' androgeny, offset only by Dick Taylor's beard.

You could speculate endlessly about how it might have been - but there was certainly a period *circa* 1965 when the Stones and the Things were on terms of fluctuating equality as belligerently unkempt degenerates, detested by adults. Even the Beatles were seen as a lesser threat to the Stones than hairy monsters like the Things, Them, the Downliners Sect and lesser lights with names like The Fairies, The Howlin' Wolves and The King Bees (whose David Bowie would revive the Things first two 45s on 1973's *Pin Ups* album).

A Beatle, see, could not be imagined urinating, committing a felony or being truly obnoxious any more than a sexless cartoon figure. By contrast, it was hard fact that three Stones were fined in 1965 for pissing against a wall, and a Fairy served time for causing death by dangerous driving. A Pretty Things road manager was prosecuted after some unpleasantness with a shotgun after an engagement in Swindon - and, remembers Phil May, 'in Stockport one night, some screaming bird tore my shirt during the first set, and Viv Prince stopped drumming to rip her blouse and bra off, and sock her in the mouth.'

Such outrages increased turn-out at bookings, even if curiosity-seekers with only the foggiest idea about the music they had paid to hear helped fill the often unsalubrious new beat clubs pocking the provinces. Yet always the Things expected their celebrity to end. Fontana did too, and rush-released an eponymous (and big selling) LP, padded with the latest hit, some derivative originals, and the expected Diddley, Berry and Jimmy Reed retreads.

No longer an overnight sensation, fading interest was confirmed when the Things bid a final farewell to the singles Top Fifty with a desperate cover of a Kinks LP track, 'House In The Country' - though, paradoxically, their music had acquired a less derivative sophistication as Taylor and May found their feet as composers, placing a greater stress on vocal harmony via the recruitment of new personnel from another Kentish combo, Bern Elliott's Fenmen. Raw blues-wailing ferocity now deferred to subtlety of structure and studied artistic progression.

A move to EMI guaranteed increased artistic freedom, manifested in self-consciously 'weird' discs born of late hours at EMI's Abbey Road complex with engineer Norman Smith as well as awareness of post-serialist composers such as Cage, Berio and Stockhausen, much hard listening to avant-garde jazz - and, on the evidence of titles like 'Trippin'' and just plain 'LSD', drug experience beyond mere pills and reefers. Taped under the influence, 'Defecting Grey', hinted at an aesthetic if wilfully uncommercial brilliance. Aswarm with jarring vignettes of music spliced together to coalesce a medley of five pieces, this 1967 single paved the way for *SF Sorrow*, unquestionably the first 'rock opera' (though, technically, a song-cycle).

However, for what remained of the Swinging Sixties, the Things' bread-and-butter depended less on record sales than on one-nighters on the 'alternative' circuit, rubbing shoulders with the 'progressive' likes of Tyrannosaurus Rex, Mick Farren and his Social Deviants, Eire Apparent, The Edgar Broughton Band and Hawkwind. Even outside this clique, Phil May lookalikes had become common enough in English country towns and the American Mid-West.

After 1970's *Parachute* achieved the dubious distinction of being the only *Rolling Stone* magazine Album Of The Year not to be awarded a gold disc, *Freeway Madness* was sufficiently well-received in North America for the Things to undertake the first of a hectic succession of coast-to-coast tours, where - in part because of Led Zeppelin's advances there - collegiate youth seemed fair game to buy anything British labelled 'heavy'.

By the middle of the decade, however, the Things were waiting, like Mr. Micawber, for something to turn up. It did in the burly form of Peter Grant who, largely at John Paul Jones'urging, signed the group to his organisation's new Swan Song label in 1974. 'It was the first time we got some attention,' said Phil, 'Led Zeppelin would fly in under assumed names to wherever we were and sit in the front row.'

John Paul Jones had been in a position to dispense no such favours, however deserved, when the Things had been up-and-coming in late 1963, and he was merely a back room boy ministering at Musicians Union rates to diverse Decca acts. Among these was Dave Berry, through which he entered the orbit of Jimmy Page - of whom he'd been aware previously as the guitarist with Neil Christian's Crusaders and on Jet and Tony's 'Diamonds'. Berry recalls both Jones and Page being present on the session for 'The Crying Game' and its contrasting B-side 'Don't Gimme No Lip Child', harsh enough to be revived by The Sex Pistols after pop wobbled into another dimension.

His biggest British hit, 'The Crying Game' was tailor-made for both the charismatic Dave's lack of obvious drama in his vocal style, and his then fully fledged cartoon spookiness that had earned him nicknames like Spider Fingers, Mr. Slocomotion, England's Herman Munster or, as Alan Price put it to Bob Dylan in the 1965 film documentary, *Don't Look Back*, the Human Sloth. The antithesis of Mick Jagger's flickering and much-plagiarised cavortings, it hinged on hand ballets, microphone *glissandos*, *kismet* supercool and a vague and surreal composite of James Dean's brooding intensity and Gene Vincent's crippled melodrama. It was, perhaps, the most original stage concept of the beat boom.

Nevertheless, though he acquitted himself admirably on stage, Berry's living still depended on the day-to-day mundanities of record sales, and the assistance of favoured accompanists, anchored by John Paul Jones'pulsation and, dependant on the needs peculiar to each number, one of two drummers. With a blithe dedication to his craft, Jones was equally at ease with R&B showstoppers that had been in and out of Berry's repertoire since the beginning, and items from the pens of assembly-line British tunesmiths as well as the songwriting 'factories' within New York's celebrated Brill Building and Nashville, the 'Hollywood' of country-and-western.

Coping with the more complex arrangements of other artists - some of them requiring more than one bass player - neither had the multi-faceted Jones any qualms about being at the disposal of Mickie Most, no longer South Africa's answer to Elvis Presley, but relocated to England as a freelance producer. Indeed, he had 'discovered' Dave Berry at a booking in Doncaster, and supervised a demo session for submission to Decca. Next, he secured hits for The Animals and The Nashville Teens. Then, with the highest calibre of London session players at his command, Most procured a rich crop of international chartbusters for Lulu, Donovan and, especially, Herman's Hermits - whose million-selling 'Silhouettes' was carried as much in its way by Jones'skilled bass pumping as Jimmy Page's invigorating lead guitar section.

Jimmy and John Paul were paid the standard session rate by Decca's accounts department for their contributions to 'Silhouettes' and other singles by this Manchester outfit fronted by Peter 'Herman' Noone. After their maiden 45, 'I'm Into Something Good', topped the domestic chart, it caught on in North America where little-boy-lost Noone could hardly fail at the apogee of the 'British Invasion'. Indeed, 'Hermania' plagued the continent throughout 1965 and 1966 as manifested by high *Hot 100* climbs for such as 'Silhouettes', 'Mrs. Brown You've Got A Lovely Daughter' and 'Listen People' before a predictable decline when new sensations arrived - notably The Monkees, four amenable fellows hired by a Hollywood business conglomerate to play an Anglo-American pop combo in a 1966 television series that was to be networked worldwide. They were also required to mime its musical interludes which would all be taken from discs on which - like Herman - they'd sung to accompaniment by the best session teams that money could buy.

Testaments to commercial pragmatism too were British-made discs by celebrities from non-pop fields who, however unmelodious their voices or dubious their abilities as composers or instrumentalists, hadn't been able to prevent themselves from immortalising their musical capabilities on disc. A combination of personal vanity and a desire to maximise public exposure has led to all manner of unlikely names appearing on records containing the two future members of Led Zeppelin.

Nevertheless, if first seen by the public at large as Len Fairclough's son in *Coronation Street*, 'Herman' Noone proved to be a capable enough pop star. Roger Moore and Bill 'Dr Finlay' Simpson, however, weren't so lucky with their respective singles. Neither was David McCallum of *The Man From U.N.C.L.E.* as apparent conductor of 1966's *Music...A Part Of Me* LP - an Andrew Oldham Orchestra-like exercise - though its 45, 'Communication' harried the lower reaches of the Top Fifty. Of like vintage was 'Kinky Boots' from Honor Blackman and Patrick McNee - but arriving too late was 1968's 'Flower Power Fred' by Harry H. Corbett in his 'Young Steptoe' character.

Lest we forget too, Jimmy Savile began as a wrestler before surfacing as the Swinging Sixties' most eye-stretching disc-jockey after his Decca recording contract expired. Further members of Equity who moved in on the beat boom included Lancastrian comedienne Dora Bryan with 'All I Want For Christmas Is A Beatle' and Peter Sellers with a cod-Shakespearian reading of 'A Hard Day's Night' - his first Top Twenty entry since 1961's 'Bangers And Mash' with Sophia Loren. Relevant to this account too is Michael Chaplin (son of Charlie) with his harmonica-led 'I Am What I Am' 45 of 1965.

Also among the hopeful, the hopeless and just plain starstruck for whom John Paul thrummed bass were Marc Bolan and Rod Stewart who were to come into their own - as Led Zeppelin did - in the 1970s. Neither seemed to have much going for them when, for instance, Bolan's second single, 'The Third Degree' made a depressing journey to the bargain bin, while Stewart arrived late at Decca's West Hampstead studio to record a number - direct from Denmark Street - with which he hadn't bothered to acquaint himself. However, largely through John Paul Jones'understanding of awkward talent, Stewart delivered a version of Sonny Boy Williamson's 'Good Morning Little Schoolgirl'[33] in his unmistakable rasping baritone.

It was to rival the faster 'surfing' arrangement of the same song by The Yardbirds, who, nevertheless, snatched the slight chart honours by spring 1965 when The Poets, a Glaswegian outfit in whom Andrew Loog Oldham was 'interested', followed up their only hit, 'Now We're Thru', with 'That's The Way It's Got To Be', which lived in a fat six-string bass sound, courtesy of John Paul Jones, who ministered likewise to further Poets A-sides such as 1966's 'Baby Don't You Do It', under the aegis of a certain Paul Raven, then *Ready Steady Go*'s 'warm-up' man, but destined to team up with Mike Leander and rule glam rock as 'Gary Glitter'.

Raven was at the end of his tether then as an entertainer, but John Paul Jones seemed outwardly content and prosperous as an indispensable backroom stable of an industry where he was becoming known too as a reliable keyboard player, and for more general abilities as an arranger since a commission in this respect on what started as a shambles of a session for 'Sunshine Superman' by Donovan, a Hertfordshire lad who'd landed the job when the hunt was up in 1965 for a British 'answer' to Bob Dylan. His recording career had commenced with two fast hits, 'Catch The Wind' and 'Colours', that presented him as a beatific, non-doctrinal Dylan. However, Donovan showed he had teeth with a best-selling EP that was accompanied by a promotional film featuring the title track, Buffy St. Marie's 'Universal Soldier', and shot on location in World War Two trenches, thus provoking image-enhancing letters of disgust to *The Times* from retired generals about this long-haired pacifist.

Before 1965 was out, however, Donovan had lost impetus in Britain - largely because of embarrassing publicity surrounding a drug bust; a long period spent in a proto-hippy commune on a Hebridean island, and, vitally, contractual difficulties that effectively put his domestic release schedule on hold for the best part of a year. However, with Mickie Most as producer, he came round again with a vengeance via 'Sunshine Superman' for which he sported a solid-body electric guitar on the TV pop series *Shindig* as it winged its way to Number One in the USA.[34]

'I happened to be on the "Sunshine Superman" session as a bass player,' recalled John Paul Jones, 'and the arranger they'd picked really didn't know about anything. I got the rhythm section together, and we went from there. Arranging and general studio direction were much better than just sitting there and being told what to do.'[35]

THE BLACKWATER SIDEMAN

*'There's an attitude of pseudo-professionalism that pervades
a lot of the entertainment unions - the syndrome where you
won't command respect unless you're totally disinterested in
the product they're working on. If you show interest, what are
you? A sissy? You've got to go back there and drink coffee with
the guys, screw the session. If there's two more bars of music to
record, and the contractor's watch goes to zero, that's it! And if
those two bars get played, it'll cost'* - Frank Zappa[36]

'You there! Guitarist!' crackled a Sandhurst-inflect-
ed voice from one metropolitan control room, 'Keep that up!
That's splendid!'

Jimmy Page, see, was using notes now with an economy
that had come from what was turning into years of three sessions a day every day, contructing his solos and riffs to integrate
with the melodic and lyrical intent of a given number. He could
play faster than most, but he preferred - in those days anyway -
not to clench his teeth and be super-flash over underlying chord
patterns. When it was necessary for him to get the blues, for example, his runs were like the contralto section of a melody, sad
in itself, but enhancing the sweetness of the whole. If handed a
basic part, he could make something of it without contributing
any stylistic individuality if it wasn't required.

Just as studio engineers would be directed over and over
again to reproduce the corrupted snare drum sound on David
Bowie's *Low* in the late 1970s, so session guitarists in the mid-
1960s were told to 'play like George Harrison'. Derided for
the publicity stunt it was, an allegation that The Beatles used a
substitute lead guitarist was made by an expatriate Texan singer
befriended by the group. He even named the changeling as
Jimmy Page. Although such practices have always been common
in pop, this suggestion can be refuted by documentary evidence
that Page must have been in two places at once if he did play on
Beatles tracks. Moreover, the lead picking on these are identical

to those on extant earlier Beatles recordings as demonstrated by the 'Til There Was You' on a Decca audition tape in January 1962 and the treatment on The Beatles first LP.[37]

Nevertheless, George Harrison would only continue to win polls as top guitarist only for as long as Eric Clapton, Jeff Beck, Alvin Lee, Stan Webb and other would-be virtuosi fermented hitless in the clubs. Yet, though 'wanted' ads for 'Clapton-type' guitarists were starting to appear in *Melody Maker*, Jimmy Page found himself called upon to emulate willingly the more attractively rough-hewn solos and riffs of Dick Taylor of The Pretty Things, say, or Dave Davies, the youngest Kink.

Producers and songwriters were further delighted with him because, though he pot-boiled the same as any other interchangeable musical technician, he was not cheese-paring about his services. Moreover, he wasn't self-depreciating about his understanding and love of pop, and couldn't be robbed of his humanity like the fourth-row violinist once witnessed yelling a maliciously gleeful 'Time's up!' in the middle of a final take, despite (or because of) sensing that it was make-or-break time for the artist concerned.

Page had none of that condescending sight-reading complacency that was the norm within that self-contained caste-within-a-caste of around twenty middle-aged middle-of-the-road musicians, who, though all good men and true, seemed to think that British pop couldn't be done in any other way or with any other players than those bound by the rigidity of Musicians Union officialdom and the 'but he's new' resentment whenever an alien element entered the equation.

This was the pervading attitude in the capital's principal studios when drummer Clem Cattini left The Tornados in 1965[38] and thus moved out of Joe Meek's orbit. Within a fortnight, a Decca single, 'No Time To Think' - B-sided by an opus entitled 'Goodbye Joe' - by The Clem Cattini Ork had been taped under the supervision of Larry Page, still clinging on as manager of the mercurial Kinks, for whom Cattini 'did loads of work, but I can't recall actual titles'.

On the boards, he presided over Division Two, a unit assembled to back The Ivy League, the close-harmony trio who were then at the pinnacle of their fame, but still available for session work and composing commissions. Clem believed that 'doing demos for them and the rest of the Denmark Street songwriters got my session career off the runway, because next I started getting calls asking if I'd played on such-and-such a demo, and could I do it again on the master? Few musicians I worked with knew I'd been a Tornado as I never used to talk about it. Maybe it was an inferiority complex, what with my background as as rock 'n' roll hooligan, and them being hardened jazzers from the Academy of Music or whatever. I came from a completely different school. I'd learnt my trade on the A1, A6 and A5. However, it was a case of sink or swim. I had to teach myself to read percussion music in a hurry.'

Another relative newcomer had been Bobbie Graham, once in Joe Brown's backing Bruvvers, who, likewise, favoured 'feel' rather than scoring. He recognised a kindred spirit in Jimmy Page, who only learnt to sight-read after Big Jim Sullivan noticed him struggling at a session, and offered to teach him the basic principals, thus beginning an amity akin to that of a liberal-minded teacher and a waywardly earnest pupil. 'Jimmy and Big Jim were brilliant together,' observed Bobbie Graham, 'Big Jim was more precise, but Jimmy had this wonderful dirty sound.[39]

Like Graham, Page's opinion had come to be valued by certain producers, songwriters and other record business folk for whom he acted as a semi-official capacity as a talent scout - and more - as he did during the 'British Invasion' of the US pop charts when many North American entrepreneurs, anticipating further demand for Limey talent, crossed the Atlantic in person to stake claims in the musical diggings.

Among them was Kentucky-born Jackie de Shannon, a house songwriter in a Los Angeles publishing company, who, like Jimmy, Glyn Johns, and The Ivy League, took pot-shots at the charts herself. In 1964, while she had yet to score as big hit of her own, she was on the crest of a wave by proxy with her

'When You Walk In The Room' smash for The Searchers, and was on the lookout for further vehicles for her compositions. During a visit to London, she was squired by Jimmy Page, with whom she penned songs for Marianne Faithfull and P.J. Proby. Jackie also contributed backing vocals to 'Keep Movin', B-side of 'She Just Satisfies'.

Through Jimmy too, she'd heard glowing reports about The Paramounts - a Southend outfit from which would evolve Procol Harum - and The Hellions, whom he'd encountered when helping out on a recording by Raynor's Secrets, another four-piece from their native Worcester. Astute enough to recognise the weathered professionalism of both The Hellions and The Paramounts, Jackie promised each an A-side. However, both The Paramounts' 'Blue Ribbons' and 'Daydreaming Of You' by The Hellions failed badly to repeat the 'When You Walk In The Room' miracle, and Jackie, her romance with Page over too, returned to California to resume her singing career.[40]

To some it was inconceivable that one such as Jackie had had an affair with Jimmy in his perpetual navy-blue donkey-jacket and 'very dull in those days,' opined Marianne Faithfull, 'Jackie was born interesting. She was brassy, a bit tarty and naturally very beautiful, but she had her hair all frizzed up and she wore tons of make-up. You could see from the moment you met her she had been distorted and thwarted by showbiz - like a beautiful woman who'd been forced into a corset and twisted.'[41]

Jimmy was only too pleased to help Jackie's best friend, Sharon Sheeley as well. To the man-in-the-street, she is most renowned for being pulled from the same Wiltshire car crash that killed boyfriend Eddie Cochran in 1960. Yet, following Ricky Nelson's million-seller with her 'Poor Little Fool' in 1957, Sharon amassed a formidable reputation as a hit writer. Furthermore, when Cochran and Gene Vincent appeared on the ITV pop magazine *Boy Meets Girls* during that fateful 1960 tour, Sheeley attracted the attention of producer Jack Good. At his urging, Decca offered her a contract as a vocalist, but 'Homework', a single taped immediately in London, was never issued.

During further working visits to Europe in the mid-1960s, Sheeley plyed wares co-written with de Shannon, which were recorded in London with not the usual people - apart from Jimmy Page - but Jeff Beck and less enduring assistants such as Chris Curtis, drummer with The Searchers, who, along with Irma Thomas, Sandie Shaw and Brenda Lee, were among the more famous acts that recorded Sheeley-de Shannon material during the 1960s.[42]

Outside the context of work, Jimmy had taken Jackie and Sharon to a recital by two of his favourite guitarists, Bert Jansch and John Renbourn. The latter was one of a surprising number of later famous axemen with roots in English art schools. At Kingston College - where *sarf* London collides with genteel Surrey - he'd been casually knowledgeable about the folk and blues bedrock that lay beneath skiffle's chewing gum-flavoured topsoil.

'The R&B craze had replaced skiffle, and the best band was considered to be Alexis Korner's Blues Incorporated,' recollected John, 'I played in an Art School R&B band for a while, Hogsnort Rupert's Famous Porkestra, using a borrowed electric guitar. I found that some of the band's riffs sounded interesting played fingerstyle on an acoustic.'

From Redhill in the same part of Surrey, grammar schoolgirl Jacqui McShee had become a leading figure in the Home Counties folk scene, backed by a guitarist named Chris Ayliffe. Running in the same pack was Hounslow's Sandy Denny, who was to both replace Fairport Convention's original *chanteuse,* Judy Dyble, and duet with Robert Plant on a Led Zeppelin opus, 1971's 'The Battle Of Evermore'. Among her credentials was guesting on a 1965 album by Scottish singing guitarist Alex Campbell. Her version of his best-known composition, long-faced 'Been On The Road So Long' was covered by Bert Jansch during Campbell's optimum artistic period in the mid- to late 1960s. While the likes of 'I'm A Rover' and 'The Water Is Wide' were the common property of countless other folk performers, how many of these first latched onto them via the Alex Campbell blueprint?

Further stalwarts of the British folk club circuit known to Jimmy Page were Ralph McTell, Mick Softley, Jon Mark and Wizz Jones who, like John Renbourn, were 'all in awe of Davey Graham'. While his singing didn't match his playing, Graham had made 1962's *The Guitar Player*, an LP of insidious impact for its finger-picked reconciliation of jazz, folk, blues with an occasional breath of the Orient - and baroque too. Some of his disciples were awaiting similar destinies as folk club behemoths - and recording artists.

In 1965, twenty-one-year-old Renbourn's time came as accompanist on blues singer Dorris Henderson's maiden LP, *There You Go*, and with an eponymous album in his own right: 'I was using an English dance band guitar - a Scarth - something of an oddity with maple back and sides, arched top, round soundhole and tailpiece. It had its little idiosyncracies: the action went up and down according to the weather, which could be counteracted by wedging a lollipop stick under the neck. It served me well - featuring on the cover of *John Renbourn* (in the traditional folk-singer-on-the-rubbish-dump pose), and on two albums with Dorris as well as the first tracks with Bert Jansch'.

Both together and apart, Renbourn and Jansch, his sometime flatmate, had emerged swiftly as attractions at folk venues, prompting brisk sales of their jazzy 1966 LP, *Bert And John*. 'The domestic record companies were getting interested in what was going on in the world of "folk",' explained Renbourn, 'Transatlantic Records used to send out their engineer with an Ampex to capture the "authentic" sounds on location in deepest south London. *Bert And John* was recorded that way - with blankets tacked up in the hallway to keep out the noise of our neighbours. When *Bert And John* came to be released on CD, one of the selling points was the "vintage" sound.'

Another was the decorative and interlocking virtuosity. 'John and Bert both had huge followings of the kind of guitar enthusiast who'd sit in the front row, watching their fingers,' observed Jacqui McShee.

'Eric Clapton was often there,' added Wizz Jones, 'when Bert and John played at the Olive Tree in Croydon'.[43] Another onlooker was George Harrison, who took particular note of the Eastern influences that were more than a trace element of Renbourn's style - betraying evidence itself of hard listening to both the eclectic Davey Graham and, to a smaller degree, John Mayer's Indo-Jazz Fusions and the 'trance jazz' of guitarist Gabor Szabo, whose LPs contained titles such as 'Search For Nirvana', 'Krishna' and 'Ravi'.

The last was a *salaam* to Ravi Shankar, a sitarist who, in 1965, recorded an album that his record company released as *Portrait Of Genius* during his seventh world tour as one of India's leading cultural ambassadors until his profile was sharpened by the interest of The Beatles. There would follow, as Ravi himself puts it, 'a sitar explosion. All of a sudden, I become superstar' (*sic*).[44]

Adjectives like 'shimmering', 'caressing' and 'atmospheric' spring to mind as well as the notion that one individual's response to Oriental classical music may be markedly different to another's - for, not meant to 'go anywhere', the sound at any given moment matters more than individual pieces, and an air of spontaneity combined with an undynamic repose akin to Gregorian chant means that some will find it hypnotic while others may be bored stiff.[45]

Big Jim Sullivan belonged to the former category, having purchased a sitar in 1964 after listening in on a session by Indian musicians at EMI's Abbey Road complex. It was to feature on an exotic arrangement of 'She Moved Through The Fair', a traditional folk melody, a 1965 single by The Jim Sullivan Sound.

It was however, *Portrait Of Genius*, when recommended by John Renbourn, that turned Jimmy Page onto Indian music. He also logged 'Blackwater Side' from Bert Jansch's 1966 album, *Jack Orion*, for arrangement for tabla and acoustic guitar on the first Led Zeppelin album, and was to cite Renbourn and Jansch's 'She Moved Through The Fair' rather than that by The Jim Sullivan Sound as the inspiration for 'White Summer', a showstopper when he joined The Yardbirds in 1966.

As, say, Them and The Equals are recalled respectively as Van Morrison's and Eddy Grant's old groups, so most consumers of today's cultured 'contemporary' pop for the over-forties have taught their children to regard The Yardbirds as less combined figureheads and *eminences grises* of 1960s pop than a springboard for the nurtured prowess and neo-deification of its successive 'guitar heroes', Eric 'God' Clapton, Jeff Beck - and Jimmy Page.

While the over-attention paid to Clapton, Beck and Page contributed to the group's self-destruction, their varying degrees of whimsical fretboard elasticity, masterful technique and outright craziness were *among* ingredients that transformed The Yardbirds from a Home Counties blues appreciation society to the point where even Simon Napier-Bell, a disgruntled former manager, found it in him to admit in an otherwise waspish 1982 autobiography, that 'there were four rock bands in the world that really counted, and The Yardbirds was one of them'.[46]

Initially, the ceiling of The Yardbirds' ambition had been modest. Record sessions had evolved into attempts to reproduce ethnic gutbucket blues on guitars and self-conscious voices. Amused by the memory, general factotum Chris Dreja recollected that 'I'd taught himself boogie-woogie piano on the family upright, but I bought an acoustic guitar for five shillings from a local pawn shop. The strings were about an inch off the fretboard, but it gave me incredible strength and steadiness in my left hand. My best friend, Tony 'Top' Topham's dad had all these great import blues records - Blind Lemon Jefferson, Robert Johnson... They kept me awake for days on end, just thinking about them - and I went ballistic when I heard the electric

sounds of Jimmy Reed. That was probably what shaped me forever - and partly what shaped The Yardbirds too because one of
the group's virtues was the amazing energy, the 'rave-ups' - that
we could never get onto tape. It came from the heart and my excitement with the music.

'I'd bring my guitar into school or skive off to Bell's
Music Shop in Surbiton where they had electric models. I was
eventually able to buy a fifteen-watt Vox and a solid-body Watkins Rapier - terrible instrument, but it looked flash enough for
Eric Clapton to borrow so that he could pose in front of the mirror with it.'

The first line-up of The Yardbirds smouldered into form,
circa 1962, with singing mouth-organist Keith Relf, drummer
Jim McCarty, Paul Samwell-Smith on - eventually - bass and
guitarists Dreja and Topham.

The five clung onto their day jobs and college courses
whilst delivering souped-up R&B in bohemian haunts around
the western edge of Greater London. Nevertheless, when student Top Topham's double life burnt the candle to the middle
in 1963, it was The Yardbirds that had to be sacrificed in the
interests of higher education. He was replaced as lead guitarist by the older Eric Clapton, nicknamed 'Slowhand' in those
days, and late of The Engineers, accompanists to Casey Jones,
a vocalist with a potentially breadwinning Scouse accent and a
one-shot single, 'One Way Ticket'. Clapton was no more elo-
quent an instrumentalist than Topham, but possessed stronger
stage presence.

As The Rolling Stones had pushed R&B-derived pop
into the hit parade, The Yardbirds were well placed to do likewise. Signed to an EMI subsidiary, their debut single, 'I Wish
You Would' sold well over a long period without actually cracking the charts - and it began a life long devotion to the group
by Richard MacKay, then an Isle of Thanet schoolboy: 'From
the moment I heard 'I Wish You Would' in 1964, I was hooked.
Every release from that point on was totally different from the

one before. This I admired as they were obviously not follow-ing the latest trends: they were setting them! Also, Eric Clapton, Jeff Beck and Jimmy Page were the best guitarists around.'

A second 45, that 'surfing' revival of 'Good Morning Little Schoolgirl', gained a toehold on the Top 50 in Octo-ber 1964 - and may have risen higher had not Keith Relf been laid low for several weeks with a collapsed lung. He was fit enough, however, for late 1964's rough-and-ready but atmos-pheric *Five Live Yardbirds* LP with himself and Eric at the forefront of the open-ended 'rave ups' that ran a gauntlet of all roots and branches of urban blues from North America.

THE LISTENER

'Not all of it was great, but all of it was worth it' -
Robert Plant's sleeve notes to his *Sixty-Six To Timbuktu* CD
retrospective

In spring 1964, The Yardbirds had landed a job accompanying charismatic Mississippi delta legend Sonny Boy Williamson[33], bowler-hatted and vulture-like in posture, on the majority of dates when he headed a bill of native attractions during
a visit to Britain. This had been organised by the British Jazz
Federation's Georgio Gomelsky, who also happened then to be
The Yardbirds' manager.

Unusually, the highlight of this expedition wasn't anywhere in London, but Birmingham Town Hall, an evening captured on tape for release many years later after it had gained
cultural (and financial) importance. The show's co-promoter
was Brian Allen, who had also been the brains behind what regional pop journal *Midland Beat* reported as 'the unusual sight
of prominent modern jazz instrumentalists playing alongside
members of The Renegades and other beat exponents'[47] during
a foggy October Monday in 1963. Thanks to Brian, rhythm-and-
blues had come to Birmingham in the form of the Rhythm Un-
limited weekly club, which complemented the Wednesday jazz
sessions within the art deco interior of Birmingham's Golden
Eagle pub in Hill Street, beneath the shadow of the Town Hall.

Next, Allen needed little persuasion from Gomelsky that
an evening of the stuff at the Town Hall on the following Friday, 28 February would more than cover costs. Thus, from the
revolving stage on that night of nights, master of ceremonies
Bob Wooler - imported from Liverpool's Cavern - completed
a mahogany-toned build-up. With 'a very big responsibility to
launch this sound on your eardrums', the first act on were 'at a
sort of turning point in their career because they have decided
that, following the show tonight, they will turn pro' (*like all the
other poor sods*) 'and we'll have them on the television screens
and nationwide tours' (*some hope*).

The Spencer Davis Rhythm-and-blues Quartet's brief spot enabled Gomelsky and his engineers to adjust the public address system levels, the better to tape on his fancy Ampex reel-to-reel the more important artists who would be coming on later. Sending Georgio's recording level off the dial would be 'the powerful rocking singing of young Rod Stuart' (*sic*) of Long John Baldry's All-Stars, who was to trouble the world further into the decade and beyond.[48]

Rod Stewart and the Quartet's two lead singers - Steve Winwood and Davis himself - were to share a microphone on the assembled cast's 'I Got My Mojo Working' finale after pedantic, repulsive old Sonny Boy's recital had climaxed with 'harmonica contortions in which he even played the instrument with his nose'.[49]

Watching from the rabble was seventeen-year-old Robert Anthony Plant. He had blown in from Kidderminster, a satellite of Birmingham and so famous for its carpets that there was a Department of Carpet Technology at its local college of further education. Then a business studies student there, Robert would be among those picking up the pieces when The Yardbirds fragmented in an unimaginable tomorrow, but for the present, he was known to Dave Hill, then guitarist with Johnny Travell and the Vendors, only as 'a local Mod with very short hair.'

When Sonny Boy Williamson's bass harmonica was stolen afterwards, Plant was a chief suspect. Presumably, the most opportune moment for larceny arrived when a caretaker, anxious to lock up, pulled the main electricity switch because all that terrible racket had over-run for half-an-hour, and degenerated into 'a late-night Twist session'[49] - 'late' in that innocent era meaning 9.30pm - 'and we are left asking, "When is the next R and B festival?"'[49]

Entranced, Robert Plant vanished into the night, lost in wonder and now fully-formed ambition. He'd become aware of the blues via Elvis Presley - and a wild dream then was to come true eight years later when, via Jerry Weintraub, concert promoter for both Presley and the record-breaking Led Zeppelin, Robert and his colleagues were introduced to the King in a Las

Vegas hotel. Elvis, it seemed, wanted to 'meet the guys who are outselling me.' He received them like deified Caesar had the Gallic peasants. There was some fidgeting and poker-faced glances at one another, but an awestruck silence was broken, apparently, when Plant expressed his admiration of Presley's gold and diamond watch - which Elvis swapped for John Paul Jones'Mickey Mouse one.

Plant was to pay vinyl respects to the late Presley on a 1984 EP - extended play - *Honeydrippers Volume One*, even though, shortly after the Las Vegas encounter, Elvis, in an astounding and ramblingly respectful letter to President Nixon, had asked to be enrolled as a Federal Agent in order to combat 'the Hippie Element' of which he considered Led Zeppelin part. Furthermore, both on tour and on disc, he was prone to sung bursts of patriotism like 'American Trilogy' and just plain 'America', some taped in grandiloquent but self-indulgent cabaret pageants where the last most people would ever see of him would be in the white garb of a rhinestoned cowboy *sans* stetson.

Yet, if Elvis Presley had shed most of his artistic load by 1960, he'd left such an ineradicable impression on fans like Robert Plant - and, generally, the complacency of post-war pop that his own later capitulation to it was dismissed initially as the prerogative of glamour. Though the world has since become wiser to his failings, his omnipotence remains such that veneration has yet to fade for countless fans in a languid daze from the fixity of gazing - figuratively anyway - at the bolted gates of his Gracelands mansion. For them, the King - who would have been seventy-one in 2006 - still rules from the grave.

Though blues - later, rhythm-and-blues - and country-and-western were his principal stylistic determination in the beginning, he drew too from light opera, folk song and like Chuck Berry, all manner of trace elements in North America's musical spectrum: gospel, bluegrass, showbiz evergreens, Zydeco, vaudeville, Appalachian, and jazz, particularly, the orchestral euphoria of Count Basie; Ted Daffan and his Texans' Western Swing ('hillbilly jazz'), and the vocal daredevilry of such as Anita O'Day and Frank Sinatra.

As Robert Plant was to discover, more explicit precedents may be heard in particular records. Examples include Hank Williams' 'Move It On Over', 'Boogie Woogie Bugle Boy' by The Andrews Sisters and, more obviously, Roy Brown's 'Good Rockin' Tonight' from 1947 plus any number of gutbucket Mississippi and Chicago blues offerings. Nevertheless, with its cowpoke pessimism, C&W was no more or less than white man's blues. The incorporation of blues into the stylistic *oeuvres* of C&W giants such as Jimmie Rodgers and Hank Williams was exemplified by vocals couched in rural black imagery and phrasing, an unusual preoccupation with rhythm, and an ineludable commitment to the spirit of their songs - and it was when contents of black and white music merged that Elvis Presley was able to advance beyond local popularity.

He was preceded by Oregon's Johnnie Ray, 'The Prince Of Wails', whose melodramatic onstage exhibitionism was derived from black R&B. A pivotal onstage moment during a Ray performance was when he lurched into his cover of Clyde McPhatter and the Drifters' 'Such A Night.' Such a whitewashing of an R&B hit for the mainstream pop charts was anticipated - even welcomed - by black recording acts of the early 1950s as it brought their music, if not their performances of it, to a parallel dimension of teenage consumers with money to waste.

In the mid-1950s, some unadulterated R&B crept into the *Billboard Hot 100* pop charts, notably in the sly lyricism of Chuck Berry and Fats Domino's ambulatory lope. Though it, like Chuck Berry's 'Maybelline', owed as much to C&W for all its springing from a blues environment, some presenters weren't keen on scheduling such a racially-integrated disc as Presley's first release - a jumped-up treatment of 'That's All Right' by black blues artist Arthur Crudup - and, equating with Led Zeppelin and Howlin' Wolf's 'How Many More Years' decades later, it would be pleasant to think that Arthur's composition of this opus will benefit his descendants because the fellow himself earned little from it.

The Presley version rose high in the US country-and-western chart. Further smashes with similar material ensured that he was both loathed and adored throughout the South. Everyone was talking about Elvis. The rest, as they often say, is history. As it would over The Rolling Stones, The Sex Pistols and the attendant stylised delinquency in succeeding decades, so adult blood had run cold at Presley and the many other 'rockabilly' entertainers who flowered in his wake. Yet, in a nonplus of repellent fascination, many teenagers were just as aghast as their parents - because rearing up before them was everything that their upbringing had taught them to both despise and fear. He didn't appear to care how badly he behaved - breaking guitar strings, spitting out chewing gum, swivelling his hips in a rude way, doing the splits, knee-dropping and crawling to the edge of the stage.

As the first photograph of him published in Britain depicted - in *Record Mirror* on 21 January 1956 - he was a hybrid of amusement arcade hoodlum and nancy boy. Indeed, Presley's dress sense and hair style were as much of an issue as his shout-singing; his girly cockage and 'cat' clothes at odds with sideburns to the earlobes, and the hetero-erotic truculence in concerts. In a time-honoured ritual of thwarted eroticism, an entranced Robert Plant - still in short trousers - placed Elvis' 1956 winter chartbuster, 'Hound Dog', on the record player in his bedroom, and arranged himself in front of the wardrobe mirror. From the opening line to the coda, he curled his lip and pretended to slash chords and pick solos with negligent ease. He flicked back his quiff - which was soon to be trimmed at his mother's behest - and mouthed the lyrics to thousands of ecstatic females that only he could see. Yet, when not miming, he discovered that 'Hound Dog' could be filtered through his own lithe, full-throated - and quite serviceable - lament.

Such episodes would be supplemented by his delving as far as he was able beneath the showbusiness veneer of Elvis and other rock 'n' rollers he admired to its nitty-gritty. The adolescent Plant wasn't that far removed from an obsessed supporter of Wolverhampton Wanderers. He was taking a blues fixation in particular so far that he cared no more about how others may have mocked it than a chimp in the zoo does about what the public peering through the bars thinks about its antics. He acquired Paul Oliver's *Blues Fell This Morning*, then a standard work[50], as soon as it was published in 1960, turning to it as a monk to the Bible. Working his way through as much of its bibliography that could be ordered from the library, and fanning out to erudite tomes concerning, say, plantation field hollers and the African roots of blues.

Almost as if he was embroiled in formal research, Robert catalogued, filed and gloated over his growing collection of vinyl treasures, finding much to study, notice and compare in sleeve notes, composer credits and so forth. Hardly any piece of information was too insignificant to be less than completely absorbing in the weekly music press either, especially *Melody Maker*, which covered jazz and blues as well as mainstream pop. He also discovered that many blues recordings could be purchased at import prices from a specialist shop off Gunmakers Walk near a Birmingham district known as Soho, much like its London namesake.

On instant replay for weeks at a time was Robert's dog-eared *Folk Blues Of John Lee Hooker* album, eventually issued in Britain in 1962. With a less lackadaisical regard for business than Arthur Crudup, an older contemporary, Hooker's career had taken off in the late 1940s with 'I'm In The Mood' and 'Boogie Chillun', million-sellers in the 'sepia' charts of *Billboard*, the US music business periodical, but meaning nothing in the parallel dimensions of 'popular' and 'country-and-western'. His biographical credentials as a bluesman were impeccable. An upbringing in Clarksville, the rural Mississippi birthplace of the legendary Robert Johnson - was followed by an adolescence spent in Memphis. Next came migration north, purchase of an electric guitar and discovery by a record company talent scout during a club residency in Black Bottom, a Detroit suburb.

After his initial brace of hits, Hooker made his US television debut in 1949 as further specialist smashes such as 'Driftin', 'Hobo Blues', 'Crawling King Snake' and a re-make of 'I'm In The Mood' established him as a major blues exponent. As such he was recognised by British bandleader Chris Barber who underwrote British tours by Hooker and other of his black contemporaries who found favour with white bohemia.

During his British visits in the early 1960s, he was often backed - as Sonny Boy Williamson was - by one of myriad native rhythm-and-blues outfits he had inspired. Among these was The Spencer Davis Group whose 1963 single, Hooker's 'Dimples', was vanquished when the original was issued to reach the British Top Thirty. In versions of 'Boom Boom', 'I'm Mad Again' and like examples of John Lee's gutbucket hollering and eccentric rhythmic shifts, The Animals, The Yardbirds, Them and other groups paid their respects too - as they did to Howlin' Wolf, possessor of the most bestial voice in pop.

Principal among Wolf's own influences throughout a Mississippi delta boyhood were those of brother-in-law Sonny Boy Williamson - the one who slew 'em at Birmingham Town Hall - who taught Wolf to play harmonica, and singing guitarist Charlie Patton. On moving to Arkansas in 1948, Wolf became a full-time musician, backed by one of the first electric blues bands in the Deep South.

In the early 1950s, he was spotted by Ike Turner, then a freelance talent scout for the West Coast record company for whom Wolf first recorded. More crucial, however, were the tracks he taped at Sam Phillips' Sun studio. These were then sold to Chess in Chicago where Wolf migrated in 1952.

Though the Windy City left an indelible mark on his style, Wolf would never renege on his rural roots as he entered the most commercially fruitful chapter of his career. Composed either by himself or bass player Willie Dixon, many of the singles he released up to 1964 would surface as set works for white artists as varied as The Rolling Stones (with chart-topping 'Little Red Rooster'), The Doors ('Backdoor Man'), Canned Heat ('Spoonful' - not the Patton song of the same title) and Electric Flag ('Killing Floor').

After visiting England in the early 1960s as part of an American Folk-Blues Festival package, the burly Wolf was feted by middle class bohemians for a stage act of sweaty intensity and earthy sexual braggadocio. A re-issue of his eight-year-old 'Smokestack Lightning' standard even made the UK chart's lower reaches in 1964. As it also penetrated the repertoires of The Yardbirds and Manfred Mann, so 'Sitting On Top Of The World', 'I Ain't Superstitious', 'How Many More Years' and other Wolf items were interpreted by later British outfits such as The Jeff Beck Group, Love Sculpture, Cream, Led Zeppelin, Ten Years After and Savoy Brown.

While an admirer of Howlin' Wolf as much as he was of John Lee Hooker, Robert Plant had been captivated too by the grippingly personal styles of post-war country bluesmen like Snooks Eaglin, Lightnin' Hopkins, Bukka White, Tommy McClennan and Peetie Wheatstraw, toast of Louisville's red-light quarter, who named himself at various times 'the Devil's Son-in-Law' and 'the High Sheriff of Hell'. Plant was, however, more obsessively fond of Robert Johnson, who inspired 'Walking Into Clarksdale', a post-Led Zeppelin collaboration with Jimmy Page. Thanks in part to revivals of his songs by such as Cream, The Rolling Stones and the late Jo Ann Kelly, critical awareness and reassessment of Johnson, despite his early death, resulted in some noted pop pundits - like Charles Shaar Murray - regarding him as possibly the greatest musician ever to walk the planet. I wouldn't go that far, but I would applaud Robert Plant as a serious student of the blues, going first and last to Robert Johnson.

Prior to joining the Beatles, Ringo Starr had considered emigrating to Texas because it was the stamping ground of Lightnin' Hopkins to whom the drummer had been introduced by an enthralled Tony Sheridan. A victim of a similar passion for Robert Johnson, Plant undertook a pilgrimage to Clarksdale in an attempt to trace a surviving acquaintance of the Great Man. He was driven to knocking on doors almost at random. 'I've never been so ridiculous in my life,' smiled Robert, 'When I was at school, I had a paper round to earn money, and I bought the original first Robert Johnson album with the gatefold sleeve and a picture of a sharecropper's shack on the front. When I heard "Preaching Blues" and "Last Fair Deal Gone Down", I was probably a year or two behind Keith Richards and Mick Jagger, but I went, "This is it!"'[51]

Robert's recreational interpretation of blues, however, was less narrow than outsiders may have imagined. It extended from the rural exorcisms of Johnson to the badlands of rock 'n' roll and soul, as exemplified by The Miracles' 'Shop Around' - the first record he ever bought - and Chris Kenner's 'I Like It Like That', an eternal favourite. He was to express an especial - and probably ironical - fondness for a form of rhythm-and-blues that evolved from fellows vocalising for their own entertainment on street corners across the post-war USA. Generally, the harmonies that resulted were bracketed by falsetto and deep bass, and had a preoccupation with lyrics that, ostensibly, were directed more towards the 'nice' boy 'saving himself' for his future bride than the pimpled fumbler of a 'cheap' girl's bra-strap.

For youths like Plant, The Mothers Of Invention's *Cruising With Ruben And The Jets*, a parody of the style over an entire 1968 album[52], was to be a novel experience, partly because the - usually black - music that influenced it had never caught on in Europe. Thus prompted to investigate compilations and even the original pressings of the genuine articles, Plant would find much to intrigue - like the almost inaudible lone guitar behind The Orioles' funereal 'It's Too Soon To Know'; the subtle entry and exit of a sax in sublime 'Red Sails In The Sunset' by The Five Keys; also in 1952, Edgar Myles of The Shaweez weeping noisily during the coda of 'No-One To Love Me'; some dingbat going 'bap-bap-bap-bap' every few bars in 'Is It Too Late' by

The Fidelitones, and a counter-tenor singing sharp so often in 1954's 'Chimes' by The Pelicans that he became convinced that it was deliberate.

When a pupil at Stourbridge Grammar School, Plant had been performing himself with a group named Andy Long and his Original Jaymen - to which his parents had nurtured a sort of neutral malevolence. After he'd come to terms with it, Robert would reconjure how his father - also a Robert - had 'cut the plug off my record player, a little Dansette, after they heard "I Like It Like That" seventeen times in one hour. It was a rocky journey with my parents. They just didn't understand it at all, any of it. In the beginning, they thought that it would pass.'[51]

Relaxing over, say, an after-dinner crossword in quiet cardigan and baggy trousers, Mr. Plant, a civil engineer, couldn't comprehend what his son found so loathsome about a decent life in an old market town - well, the upmarket and village-like Hayley Green suburb where his family lived - that tended to exhibit a certain insular superiority towards its big city neighbour, aligning itself more with Wales, whose forested marches were only an eight-mile hike away, and the West Country. What did Robert find so objectionable about a true gentleman's name appearing in the *Kidderminster Times* only on the occasions of his birth, baptism, marriage and when he shuffled off this mortal coil?

This was the heartland of a strait-laced Britain that was to oblige Billy Fury to moderate his Presley-esque gyrations. Moreover, burghers in Gloucester, less than thirty miles south, were to bar The Sapphires, an Evesham-based pop group, from ever defiling its Guild Hall again because lead vocalist Rodney Dawes' trousers were deemed 'crude' round the thighs and crotch.

Every effort by his parents to nip in the bud anything similarly untoward in Robert Plant would be in vain. You only had to look at him to see what he was like. Take when he started growing his hair perhaps an inch or so beyond the short-back-and-sides that marked sobriety and masculinity. Then there was his rejection of dictates about what and wasn't 'nice' music. At best a passion for pop would bring puffy smiles to the lips of the most open-minded do-gooders in cardigans, who presided over botany, charity work, the great outdoors and further hearty pastimes intended to distract young minds from what Lord Baden-Powell described in *Scouting For Boys* as 'the secret sin of beastliness'.[53]

The atmosphere in the Plant home intensified even when Robert started a busness studies course at Kidderminster College. Although he was socialising with bohemians from Stourbridge Art School, there was little as yet to indicate vocational possibilities for him other than in secure desk-bound jobs. Any attempts to discuss a different future with mum and dad proved pointless. Variations on the same theme of prevarication would just come up over and over again, and end, as likely as not, with a blazing row, bringing to the fore not only how contemptible they considered his aspirations might be, but whether he had any that could be taken seriously. How could you take seriously anyone with hair like his?

From a nearby neighbourhood, Walsall, the mother and father of Neville 'Noddy' Holder, a fellow two years Robert's senior, encouraged their only child's activities with a zeal that Mr. and Mrs. Plant might have thought excessive to the point of insanity, but then, unlike the nicely-spoken Plants, that brood spoke in an intonation that many regard as the vilest in the English language. Yet, while a Royal Shakespeare Company director might baulk at casting a Walsall-accented actor in the male lead of *Romeo And Juliet* ('Saft! Wot loight on yonduh windaw braiks...'), there is no finer way of saying 'you daft bastard'.

Mr. and Mrs. Holder supported with relative vivacity, therefore, every more glamorous ambition that their Neville had beyond dwelling until the grave in the lugubrious suburb where both he and they had been raised. In 1966, when Noddy had just left a group called Steve Brett and the Mavericks, and was waiting for opportunity to knock in another parochial outfit, The 'N Betweens - in which the line-up of 1970s hitmakers Slade found each other - he was to serve Listen, one of Robert Plant's later groups, which contained two of Holder's school friends, as a road manager.

Groups containing both Plant and Holder surfaced as regularly as rocks in the stream in *Midland Beat*, launched in October 1963 and modelled on Bill Harry's celebrated *Mersey Beat*. It also chronicled the grassroots struggles of other beat groups from whence would spring the industrious pragmatism of the Rockin' Berries; The Moody Blues' initial home-made passion, and the nascent vision of The Move. Furthermore, individuals in such groups might have racked up heftier achievements since but many locals had caught them mastering their assorted crafts in the pre-Merseybeat likes of Mike Sheridan and the Nightriders, Gerry Levene and the Avengers, Johnny Neal and the Starliners, Danny King and his Mayfair Set - and Keith Powell and the Valets who would metamorphose into Carl Wayne and the Vikings after their first three singles lead to a transfer from EMI to Pye - and a sundering whereby Powell commenced a solo career, and Wayne - featured singer whenever Keith's voice needed a rest - assumed command of The Valets, and renamed them.

If respected - even adored - in the West Midlands, none of these somebody-and-the-somebodies acts were able to brag that they'd legitimately Made It, without resorting to logical blindness and retiming of the truth when questioned in the pages of *Midland Beat*. Its editor was a Dennis Detheridge, who operated from an office overlooking playing fields in Moseley. That such a sixpenny gazette had to reprint after selling out within hours demonstrated a strength of demand for its 'complete coverage of the Midlands Beat and jazz scene'.[47] The main feature of the first edition, however, was an interview with John Lennon 'one of The Beatles', but 'otherwise the entire content is restricted to Midlands items' for, according to Detheridge, 'Liverpool started the ball rolling. Now the Midlands is ready to take over.'[47]

Yet December's frustrated editorial was to cry, 'Why has the Brum Beat failed to gain a place in the Top Twenty.'[54] Perhaps it was because Detheridge had overestimated the cohesion and depth of the region's pop scene. His was an easy mistake. After all, dozens of beat groups - most less than a year old - infested every borough, many bending over backwards in their hyperbole. The best of them tended to be derivative if competent - for reputations were won by duplicating Top Twenty favourites in the Carlton, the West Bromich Adelphi and like ballrooms which provided a link between youth club bashes and contracts with leisure corporations like Top Rank or Jaycee.

Right up to the final edition in August 1967, the *Midland Beat* reader could select a night out from a vast array of local jive hives because, for hot Midlands combos who failed to gain a recording contract, let alone breach the charts, there was consolation in the guarantee of a full workload within easy reach, and recurring dates within a *Midland Beat* circulation area defined roughly as mid-Wales to East Anglia, Derby to as far south as Beaconsfield, home of the imaginatively-named Beaconsfield R&B Group, namechecked in issue number nine.

Into the bargain, the BBC Light Programme's two-hour pop show, *Saturday Club*, was recorded in Birmingham and broadcast nationally, as were dozens of ITV programmes via Sutton Coldfield's transmitter, the first to be built outside London. The jewel in ITV's pop crown was *Thank Your Lucky Stars* but also showcasing pop were *For Teenagers Only* - on which Noddy Holder made his televisual debut as one of Steve Brett's Mavericks - *Pop Shop, Midlands At Six* and, at the bitter end, *Lunch Box* - hosted by Noele Gordon, then awaiting her fate as *Crossroads grande dame*.

Avid surveyors of the hit parade, some groups and their devotees were elated when, spurred on by scattered spins on the Light Programme and Radio Luxembourg, the odd single began a yo-yo progression into the lower reaches of the Top Fifty. The Marauders had lived up to *Midland Beat*'s 'Pride Of The

Potteries' citation by thus irritating the charts in August 1963 with their Decca 45, 'That's What I Want' - and The Cheetahs from Erdington were to bring off a similar feat *twice*, a year later.

The first venture to the Top Twenty interior by a Midlands beat group had come in spring 1964 when the red-smocked Applejacks were visualised by Decca as harbingers of a 'Solihull Sound'. This had been a signal for London talent scouts to descend on the Midlands with the promptness of vultures during the frenzied search for the next titans of teen - and why not? Already, Pye recording manager Tony Hatch had thought twice about Denny Laine and the Diplomats, who had supported those very Beatles at Wolverhampton's Old Hill Plaza as 'Love Me Do' left a tide mark at Number Eighteen in 1962. In rejecting Laine, did Hatch miss something? Better late than never, that mighty Cerberus the *TV Times* thought, in a roundabout way, on 4 February 1965, that he might have done. This opinion was based on the climb of 'Go Now' by The Moody Blues - fronted by the selfsame Denny Laine - to Number One a month earlier.

Sounder argument for this judgement, both then and now, is more deeply rooted. For example, The Steve Gibbons Band, whose optimum commercial moment was in the late 1970s, can be traced back to The Dominettes, an Edgbaston combo who appeared frequently in that suburb's Cecilia coffee bar in the late 1950s. By 1963, they'd become The Ugly's (*sic*) - from a sardonic nickname given to two impossibly handsome Mods who ran a city club. 'The name - its curiosity angle - was a big advantage in terms of getting us gigs,' reasoned Steve.

The Ugly's were distinguished too by their employment of an electric harpsicord. From touting for work in *Midland Beat* small ads - 'anything considered' - they enjoyed qualified and intermittent commercial triumphs, notably by one of these strange variables that intrude on pop when airplay for their maiden single, 1965's self-penned 'Wake Up My Mind', snowballed in Australasia, pushing the disc high in Top Tens throughout the continent. 'They should have sent us out there straightaway,' sighed Steve, 'It did nothing for us financially as we'd signed such pitiful deals - something like a farthing off every record sold between all of us - but at least things were starting to happen.'

Though subsequent releases didn't leave the runway to anywhere near the same degree as 'Wake Up My Mind', The Ugly's - as much in their way as The Applejacks and The Moody Blues - had extended the commercial yardstick by which the humblest local would-be pop star like Robert Plant could judge himself - and often conclude that he was better than a lot of those who'd become suburban heroes in yet another rash of new clubs that had been created by ripping the guts from old factory premises, clearing out cellars and extending licenced premises. Clasping pop to its bosom as far back as 1961 was the Hereford Lounge which accommodated the Twitch Club, immortalised in a Rockin' Berries B-side as The Big Three's 'Cavern Stomp' had the more illustrious Liverpool venue. Moreover, 'Top Local Groups Four Nights A Week' could be heard at the inevitable Brumbeat Cavern near New Street station.

With much the same avaricious haste after 'She Loves You' swept to Number One in September 1963, another entrepreneurial cabal jumped in with the Kavern in Small Heath, which was lent an authentic sheen by dim lighting, low ceiling and the presence of The Searchers at its inauguration, lording it over locals Danny King and the Royals, The Defenders and Ace Kefford's Chantelles 'shortly before disbanding'.[54] Its half-a-crown membership ballooned to five hundred within a fortnight.

There were beat clubs in every vicinity engaging groups of every size and variety enjoying regional fame. So much had the post-Merseybeat explosion impinged on the national consciousness that the *Birmingham Evening Mail* as well as *Midland Beat*, were inundated with advertisements for musicians, groups and venues.

This rich, vast stamping ground was, however, symptomatic of the landlocked mediety that deprived Brumbeat - a convenient term for the entire Midlands pop scene - of the greater unity and independence that had been Merseyside's. Though widespread, it was devoid of regional identity. Moreover, though Brumbeat was as unstoppable as the Black Death, it grew in impact *after* rather than *with* Merseybeat. Adhering to the two guitars-bass-drums archetype, some groups like The Cheetahs, The Marauders and, especially, The Applejacks were fortunate enough to get chart placings but, each group waned within a year. Of a rapid second wave of chart contenders, only The Rockin' Berries, The Spencer Davis Group, The Fortunes and The Moody Blues enjoyed lasting prosperity - and almost all they had in common was that they were from the same part of the country.

Of all these acts, the one that opened Robert Plant's - and Noddy Holder's - eyes widest were The Spencer Davis Group. Their origins are traceable to singing vocalist Davis beginning a degree course in German at Birmingham University in 1960 where he became such a power on the entertainments committee that he was able to book himself for bar functions - and, when sitting in with The Excelsior Jazz Band, Spencer's four-song intermission spot became the highlight of the set.

At a vocational crossroads in 1963, he had vacillated between music and teaching after his wife presented him with a daughter at their Sutton Coldfield home that December, and a Monday night residency at the Golden Eagle seemed set to continue indefinitely. From a pool of players that he knew, Davis managed to find some kind of combo to back him every week. The most reliable stand-in whenever his voice needed a rest was this slip of a lad named Steve Winwood. Finding the rapid turnover of personnel prohibitive in his campaign for more bookings, Davis proposed that he and Steve could form a permanent group. With drummer Pete York from The Excelsior Jazz Band plus Winwood's elder brother, Muff, on bass, the new outfit first cast its net at a students union dance in April 1963.

They became known eventually as The Spencer Davis Group but the more obvious talent of Winwood Minor with his instinctive feel for black vocal stylings, and rapid command of any fretboard or keyboard instrument put in front of him was the

wellspring of Spencer's gradual demotion from the main spotlight, though he remained the *de jure* leader of the Group, and
continued to be rated as a competent, even distinctive singer and
guitarist.

It was, however, his misfortune that young sidekick Steve, if acned and pop-eyed at the microphone, was in another
league - as illustrated by Noddy Holder's gut response to the
Davis outfit in 1964: 'Of all the bands I saw in those days, they
were the ones who impressed me most musically. They were
very unassuming on stage - and then this kid on the organ suddenly opened his mouth and screamed, "I love the way she
walks..." and launched into that old John Lee Hooker number,
"Dimples". Gosh, my mouth fell open, and I felt a chill down
my spine. That was the night I discovered rhythm-and-blues for
the first time.'[55]

Many will always believe with Spencer Davis that 'Steve
never sounded so good as he did with us'.[56] It helped that these
prodigious antics were framed by thoroughly road-drilled accompaniment from Muff, Davis, and, especially, the gifted Pete
York, all ministering to an often thrilling overall effect bereft
of the squeaky-clean complacency that continues to mar the autumn of the Boy Wonder's career.

Robert Plant had yet to spit out the nicely-spoken Hayley Green plum, but both Holder and another Kidderminster
lad, Jess Roden, possessed a similar Ray Charles-with-a-hernia
voice to The Spencer Davis Group's X-factor and those of other
spotty herberts like Eric Burdon, Mick Jagger, Van Morrison,
Rod Stewart - and Phil May of The Pretty Things whose stage
act was more open-ended than most; becoming at one point a
continuous performance underpinned throughout by Bo Diddley's shave-and-a-haircut-six-pence beat, and May extemporis-
ing from full-blooded screech to *sotto voce* intimacy. If barely the Mannish Boy that Muddy Waters bragged about being,
Phil's straining attack was not unattractive, even gruffly charming, as, with spontaneity overruling expertise, he warped a limited range and natural coarseness to his own devices.

As the Swinging Sixties got out of neutral too, most R&B performers who imagined that they had a black soul within a white skin kept eagerly abreast of the latest developments among the James Browns, Tina Turners and Marvin Gayes of North America. Of few white British vocalists capable of mining this seam of 'soul music' without losing any of the overriding passion were Tom Jones, Dusty Springfield, Steve Winwood again, Chris Farlowe and Cliff Bennett.

Robert Plant was yet to become capable of taking on black rhythm-and-blues and its soul and rock 'n' roll derivations without such a loss. Though the spirit was willing, he - like most of the others - tended to be merely raucous if he got as far as shedding enough of their inhibitions to cut up rough. The stumbling block was bigger *sur le continent* as rock 'n' roll had developed into an English-language music, and would remain so for all time. Even on static-ridden radio, reproductions of wordy Chuck Berry did not, therefore, sound anywhere as accurate as they did past the Straits of Dover where 'Carol', 'Reelin' And Rockin'', 'Memphis Tennessee', 'Little Queenie' and all the rest of them were prominent in the repertoires of all British beat groups that counted - and Berry items were often the redeeming features of many that didn't. Recalling Bern Elliott and the Fenmen, the Medway Towns' 'answer' to Cliff Richard and the Shadows, Pretty Thing-in-waiting Phil May 'used to go and watch them, but we would wait for them to play their two Chuck Berry numbers.'

Berry numbers freighted the Things' early performances - and those of The Beatles, Dave Clark Five, Gerry and the Pacemakers, Rolling Stones, Animals, Downliners Sect, Kinks, Rockin' Berries, Yardbirds, Troggs, you name 'em. The Five were to penetrate 1965's Top Thirty with a definitive 'Reelin' And Rockin'', and Steve Gibbons' time would come with a revival of 'Tulane', a 1977 single that shinned up the domestic Top Twenty - as The Electric Light Orchestra had done four years earlier with 'Roll Over Beethoven'.

The night that Robert Plant and Noddy Holder saw The Spencer Davis Group, they heard two Berry numbers which were, along with The Coasters' six-year-old 'Searchin', the Group's most irresistable concessions to anything approaching mainstream pop. Robert learnt also that Steve Winwood, still a pupil at Great Barr Comprehensive, was only fractionally older than himself. More pragmaticially, the cash flow from engagements was such that the three older members of the Group were thinking seriously of packing in their day jobs.

Apart from the fly in the milk-jug of his parents, Robert could be, so he contemplated, in the right place at the right time. For the publicity it gave deserving acts, *Midland Beat* served as a stepping stone between rehearsing in front rooms and the-day-we-went-to-a-recording-studio for all sorts of amateurs, bending over backwards in their hyperbole, providing false information about impending success for local pop newshounds. Who would admit, for example, that they'd taken the stage the previous evening before only the hall caretaker and his barking dog? *Midland Beat* missed a lot of great moments apparently.

It didn't matter how far-flung you were either. In Robert Plant's part of the world, The Sundowners represented Great Malvern[57] during an era when every area in the kingdom was supposed to have a 'beat' or a 'sound'. They'd made ripples of a sort when their shot at 'House Of The Rising Sun' was eclipsed totally by that of The Animals everywhere outside loyal Worcestershire. Nevertheless, they didn't do particularly well when *Midland Beat*'s readers poll in May 1964 to find the region's most popular group showed The Talismen from distant Cheltenham on top. The following year's nine-day-wonders would be The Moonrakers from Henley-on-Arden who, by fair means or foul, presided over a tabulation which slotted The Spencer Davis Group and The Moody Blues - each with records in the Top Fifty - between twelve and twenty.

THE SPIDER

'Drumming was the only thing I was any good at' - John Bonham[1]

Like provincial football teams, home-grown alternatives to chart pop in the mid-1960s would acquire a tremendous grass-roots following. Then fans would recount bitterly how, with record success, this singer or that group later betrayed them by defecting to London and beyond. Yet it is notable how many performers from the West Midlands chose to remain within its environs, regardless of whether their individual storms broke.

Jimmy Page and Peter Grant were to be, therefore, spoiled for choice when their search for New Yardbirds fanned out from London to the Second City and its suburbs. When short-listing bass players, the two may have thought twice about Dave Pegg, future cornerstone of Fairport Convention, but then in The Way Of Life, a heavy rock outfit popular regionally if nowhere else. Drumming for him like a rhythmically-integrated octopus was twenty-year-old John Henry Bonham from Redditch, a dormitory outpost of Birmingham, south along the A441.

At odds with a self-image as a streetwise hard case, and speech laced with incessant swearing, John Bonham's upbringing was comfortably working-class posh. He knew how to behave when among other folk of the same 'decent' social standing. Through his father's income from his own building firm - which John, the eldest of three, was expected to join - and mother's from a corner shop, he was privately educated. John was not academically inclined, but, if he left school without formal qualifications at sixteen, he had become as known for his instinctive ability as a percussionist as the school bully and football captain were in their chosen spheres.

His hand had been the first to shoot up when the teacher sought volunteers to rat-a-tat-tat the rhythmic pulse to 'Donkey Riding', 'Down In Demerara' and other selections from the standard *Singing Together* pupils' handbook distributed by the monitor during cross-legged music lessons round the upright piano in the main hall. At home, while he'd taught himself the rudiments of guitar,[58] and was able to follow musical script, he found it more fulfilling to smite furniture and kitchen utensils before his parents bought him a snare drum and, shortly before he entered the world of work, a second-hand kit.

John attacked his present with gusto, showing no signs of ever stopping. Pondered trial-and-error, however, brought forth sound hand-and-foot coordination, accurate time-keeping, a roll faster than *moderato* and an impactive - if dinning - personal style. Before admitting to himself that he was an unadulterated rock 'n' roller, he'd developed a liking for the more flamboyant mainstream jazz sticksmen like bandleader Buddy Rich - every smart alec's notion of percussive splendour - and Gene Krupa, such a legend that he was to be the subject of a 1960 bio-pic. Bonham also half-liked US swing band drummer Lionel Hampton, twirling his sticks gratuitously and whose raucous nod to rock 'n' roll during a 1956 concert at the Royal Festival Hall prompted jazz purist Johnny Dankworth to voice his disgust through cupped hands from the audience. Nonetheless, like Rich and Krupa, Hampton was capable of commanding the stage alone under a voodoo spell for minutes on end.

Ministering more unobstrusively to overall effect was another boyhood idol, Joe Morello, best known to the man-in-the-street for accompanying Dave Brubeck, one of few modern jazz pianists to reach the British pop charts without compromising his stylistic determination.[59] Bonham's adolescent imagination was particularly captivated by Morello's occasional habit of abandoning his sticks and pounding the tom-toms with the flats of his hands.

Of British drummers, Bonham came to admire Clem Cattini, who, like John Paul Jones - and Tony Sheridan - had had an opportunity to join The Shadows. 'Bruce Welch and Hank Marvin were friends of mine, and they asked what I was doing next week. They wanted me for a rehearsal with Cliff, but I was off to a gig in Manchester with Terry Dene, and I felt bad about letting him down. *Que sera sera.*'[60]

1959 had finished with Clem in The Beat Boys, backing ensemble common to Billy Fury, Duffy Power, Dave Sampson, Dickie Pride and similar entertainers guided by either or both Larry Parnes and Jack Good. The group was also on hand for auditions by newcomers like Georgie Fame - on whose 'Ballad Of Bonnie And Clyde' chart-topper would drum in a future that was a paradox of faraway and close at hand.

Cattini's commercial discography began, however, as one of Johnny Kidd's Pirates, whose chart placings had not then superceded summer 1959's high of Number Twenty-Five with 'Please Don't Touch'. However, coinciding with Cattini's arrival, the highest peak of all was scaled via 'Shakin' All Over'. Yet, despite it knocking Cliff Richard's 'Please Don't Tease' from Number One in August 1960, 'Shakin' All Over' netted Cattini only EMI's standard session fee. Within a year, Johnny and the Pirates were becalmed outside the Top Fifty again, and reduced to support spots and one-nighters.

By the end of 1961, however, Cattini had landed on his feet in The Tornados at Joe Meek's Holloway studio, remaining with both the group and Joe throughout their period of optimum commercial magnitude and subsequent decline until 1965 when 'I was sitting in a dressing room somewhere with Stuart Taylor, the guitarist for the previous two years. The hall was empty, and that was the end of instrumental groups. Stuart told me he was leaving, and I told him that I wasn't prepared to carry on with The Tornados as I'd had enough too.'

While Clem and The Tornados ran out of ideas and motivation, John Bonham listened and learned nearer to home from Bev Bevan of Carl Wayne's Vikings and Pete York from The Spencer Davis Group, who was to write a regular column in *Midland Beat* containing valuable tips from his own strict practice rota plus erudite critiques of the latest kit accessories. Yet, of all 1960s drummers within the sphere of pop, making the most irradicable impression of all on Bonham was Peter 'Ginger' Baker, then of London's Graham Bond Organisation, plotted as a tighter, jazzier take on Blues Incorporated. Seated behind a largely self-constructed kit of perspex and *bona fide* African 'talking drums' of thick, shaven animal skins, Baker was rated as 'bloody good'[61] by no less than percussion aesthete Charlie Watts of The Rolling Stones, whose heart - like that of York - would always remain in jazz.

When Baker and the Organisation's former bass guitarist, Jack Bruce, were forming the Cream 'supergroup' with Eric Clapton in 1966, John Bonham was resisting overtures to join The Move. Before that, there'd been an approach from Gerry Levene and the Avengers among many other outfits for one who, even as a schoolboy, had emerged parochially as a sensational drummer, albeit one given to boozy lunaticking, on-stage and off.

It's intriguing to speculate how different Bonham's life might have been had he stuck it out to the bitter end with either outfit - which may have been epitomised by Roy Wood, composer of all Move A-sides and ultimate controller of the group's destiny, touring Britain in 1993, and the show getting off to an unpromising start with The Jim Onslow Experience, a trundling if competent rock 'n' roll revival act lacking both the appropriate attire and haircuts, but enshrining what was left of Gerry Levene and the Avengers.

Like singing bass player Onslow, Wood had served Levene back in Birmingham when the world was young. The story went that, judging by volume of applause from an admittedly partisan crowd, The Beatles, then not much more than an outfit of comparable popularity in Liverpool, had *lost* a 'Battle of the Bands' tournament with Gerry and the Avengers on 19 November 1962, at West Bromwich's Adelphi Ballroom. Things were looking up for both groups; the Merseysiders' first single, 'Love Me Do', had just been released while Gerry's boys' booking schedule was such that what had signified a month's work a year before had become a week's.

Then paths diverged; after that Greatest Night Anyone Could Ever Remember, Levene and his boys plodded an infinitely drearier path, culminating in The Jim Onslow Experience giving 'em the same numbers that had been in the set when the long-departed Gerry formed the group in 1959. The Beatles, however, went on to international stardom - and so, to a more qualified degree, did Roy Wood. After 'California Man', The Move's Top Ten swansong, he'd form The Electric Light Orchestra - ELO - and then Wizzard as well as sustaining a parallel and similarly chartbusting solo career.

Alternatively, Bonham might have followed Dave Pegg into Fairport Convention, who became not so much a premier folk-rock ensemble as one of the most English of veteran rock groups. At 1997's Cropredy festival - the ensemble's annual knees-up since the early 1980s, drawing tens of thousands from as far away as Australasia - representatives of all trackways of the Convention's numerous line-ups pitched in for the group's thirtieth anniversary celebration. With Fairport presiding, Cropredy's artistic brief also enabled the sharing of the stage by the most unlikely combinations - or not so unlikely in the light of Sandy Denny's duet with Robert Plant on *Led Zeppelin IV*. Plant starred at Cropredy as did Roy Wood - whose all-female horn section blasted out 'I Heard It Through The Grapevine' (with former Convention guitarist Richard Thompson on lead vocals).

Less trumpeted that particular year was a similar bash at Dudley Town Hall on 2 November 1997 to celebrate Dave Pegg's half-century. Overflowing with 'special guests', it covered the expected folk-rock as well as 'Johnny B Goode' and further standards from the birthday boy's Brumbeat genesis. In an opening address, Dave referred to his beginnings in the youth clubs of Yardley as a lead guitarist with The Trespassers, whose stock-in-trade was the Top Twenty and instrumentals by the trailblazing Shadows .

Every vicinity in the West Midlands seemed to contain groups like The Trespassers, enjoying parochial fame, albeit often via a makeshift ingenuity. In Steve Gibbons' Dominettes, for example, the drummer's meagre kit lacked a kick-bass, thus obliging him to thump the floor with his foot. Two six-strings and Steve's microphone were all plugged into one twelve-watt amplifier. There was no bass player until one of the guitarists volunteered to put bass strings on his Club 60 semi-acoustic.

The Dominettes tussled with The Modernaires, The Mysterons and The Jaymen among other Edgbaston outfits for local bookings. A few bus stops south-east, The Chantelles ruled poor streets, where terraces had gloomy tunnels through them to get to the backs. Their bass player was Ace Kefford, who, after he was a prime mover in the formation of The Move in 1966, was to be the still-struggling John Bonham's most famous celebrity intimate. Moreover, if Roy Wood was the mind of The Move, the charismatic bass player - blond Norse god androgeny with underlying dread was its face - and also its James Dean, its Jet Harris, its Brian Jones and, ultimately, its Pete Best.

As Bonham's best friend - albeit an increasingly more distant one - it is educational to trace Kefford's early career in his own words: 'At Yardley Wood Secondary Modern - a dump, very rough - I got into James Dean, the way he looked. My school uniform was cheap black jeans sown up as tight as I could get 'em, black shirt, red waistcoat off my grandad, greased-back hair.

'My family came to recognise that how you dressed was part of a musician's job. My saving grace, you see, was getting into rock 'n' roll because we had a gang at school with names like Chunky, Spooky, Huker, Scratchy - real dead end kids who broke into shops and pinched cigarettes, but I think that's how a lot of groups started in those days - as an extension of that.

'My Uncle Chris - who was only nine months older than me - and I were both into The Shadows, The Packabeats, The Hunters, The Tornados - all the instrumental groups that we went to see at Birmingham Town Hall. We used to sit in the house, playing guitars together. We got another guitarist, Mugsy Morgan, and a drummer, Barry Smith, to join us - though Graeme Edge, later of The Moody Blues, drummed with us for a while. When my other uncle, Reg, wanted to be a singer, we became Steve Farron - Reg in a gold *lame* suit - and the Chantelles, and started getting pub gigs, making some money and building up a following.

'I worked in the fruit market for about a year. As I started at five in the morning, I'd often clock-in straight from a gig - especially if it was something like an all-nighter in Kidderminster - still wearing stage gear, and causing comment. That hardened me up, working there, especially when I started combing my hair in the Beatle style.

'Lead vocalists who didn't play instruments didn't seem necessary anymore. Reg left, and we started doing "Love Potion Number 9", "Some Other Guy", Chuck Berry - the stuff the Liverpool and Manchester bands were playing. That's when I first began singing.

'The Chantelles disbanded in December 1963, and Barry, Chris and I put a group together with Danny King as Danny King and the Jesters. You ask Carl Wayne, Denny Laine or anyone, who was the greatest singer in Birmingham, and they'll all tell you it was Danny. He had a voice like nobody else - a brilliant high-pitched vibrato - but Danny didn't want to get involved in the mainstream pop business. He only performed when he felt like it.

'By then, we were on the night club and ballroom circuit, but I still had to work as a builder with my uncles. One night, I got home and my dad said that a guy called Spencer Davis had come round. I'd heard that his group did this stuff called rhythm-and-blues. Anyway, Spencer came back later to say that his bass player, Muff Winwood, was going off to see The Modern Jazz Quartet in London, and I'd been recommended as a dep. So I went along to the gig at the Whiskey-A-Go-Go above a tailor's near New Street station. Stevie Winwood must have been about fourteen then. I did two nights with them - and that turned me onto rhythm-and-blues. I just fell in love with that black sound.'

So did Dave Pegg, though the observations of others contradicted this when after The Trespassers came Dave and the Emeralds who, embracing the same two guitars-bass-drums line-up, 'were actually quite slick. We wore the same outfits - brown blazers and grey-striped trousers - and did the Shadows' leg movements and high kicks routines.' By day, Pegg was an insurance clerk at the Royal Exchange in Temple Street where

Dave Peace, a keyboard-playing vocalist, was a trainee - with Denny Laine - at Rackham's department store. Like many mainstream pop musicians, Peace, Laine and Pegg had been attracted to the earthier sounds of black R&B by 1963. While Denny was yet to join The Moody Blues, the two Daves formed The Crawdaddies. 'There was a lot of interest in R&B,' remembered Pegg, 'and a lot of places to play. As a Crawdaddy, I played five nights a week for around fifteen quid compared to seven at the office where I worked.'

He packed in his day job shortly before defecting from The Crawdaddies to The Blueshounds, who were booked for the inaugural night at The Elbow Room, a club that, arguably, was more like Liverpool's Cavern than the Kavern and the Brumbeat Cavern were ever to be. Yet Beatle-sized acclaim was not on the agenda for The Blueshounds who were to touch the ceiling of their professional accomplishments as runners-up in *Melody Maker*'s national talent competition in 1966, and as accompanists to Jimmy Cliff. More soul than reggae then, this Jamaican entertainer's time was to come with a UK chart debut later in the decade.

A few commercial rungs above The Blueshounds, The Ugly's had enjoyed spots on *Ready Steady Go* and *Thank Your Lucky Stars* at home. By 1966, however, the group was troubled by personnel problems. These were resolved by enlisting Dave Pegg, who switched to bass - 'the best thing that ever happened'.

Owing to long absences from the area, The Ugly's were not especially high in the hierarchy of local pop. 'Carl Wayne and the Vikings were Birmingham's top group then,' calculated Ace Kefford, 'They were managing up to twenty bookings a week, doubles and trebles, getting forty or fifty pounds each when my old man was on twelve as a plasterer. As I was also getting crap money as a labourer then, I snapped up the job as their bass player late in 1963, even though I wasn't too happy about the shirts, ties and velvet-collared suits they wore on stage - or their music, mostly Top Twenty and a lot of smoochy ballads like "My Prayer". Even when they did Chuck Berry, it was all very polished. There was no raw Rolling Stones-type sound.

'The drummer was Dave Hollis - who came before Bev Bevan, who I first knew as one of Denny Laine's Diplomats. I got Bev into the group. He came in the week before we went to Dusseldorf for a couple of months before moving on to the Storyville in Cologne.'

Scanty parochial opportunities had already driven many other Midlands groups to the clublands of West Germany where there was continued demand for overseas talent. Nevertheless, returning to Birmingham in November 1963, Ray Thomas of The Krew Kats had been astonished to find the local scene 'in total chaos. There were about two hundred and fifty groups, half thought they were Cliff Richard and the Shadows and the other half thought they were The Beatles'.[62]

In the wake of that watershed year's Merseybeat explosion, the Second City and its tributary towns, midway between Liverpool and London, had been high on even the most slow-witted metropolitan talent scout's hit list. As The Beatles had slid from Decca's then unconcerned clutches the previous year, the company began saturating itself with beat groups in the hope that one of them might catch on like their failed Scouse supplicants had to teeth-gnashing effect when signed by arch-rival EMI. Hence the issue in 1964 of such as a *Brumbeat* compilation LP on Dial Records, containing as many of the area's groups as were deemed suitable after a couple of days in a hired local palais with a mobile recording unit.

Yet it had been two years earlier that the first 'Brumbeat' single - 'Sugar Babe' by Jimmy Powell - had been released by Decca with, incidentally, Jimmy Page and Clem Cattini among his accompanists. Powell's performances on the boards had won him the strongest possible local following before he and his accompanying Five Dimensions undertook the next logical step of hurtling, shoulder to shoulder, towards Coventry and down the unfinished M1 to re-locate around the capital. While they still accepted engagements in old haunts, their Midlands origins were not stressed as they followed that R&B trail to Richmond where they'd been hired by promoter Georgio Gomelsky as the intermission act and, in September 1963, replacements for The Rolling Stones at the celebrated Crawdaddy club.

Passing through the Dimensions' ranks during this period was Londoner Rod Stewart, a few months before he sang at Birmingham Town Hall with the Sonny Boy Williamson package. Like Stewart, Jimmy Powell's gravelly ranting betrayed a gruff charm, in retrospect, more Joe Cocker than Robert Plant. Certainly, he sounded as if he'd got the blues from Birmingham, Alabama rather than England's Second City.

Whilst enthralling 'young people' - as opposed to 'youths' - in genteel Surrey, Powell created a stir too among the Mod clientele in Soho's Flamingo and the less fashionable Marquee where he came to be regarded as on a par with other incumbent showmen like Georgie Fame, Zoot Money, Herbie Goins and Chris Farlowe who likewise kept abreast of what was now known as 'soul music'. Acting on intelligence about the new paragon of pop, Pye signed up Jimmy in May 1964 - as, in parenthesis, the company did Carl Wayne and the Vikings that same month - for two singles. The first of these was the self-penned 'That's Alright' - which had all the qualities of a hit but none that actually grabbed the public. Nevertheless, Jimmy - and the Dimensions - made the charts indirectly when, at the height of the bluebeat craze, they supplied accompaniment to Millie's 'My Boy Lollipop'.

Powell's Pye swansong, 'I've Been Watching You', was on its way to the deletion rack when The Rockin' Berries and the chart-topping Moody Blues appeared on the same edition of ITV's *Ready Steady Go*. As their name implied, The Rockin' Berries appealed to Rockers as Jimmy Powell did to Mods. Having spent much of the previous two years in Germany, getting a hit record had been a far-fetched afterthought, but in autumn 1964, the throbbing ballad 'He's in Town' - their fourth single - carried them to Number Three in Britain.

A month after 'He's In Town' left the charts, The Moody Blues were on the way up - indeed, all the way up - with 'Go Now', their second 45. Drawn from several different Midlands beat groups - including The Krew Kats and Denny Laine and the Diplomats - they had chosen their collective name in 1964 either after a Slim Harpo instrumental entitled 'Moody Blue' or for the initials, in vain hopes of sponsorship from Mitchell and Butler, a well-known regional brewery.

On first glance at most Moody Blues publicity photographs, the first face you were drawn to was Denny Laine's, who, disinterested in academic subjects at Yardley Grammar, had been enrolled in a suburban stage school which provided *in situ* training with public presentations such as pantomimes and cabaret at works parties. 'I never went in for acting so much,' recalled Denny, 'the music sort of took over.'

On buying an electric guitar, Laine joined his first group, Johnny and the Dominators as the outfit's Buddy Holly specialist, but in 1962, he formed Denny Laine and the Diplomats with Bev Bevan. They sought attention initially by wearing matching Italian suits and peroxiding their hair. They were also one of few Birmingham beat groups to try self-composed items, even if, as everyone knew, this usually caused dancers to sit them out. However, some were more intrigued than the musicians thought. 'John Bonham used to watch me and the Diplomats at the Wednesbury Youth Centre,' recounted Denny, 'Years later, he stayed at my house, and, though I couldn't remember any of the original material the Diplomats did to save my life, he could. We got a bit drunk, and he started singing "Why Cry", "A Piece of Your Mind" and others we did. He knew all the words and everything. Unbelievable!'

Rather than any idiosyncracies in their music, it was because the group toed a smooth, amiable, clean-looking line that they made a televisual debut on topical *Midlands At Six*. Denny and the Diplomats were hired too for *Pop Shop* and *For Teenagers Only* - and as token pop act on *Lunch Box*.

In April 1964, however, the ambitious Laine left the Diplomats to fend for themselves. Prospects looked rosier in the assembly of a new group from key members of others. 'The Moody Blues nicked members from top bands in Birmingham,' smiled Denny, 'I pushed the group in the direction of the blues- and jazz-based London bands. Also, we'd gone to see The Spencer Davis Group, and I was knocked out by them. I thought that if they could get away with it, we could - and that convinced the other lads.'

The Moody Blues came to be appreciated as a 'group's group' by the students and bohemians that patronised rhythm-and-blues evenings in, say, the Golden Eagle or, less regularly, in the nearby Town Hall where, on 11 September 1964, ravers could twist the night away to Blue Sounds from Leeds, the jazzy Sheffields and, as the headlining act, Alexis Korner's Blues Incorporated. Representing the Second City itself were The Spencer Davis Group and, wrote *Midland Beat*, 'the much-improved Moody Blues Five' (*sic*).[63]

Yet where did such crazy, far-out music get you? As everybody knew, reputations were made playing non-specialist pop in the ballrooms that were the domain of the 'somebody and the somebodies' likes of Carl Wayne and the Vikings, Johnny Neal and the Starliners, Keith Powell and the Valets, Danny King and his Mayfair Set, Gerry Levene and the Avengers, Pat Wayne and the Beachcombers, and Mike Sheridan and the Nightriders.

While the rest of the West Midlands slept, these and other of the county's beat combos, mainstream or otherwise, would congregate and unwind at Alex's Fleur De Lys mobile pie stall opposite the central Albany Hotel in Birmingham for a snack after Saturday night performances. United by artistic purpose and mutual respect, as they ambled past the rows of vans parked along Smallbrook Queensway, rivalry would often dissolve into easy cameraderie as exemplified by Danny King of The Mayfair Set penning Carl Wayne and the Vikings' second A-side. 'He sang "This Is Love", to us,' recalled Ace Kefford, 'and Carl said, "Can we have that one, Danny?"' On such evenings too, musicians small-talked, borrowed equipment, schemed and provided - usually exaggerated - information about impending

Led Zeppelin 1971. Photo by Chris Dreja of The Yardbirds.

Jimmy Page in relaxed mood.

Bonzo in similar pose.

Robert, concentrating.

JPJ, between the two.

Clockwise from top: Jimmy on TV aged 14; with Neil Christian and the Crusaders; with Mickey Finn's band; with Keith Relf and Andy Warhol.

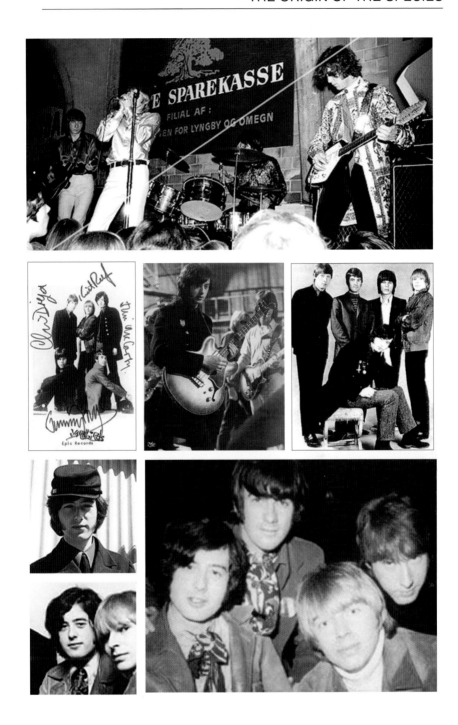

Jimmy with The Yardbirds 1966–68.

Top: the young Robert Plant. Bottom: Robert with Band of Joy, 1968.

Top: 'Percy' Plant with and without lip hair. Bottom: Percy
stands up for his rights.

The changing face of John Paul Jones...

...and of John Bonham (pictured with The Way of Life, top
right).

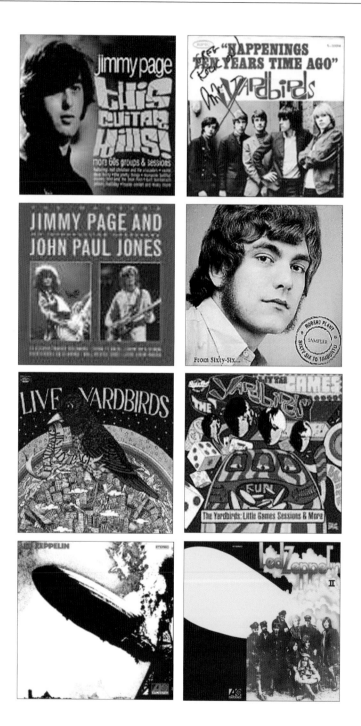

The records that led the way.

The posters that said it all.

The coming together...

...and changing the world.

LED ZEPPELIN – THE ORIGIN OF THE SPECIES
THE FILM – AVAILABLE ON *DVD* NOW

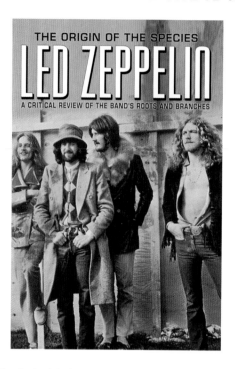

This 75 minute film is the ideal accompaniment to this book, also covering, albeit in greater depth, the years that the future members of Led Zep were struggling in the session studios and amateur band scenes of the 1960s, moving through the modest success of outfits like The Yardbirds and Band Of Joy and culminating in Led Zeppelin's first two albums as a group verging on huge global domination.

Features Include

Rare musical performances - Obscure footage, rare interviews and rarely seen photographs - review, comment, criticism and insight from: the author of this book and of *The Yardbirds,* **Alan Clayson**; *Melody Maker* journalist, **Chris Welch**; ex-1960s *NME* Editor, **Keith Altham**; Yardbirds guitarist, **Chris Dreja**; musicians and performers (all of whom worked with Led Zeppelin's future members in the 1960s) such as, **Chris Farlowe**, **Dave Berry** and **Clem Cattini**, journalists **Barney Hoskins** and **Phil Sutcliffe** and others.

Extras Include

Special feature: **The Story Of The Yardbirds -** Interactive gaming feature **'The Hardest Led Zeppelin Quiz In The World Ever' -** Contributor biographies.

AVAILABLE NOW

at all good music and DVD stores – including HMV, Virgin, Borders and many more, online stores Amazon, Play.com and most others, or from **WWW. CHROMEDREAMS.CO.UK** – where you can also find other Led Zeppelin items amongst over 1,000 titles on DVD, CD and in book format.

success. 'There was a great atmosphere - sort of all mates together, pursuing the same dreams,' grinned Bev Bevan, 'I think a lot of bands formed, changed line-ups and broke up at Alex's pie stand.'[62]

Drummers talked drums with other drummers. Sometimes, John Bonham, yet to pledge himself to any particular group, sought the company of Bill Ward of The Rest, a sober-suited quartet from Erdington. 'I grew up with John,' reminisced Bill, 'Me and him had traded licks since we were fifteen. When he was doing the out-of-town gigs, sometimes I'd end up supporting him. Sometimes too, he'd support whatever band I was in. We were always crossing paths in those days. It was always, like, "How you doing, Wardy?", and I'd say, "Doing all right. How are you?" We weren't particularly good to each other when we were drinking. We were rude to each other, but we still remained very respectful, very professional, congenial friends.'[64]

Another instance of Brumbeat's *esprit de corps* was Robert Plant, now a regular drinker at the Star-and-Garter in Halesowen, leaping up to sing a couple of numbers with the resident group. Plant was also becoming a familiar figure at midnight gatherings round Alex's pie stand before sauntering round to, perhaps, The Elbow Room, the Rum Runner, Club Cedar or some other watering-hole that stayed open into the graveyard hours. It was through the cigarette smoke at one of these watering holes that his eyes met those of John Bonham. Neither of them had any way of knowing then to what degree their lives were to interweave as, from loose, simple patterns, both the nationally famous and those unknown beyond the Black Country might then unwind in often unlikely combinations on small stages. 'Birmingham was and still is a place where everybody sits in with everybody else', observed Steve Winwood - to which he added a sweeping 'There are no rigidly exclusive groups'.[65]

Such a situation and its attendant problems would have caused many talent spotters to leave their scotch-and-cokes half-drunk on the bar after eliminated such-and-such an act from the running after no less an authority than Cliff Richard's elderly producer Norrie Paramor - on liaising with Mary 'Ma'

Regan, a notorious local promoter - had pontificated that 'the Birmingham groups I have signed have a lot of potential. The Beat Boom is subsiding and I think Birmingham will keep it flourishing.'[47]

In the same *Midland Beat* editorial as this quote, Dennis Detheridge affirmed that 'we are appointing top musical journalists as correspondents in every Midlands county.' Perhaps the most tireless of these was a B.P. Finch who, from the onset, scooped the Worcestershire scene - which embraced John Bonham's Redditch. Deemed worthy of a special section - 'Worcester Whisperings' - there was much to occupy Our Man Finch. By 1965, some of the shire's beat groups had already tilted at the national charts. As well as The Sundowners' ill-fated 'House Of The Rising Sun', The Cherokees, a Whittington unit, had had a moment of glory when their trudging 'Seven Golden Daffodils' spent five weeks in the Top Forty, almost outpacing a version by the better-known Mojos.

Without exception, however, they all faded away. So bitter was The Hellions' poverty, for example, that they were compelled to organise a jumble sale to cover accumulated parking fines. The final blow was the liquidation of their fan club in 1966. Dominating B.P. Finch's Whisperings by then were New Sense, The Daleks, The Buzz, Censored!, The Banned and The Crawling King Snakes. That New Sense had once been The Phantoms best exemplified the passing of the old order.

Reborn as 'Deep Feeling', The Hellions had attempted to crack the bigger nut of Birmingham. However, while the most western extreme of Worcestershire was less than an hour's train ride from New Street station, the traditionally greater affinity to the West Country and Wales had provoked The Vampires to become The Severnbeats, while Worcester's sixteen-odd big-time groups were as likely to play Swindon's X Club or the Rock Garden in Llandrindod Wells as Erdington's Pandora or the Moat 'Twistacular' in Wythall. Moreover, *Midland Beat* reported that one local agency - Landsdowne - was 'formed with the sole intention of stopping Brum groups playing at Worcestershire venues'[47] - an embargo extending even to Denny Laine's Diplomatic Sunday show at Kidderminster Playhouse in October 1963.

Among other acts on the bill were Redditch's boss group, Terry Webb and his Spiders - who were to enlist John Bonham a few months later, and oblige him to don their stage costume of bootlace ties and purple jackets (with gold *lamé* for the lovely Terry). One of the highlights of their performances at the Dragoon pub in Bromsgrove, their principal stamping ground, was Little Richard's 'Good Golly Miss Molly', the drum pattern of which was to be grafted onto *Led Zeppelin IV*'s 'Rock And Roll'.

Spurning requests from Dragoon customers to play quieter, Bonham's stint as a Spider was followed by one with The Nicky James Movement, fronted by a vocalist who continued defiantly hip-shakin' and oiling his gravity-defying cockade throughout the Mod-dominated beat boom. His local appeal was such that a soaring to the very pinnacle of pop seemed a certainty - but so many other lads like Nicky carried that self-belief even after a final demand from a hire-purchase firm poised to cart their equipment away.

Moving on, Bonham replaced Bev Bevan in The Senators, and was heard on their 1964 single, 'She's A Mod' on Dial Records, which was a hit in Australasia when covered by New Zealand's Ray Columbus and the Invaders. When the next Senators 45, 'When Day Is Done', was issued later that year, John had quit, and was sitting in non-committally with other outfits. When their usual drummer was indisposed, he beat the skins with, say, Steve Brett and the Mavericks when Noddy Holder was among them.

More enduring was a spell with Pat Wayne and the Beachcombers, who were to record ten singles - three by Wayne alone, two by just The Beachcombers - for EMI, beginning in 1963 with 'Roll Over Beethoven', the Chuck Berry opus that began side two of The Beatles' latest LP. It was, so their local fans understood, a hit in Scandinavia, but this wasn't sufficient for drummer Brian Sharp to hold on hoping. On giving notice, he recommended Bonham, who auditioned at Walsall's Three Men

In A Boat. The session kicked off with a number everyone knew, 'Roll Over Beethoven'. On the count-in, the newcomer brought his sticks down on the snare and hi-hat - 'and then *whoosh!*' gasped Pat Wayne, 'Off he kicked - and how!'[66]

Perhaps a more pragmatic reason for accepting Bonham as a Beachcomber was the use of his father's Ford Anglia delivery van to transport the drum kit as there was little room for it in the group's Bedford. However, after proceeding directly from the tailor's where he was working as an assistant to follow the others to his very first engagement as a Beachcomber, John overturned the vehicle into a ditch along a country lane. Somehow, the drums and John were crammed into the Bedford, and an uncomfortable journey to the Golden Diamond in Sutton-in-Ashfield in the next county was continued.

There, Bonham's new colleagues made an alarming discovery. 'John's drumming was magnificent,' agreed Pat, 'but we couldn't make ourselves heard above it all. The manager of the Golden Diamond commented that the Beachcombers had become a "drum show".'[66]

It wasn't long before Bonham was replaced by Mike Kellie from The Blueshounds, who, unlike him, kept in trim by laying off the beer. However, Bonham's parting from Pat Wayne and the Beachcombers was amicable enough for Wayne, readying himself for a bow-tied cabaret engagement in a Stockholm hotel on 6 March 1973, to receive a telephone call from Bonham to invite him to a Led Zeppelin bash in the Swedish capital's principal auditorium later that night, and be allowed past backstage security for companionable reminiscence and coded hilarity about the dear, dead Brumbeat days when the world was young. It seemed so far away now: the Rum Runner, Ma Regan, Alex's pie stand, Gerry Levene and the Avengers, beehive hairdos, 'Roll Over Beethoven' and poor old Ace Kefford, the boy who'd had everything it took. His head thrown back with laughter in the beer-sodden jollity, how could John Bonham have known that he had only seven and a half years left, and that Pat Wayne was to attend the memorial service at Rushock parish church, equidistant from Kidderminster and Redditch.

THE FACILITATOR

'If I hadn't known Eric or if I hadn't liked him, I might have joined' - Jimmy Page[9]

While not entering the album list, the in-concert *Five Live Yardbirds* from the Marquee in central London still shifted sufficient copies to serve as a holding operation during the months preceding a final recording session with Eric Clapton - for whom the blues was a craving, almost a religion. Even before Eric had joined The Yardbirds, there'd been the axiomatic 'musical differences' with the others, especially Samwell-Smith, co-producer of 1965's catchy 'For Your Love', a domestic Number One and world million-seller.

It had been decided that live, the harpsichord on the record was to be approximated by a twelve-string guitar clanged near its bridge for maximum metallic effect - but not by Eric Clapton. Before 'For Your Love' had even penetrated the charts, he was preparing to hit the road with John Mayall's Bluesbreakers, though his departure from The Yardbirds was not as acrimonious as has been supposed - as exemplified by his 'sitting in' with the group one evening at the Marquee in 1966.

'When he was a Yardbird, no-one had been under the impression that Eric was about to become a world-class musician,' believed the late Vivian Stanshall, chief show-off in The Bonzo Dog Doo-Dah Band. Even today, if Eric appeared in disguise at your local venue, how would you rate his playing? OK but nothing brilliant? You may think I'm terrible, but my opinion after seeing him with Blind Faith in 1969 is unaltered. I felt it then and I'll say it now: not only as a guitarist but as a singer and songwriter, he's all right, I suppose. Moreover, on *Five Live Yardbirds* anyway, Keith Relf, not Clapton, was 'God'.

Yet Eric was to earn swiftly the exalted status of not so much a deity as 'best guitarist in the country - and so unaffected,' according to the discerning Steve Winwood[67], following the issue of *Bluesbreakers*, Clapton's *piece de resistance* when with John Mayall.

By then, the question of The Yardbirds' new lead guitarist had long been resolved. Jimmy Page had been the first choice, but he wasn't so dazzled by the beat boom to think that its groups were immortal. Besides, a mild recurrence of his glandular fever provoked flashbacks of how dreadful life on the road had been with Neil Christian and the Crusaders. Anyway, why expend such effort when, while 'For Your Love' was in the Top Ten, Page was in the same list three times over - on Them's 'Here Comes The Night', 'I Can't Explain' by The Who and 'It's Not Unusual' by Tom Jones.

Almost despite himself, Page was becoming something of a pop personality in the pages of such as *Beat Instrumental, Melody Maker* and like periodicals less beglamoured than others by a given star's looks and posturing. Indeed, in the guitarists section of a *Beat Instrumental* readers poll in December 1965, he was to be placed tenth, just below Dave Davies, subject of unbroken pop media visibility since his Kinks' chart breakthrough eighteen months earlier.

Granting the occasional interview, Page was quite willing to pass on tricks of the trade - such as his practice of winding on a top E string where a B should be, and a banjo octave string for E. Received wisdom from Joe Brown-via-Eddie Cochran was his habit of using an extra-light third string, the key to his agile bending a middle-register 'blue' notes.

Yet, while being far too important and busy to take up The Yardbirds' offer, Page recommended Jeff Beck, then of The Tridents, a Middlesex unit active on the southern counties R&B circuit. Just a few months younger than Jimmy, Jeff was also veteran of a succession of fly-by-night Surrey groups, some just like The Shadows - though Beck was less impressed by Hank B. Marvin than the more abandoned Cliff Gallup of Gene Vincent's Blue Caps, and the guitarists on albums like 1963's *Folk Festival Of The Blues*, an aural souvenir of a Chicago concert the previous summer showcasing Muddy Waters, Howlin' Wolf, Buddy Guy and one of the Sonny Boy Williamsons.

Jeff and Jimmy had met via Annetta, the former's elder sister who'd knew Page as a fellow art student. 'He came round my house with a home-made guitar,' recalled Jimmy, 'and played the James Burton solo from Ricky Nelson's "My Babe" - and we were immediately like blood brothers.'[12] The two began tinkering on guitars together and, according to Jeff, 'were probably the closest two friends that could ever be, although there was this amazing rivalry.'[12] This tended to come to the fore in public situations - such as a remarkable jam session at Eel Pie Island on 6 May 1964 with a shower that included Bill Wyman on bass and Ian Stewart, another Rolling Stones associate, on piano. Everyone took turns on lead vocals, but the essence of this impromptu display was Page and Beck breaking sweat on duelling six-strings.

Yet when Page was consulted by Neil Christian about a replacement for Albert Lee in the Crusaders, Beck's was the name that tripped most instantly off his tongue - as it would when The Yardbirds were after a new lead guitarist. To sub-flavour the group's 'Heart Full Of Soul', the single that followed 'For Your Love' up the charts, Jimmy lent Jeff the new-fangled fuzz-box that had been custom-built by a mutual Surrey friend, Roger Meyer - and bought a sitar, a nine-stringed instrument with moveable frets and vibrating under-strings, from an Indian musician present.

Chuckling, the group's then-manager Georgio Gomelsky would recollect, 'Our friend Jimmy Page was visiting us. He and Jeff got an amp set up in the bathroom of the studio, the only place available, in an attempt to come up with some trickery to imitate the sitar sound on a guitar, and every ten minutes or so I would check on what they were doing. Time was running out. We needed a bit of luck. Miraculously, Jeff came up with something we could use, and we politely parted company with the rather puzzled Indian musicians - who had never been in a studio before - but not before Jimmy, wildly enthusiastic about the sounds emanating from it, bought the sitar (and the piece of carpet it was wrapped in) from them. I shall never forget watching him walking down the street with that strange shape under his arm.'[68]

If making the debatable claim that he was the first British rock 'n' roller to own a sitar, Jimmy treated it initially as if it was a fancy guitar, but he had become sufficiently masterful of his purchase for a Page sitar *obligato* - rather than a busking saxophone - to gnaw at Mick Jagger's 1967 production of Chris Farlowe's revival of the jazz standard, 'Moanin', after Jimmy, like Mick, had been taken on as a freelance producer by Andrew Loog Oldham's Immediate, the country's most successful independent record company of the 1960s.

Three years earlier, Farlowe had been a struggling solo singer in an age of groups, albeit backed by musicians of the calibre of Albert Lee, fresh from the Crusaders. Before Albert's arrival, Chris had made casual enquiries about the availability of Jimmy Page - and this Jeff Beck bloke. Who'd still been a Trident when Page and Glyn Johns oversaw a studio session in December 1964 that spawned several instrumentals featuring Beck. By then, The Tridents had washed up as far from the blues as they could be on lumbering themselves with the task of backing Craig Douglas, one of the UK's Bobby-ish boy-next-door luminaries of the early 1960s. This lucrative if brief stint prompted The Tridents to approach Fontana, Craig's record label, with an acetate that was rejected not for Jeff's tyro lead vocals, but because 'the guitar sounds distorted'. Beck was also prone to 'going off on a tangent, and everyone would laugh and say, "Play some proper blues"'[12] as he tossed in *leitmotifs* that alternated Oriental-sounding exotica with hackneyed clichés of showbiz cabaret.

The boy deserved attention - and after a deputation from The Yardbirds looked in at a Tridents' engagement in Twickenham, an audition the following afternoon was a mere formality. Noticing albums by The Four Seasons, The Beach Boys and Julie London in Jeff's Balham flat, his new confrères concluded correctly that he was less committed to the blues than Clapton.

Furthermore, as well as being willing to participate in crass promotional necessities, Beck's solos and riffs - in common with the likes of George Harrison, Ian 'Tich' Amey, The Dave Clark Five's Lenny Davidson and Tony Hicks of The Hollies - were constructed to integrate with the melodic and lyrical intent of a given piece. This approach seemed attractively unfussed to anyone attuned to the more obvious aesthetics of a song than a reaction principally to underlying chord sequences with high-velocity flash - as dispensed by Clapton on, for instance, 'A Certain Girl', The Yardbirds' maiden B-side, in which his break had almost a separate life from the rest of the number.

Beck was both more experimental and more direct in style too than either Clapton or the mainstream pop guitarists. 'You could never get him to tune up,' laughed Keith Relf, 'He'd go on stage with his guitar totally out of tune and bend the strings. He never really played chords - just all bendy notes - but he never once played out of tune.'

Running in the same pack as The Yardbirds before 'For Your Love' changed everything, The Downliners Sect were well-placed to likewise climb the charts as, from a rhythm-and-blues core, they too had started to sound and look alarmingly like a pop group during a lengthy 1964 residency at Eel Pie Island. Jimmy Page had known and liked individual members since the group's emergence from where outlines dissolve between Surrey and Middlesex, after treading warily amidst official disapproval of rock 'n' roll at Gunnersbury Grammar School.

A Sect recital was an education too for Rod Stewart and Steve Marriott. Moreover, Van Morrison's longtime collaborator, Herbie Armstrong 'remembered him asking if he could blow harmonica with them, but they said it was too late. I think Van had had the idea of forming an R&B group before that, but when he saw The Downliners Sect, he said, "That's the sort of group I want to have!"' Morrison himself corroborated this statement with 'the first British R&B group I heard was The Downliners Sect. It was at the Ken Colyer club. They were really doing it then. I heard The Pretty Things, but the Downliners Sect were *it*.'[69]

Yet British R&B deduced Sect bass player Keith Grant was 'a very strange animal' - and who could argue when listening to The Sect? Beyond merely sucking Chuck Berry into the vortex of blues as the Stones *et al* had, a typical Downliners set might veer fitfully from 'Too Much Monkey Business' to a skiffle stand-by like 'Wreck Of The Old '97' - and on to 'Green Onions' before exploring Screaming Lord Sutch territory with, say, the repulsively amusing 'I Want My Baby Back'. In R&B haunts, they trod on thinner ice with the likes of 'May The Bird Of Paradise Fly Up Your Nose', a country-and-western novelty.

Administering the R&B medicine far neater, John Mayall has carved a niche of true individuality in perhaps pop's most stylised form for nigh on half a century - after his blues came down from Cheshire. When he added harmonica to his keyboard, guitar and vocal abilities, Mayall's London debut in 1962 was preceded by publicity comparing him to multi-instrumental jazzman Roland Kirk. A year later, he and his Bluesbreakers cautiously went pro.

Clapton, the most illustrious of Mayall's later sidemen, recorded informally with Jimmy Page on two occasions in June 1965, not quite three months after his departure from The Yardbirds. In Page's electronic den in Surrey, the two improvised round blues structures - given titles afterwards like 'Tribute To Elmore' and 'West Coast Idea' - after microphones were positioned and the valves of Jimmy's two-track reel-to-reel warmed up.

These rambling instrumentals were for seemingly non-specific purposes and were not, in the first instance, intended for public ears. Nevertheless, following the superimposition of drums and bass - courtesy of Bill Wyman - in a hired studio, most of them were included on volumes one and two of *Blues Anytime*, 1968 compilations by Immediate. The original tapes by the two guitar heroes were sold for a vast sum at Sotheby's in 1988.

THE BLACK SNAKE MOANER

*'I only dared go home at night because my hair was so long.
So I left home and started my real education, moving from
group to group, furthering my knowledge of the blues and
other music which had weight'* - Robert Plant[9]

The truest *Midland Beat* popularity poll result would
come in 1966, when the journal's catchment area was at its
widest. This time, The Spencer Davis Group swept the board
- number one group, Davis as top rhythm guitarist and Steve
Winwood ruling the lead guitarist, male singer and organist sections. Faintly ludicrous, however, was percussion aesthete Pete
York - commissioned by *Midland Beat* to pen a regular advice
column - as joint top drummer with ex-Sunday School Teacher
Gerry Freeman of The Applejacks - whose star by then had returned to its former obscurity.

Possibly, The Applejacks might have held their demise
at arm's length by ditching the stage suits and big smiles for
the hirsute, motley taciternity of groups in artistic debt to The
Rolling Stones, Manfred Mann, The Pretty Things, the 'most
blueswailing' Yardbirds, Them and other outfits who'd first entered the Top Twenty without much compromising such an image. All discernable as 'rhythm-and-blues', they'd mined - like
The Moody Blues and The Spencer Davis Group - less confined
seams than those of Alexis Korner's Blues Incorporated. Yet it
was Alexis himself who blazened the oddest symptom of R&B's
new acceptability when he led the resident band on the ITV
children's series, *Five O'Clock Club*. The memory of the programme's glove-puppet compere, Pussy Cat Willum introducing
Korner's gritty rendition of Ma Rainey's 'See See Rider' isn't
easy to forget.

Back in the beat clubs that were now pocking the Midlands, Kidderminster's Javelins, who'd milked audiences with
fab-gear Merseybeat favourites, played a farewell engagement early in 1964 before reforming the following week as The
Crawling King Snakes, named after the John Lee Hooker opus.

More prosaic were The Rhythm-and-blues Group all the way from Grantham. Then there were The Boll Weevils from *dem ole* cottonfields of Erdington, and, from Kidderminster again, The Shakedown Sound who, prior to mutating into Mott The Hoople, backed the ubiquitous Jimmy Cliff, and often supported major R&B attractions at the newly refurbished Whisky-A-Go-Go, on a par with London's ultra-trendy Flamingo, near Birmingham city centre.

That such a policy proved efficacious in the long run won such groups respect from less sophisticated brethren who, if more immediately popular, tended to be derivative if competent. The Grasshoppers, say, were 'Meridan's answer to The Beatles' while Yardley's fave raves were now The Chindits whose vocalist copied Mick Jagger. Moreover, in an era of groups rather than lone wolves, the big-voiced likes of Nicky James and Danny King were unable to find a niche despite a flexible vocal command, commercial material and easy jack-the-lad stage projection.

Arriving at much the same soul-destroying roadblock, Johnny Neal vanished from the pages of history in 1965 with a workmanlike revival of olde-tyme rock 'n' roller Charlie Rich's 'Walk Baby Walk' - while Keith Powell, also a square-jawed throwback to the 1950s, had bid a more protracted farewell after his three singles lead to a transfer from EMI to Pye as a solo artist. Great things were expected of Keith, even though all his EMI singles with The Valets had crash-landed in the bargain bin, but, on Pye, he fared little better.

As Keith Powell was Birmingham's, so The Hellions were Worcester's. So vital a pop Mecca was this county town that, as well as 'Worcester Whisperings' in *Midland Beat*, it even had its own shoestring record label, Impression, responsible for The Jaguars' 'Opus To Spring', a 45 that had exhausted an unrepeated run of five hundred copies. Led by guitarist Dave Mason, this instrumental group sometimes accompanied Jim Capaldi, a saturnine Elvis Presley imitator from Evesham. He was to retreat from the front of the stage to become drummer with those scandalous Sapphires.

A decent interval after the disgraceful incident in Gloucester over Rodney Dawes' trousers, Jim formed The Hellions, who, noted *Worcester Whisperings*, were soon 'quietly becoming a most important force on the local beat scene, establishing themselves more by personal recommendation than by force of personality'.[49] That they were an unprepossessing bunch is borne out by the brooding intensity of publicity photos taken after they recruited Mason in 1964.

Now full-time musicians, The Hellions backed Walsall's Tanya Day - who had a Polydor single and attendant *Thank Your Lucky Stars* slot to her credit - for a residency at Hamburg's Star-Club. Among familiar faces working split-shifts on the same bill were Kidderminster's Shades Five - and The Spencer Davis Group, a cordial encounter and one which had a bearing on Jim and Dave's future lives.

When The Hellions returned to Britain in autumn 1964, they were able to place 'Shades Of Blue' - a group original - on The Rockin' Berries' *In Town* LP, and with George E. Washington, a Decca artiste. Heartened by this syndication, The Hellions convinced Piccadilly, a Pye subsidiary, that another self-composition would make a saleable single. Yet, in spite of plugging on the Light Programme, 1965's 'Tomorrow Never Comes' fought shy of the charts - as did the follow-up, 'A Little Lovin' - not, incidentally, The Fourmost's hit of the same title.

Mason was first to leave the sinking ship. As 'A Little Lovin' bit the dust, so too did a chance to plug it on *Ready Steady Go*. Finally, while their Star-Club friends, The Spencer Davis Group, reached Number One with 'Keep On Running' in January 1966 - prompting the *Birmingham Mail*'s 'City Group Top Of The Pops' headline - The Hellions signed off after their farewell single, 'Hallelujah', was released under an alias - The Revolution.

Before the year was out, however, Mason, Capaldi and woodwind blower Chris Wood, from Locomotive, gladly combined with the gifted Steve Winwood in Traffic, who, said their publicist, would 'get it together' in a remote rural cottage. With the debut single, 'Paper Sun', embracing a faint reminder of 'Shades Of Blue' in its coda, for as long as Traffic survived, so, by proxy, would The Hellions.

Traffic had been hatched over drinks and during customary *ad hoc* jamming at The Elbow Room. Likewise, the *dramatis personnae* of The Move came together at Club Cedar on Constitution Hill. While Traffic, The Move and a reborn Moody Blues were to bask in Brumbeat's Indian Summer, Dame Fortune smiled less brightly on numerous 'nice little bands' such as Listen, The Idle Race, Lemon Tree, The Dog That Bit People, Tea-And-Symphony, Slenderlorrif and Young Blood. Often self-consciously 'weird', these haunted newish venues like Erdington's fêted Mothers (where The Pink Floyd were to tape an in-concert album), Birmingham Arts Lab or the 'Contemporary Music Club' above the Jolly Sailor, where customers sat cross-legged and discussed over a reefer afterwards how 'interesting' it all was.

It was the advent of 'bands' - not groups - of such 'progressive' persuasion, beginning in late 1966, that accelerated Midlands pop's coming of age, many of its executants having spent years in the ranks of ensembles as diverse as Gerry Levene's Avengers, Mike Sheridan's Nightriders, The Hellions, The Ugly's, Carl Wayne and the Vikings, The Rest and Danny King and his Mayfair Set.

A more-than-generous fistful of 'bands' came from outside Birmingham. Bearing the same relationship to the city as, say, Windsor, Slough and Staines do to London is the Wolverhampton-Kidderminster-West Bromwich triangle and its environs, which cradled a pop scene as self-contained in its quieter way as Merseybeat. Against the odds, Kidderminster alone had already spawned hit parade contenders in Peter Wynne, one of svengali Larry Parnes' 'stable' of principally male pop singers - and former carpet manufacturer employee Roger Lavern, organist with The Tornados. This town and adjacent pivots of industrial enterprise were also to produce -

albeit belatedly - world-class outfits in Slade - and the Robert Plant-John Bonham half of Led Zeppelin. Trapeze burst out of Kidderminster as well, but global fame proved elusive.

Today, whenever certain residents of Kidderminster and thereabouts of a certain age gather in licensed premises, they speak of many things - of, for instance, the jiving in the aisles when *Rock Around The Clock* reached the Central cinema; the opening night of the Friday Pop Club at the New Meeting Hall in September 1960; The Rinki-Dinks' trip to France with glamour puss Dinah Clunes satisfying a contract stipulation about a female vocalist; the non-arrival of the rhythm guitarist when The Ramrods were in the finals of the Big Beat Contest at the Gaumont; Mack Woolley's dance band playing alternate nights at Willenhall Baths and the Three Men In A Boat - a lot of groups used to rehearse in the back room there - that punch-up at Highlands Secondary Modern when Nick and the Axemen were on; The Rolling Stones having to change their name to The Ward Five because of that other lot in London; The 'N Betweens supporting The Spencer Davis Group and Zoot Money's Big Roll Band at the Civic Hall early in '65; Johnny Travell and his Vendors coughing up for a session at Domino Sound behind a radio rental in Albrighton; a great night dancing to Jess Roden's Shakedown Sound at the Blue Flame before it became the Lafayette; Roy Grant of The Strollers, who sang just like Roy Orbison, and do you remember when Robert Plant was with The Banned? He could wail a very convincing harmonica, you know. He was no slouch as a guitarist either, but, very professionally, he left his instrument at home so he could concentrate on vocals.

Who were that bunch from Walsall? Rowdy and the Drovers! They became The Mark Dean Combo. Their big moment was backing Mike Sarne for three gigs when he was at Number One with 'Come Outside'. One of them married Janice Nicholls. She passed judgement on the latest discs on *Thank Your Lucky Stars*. Her catch-phrase was 'I wouldn't buy it, but I'll give it five' - the maximum score - in her Wednesbury monotone. In 1964 she cashed in with a single of near enough the same title.

Tony Dangerfield, Mark Dean's bass guitarist, auditioned for Carter-Lewis and the Southerners, but he was in Brian Gulliver and the Travels on *For Teenagers Only* on two consecutive Thursday nights with Steve Brett and the Mavericks. Their bass player was Dave Holland. He was later with Miles Davis, but it was Tony, wasn't it, who gave him his first lessons in a bedroom above his mum's sweet shop? Did you know Tony took over from Ricky Brown in Screaming Lord Sutch and the Savages? By 1966, mind, he was back in the Black Country, and was rehearsing a band with Jeff Lynne and Martin Barre (who replaced Mick Abrahams as guitarist in Jethro Tull). John Bonham was involved too, but he'd given cheek to his dad, who confiscated his drum kit.

Another act that broke loose of the local orbit briefly were Shades Five who, in August 1964, began that Hamburg season with The Hellions and The Spencer Davis Group. Though foreordained for chart success too, Stan Webb, the Five's lead guitarist, had been considered too young to go, now that the law was no longer as lax about minors in Reeperbahn night spots giving Wee Willie Winkie apoplexy. Decades into the future, however, Germany wouldn't be able to get enough of Stan Webb.

Yet back in 1964, the boy's heart had sunk with the knowledge that the others were managing without him over the North Sea - and with every reason to suppose that Shades Five would remain *sur le continent* indefinitely - who could blame him if he tried his luck with another group? At seventeen, Webb was already an experienced entertainer. When barely out of shorts, he'd been strutting his stuff at wedding receptions, birthday parties and fêtes before graduating to receiving actual money in pubs and working men's clubs. On leaving school, he pledged himself eventually to The Blue Four, formed from denizens of the Seven Stars Blues Club in Stourbridge, and who expanded into Shades Five.

When the Star-Club opportunity arose, Stan insisted that the other lads pack their cases with his blessing. Attractive in his matter-of-fact candour, he had noticed that the local music scene, if not quite exploding, had grown immensely, and may have ascertained from an intangible buzz in the air that his time was about to come.

It came in the form of David Yeats, who asked Webb to fill a vacancy in his Sounds Of Blue - a sextet that satisfied the artistic requirements of one bored with mainstream pop. 'The material was not the kind of stuff other bands were doing at the time,' discovered Stan, 'We did material by Mose Allison, Chuck Berry, Bo Diddley and that stuff'.[70] Within weeks, Stan Webb emerged as a guitarist of the same standing in Kidderminster as Alvin Dean (later, Alvin *Lee*, mainstay of Ten Years After) of The Jaybirds over in Nottingham, 'considered by many, the best in the Midlands', according to *Midland Beat*.[54]

Sounds Of Blue were advantaged too by the abilities of Stourbridge blues *chanteuse* Christine Perfect. She'd studied at Mosely School of Art with a guitarist named Chuck Botfield, who'd invited her to sing with his outfit, The Rockin' Berries. Nowadays, she doubled on piano, and had once functioned as half of a duo with Spencer Davis - plus, on woodwinds, Chris Wood, ostensibly studying at Stourbridge Art College, but able to cope with up to four bookings a week within the small world of Black Country pop.

That male onlookers focussed nearly as much on Webb and Wood as tall, blonde Miss Perfect was reflective of the burgeoning respect felt for instrumental virtuosity. Nevertheless, when Shades Of Blue became Chicken Shack in 1965, there was no place for Chris Wood - who was to land on his feet eventually in Traffic. Christine Perfect quit too - for a post as a window dresser in London.

Named because they used to rehearse in a poultry shed belonging to the bass guitarist's parents, Chicken Shack traced the Shades Five scent to the Star-Club for a three-month stretch which was, reasoned Edgbaston booking agent Jim Simpson, 'rather like training a thousand-metre runner by sending him on five thousand-metre courses'. This encounter with the Fatherland certainly bred a new confidence in Chicken Shack by the time they returned with the outside of their van defaced by the frauleins' affectionate messages.

Toughened for less demanding tasks in Britain, they had also increased vastly in volume. 'We were one of the first bands with great stacks of Marshall amps behind us,' recalled Stan with quiet pride, 'We were so bloody loud, we could - and did - get away with murder, doing a mix of blues and R&B, featuring lots of Muddy Waters and Howlin' Wolf'.

The success of Chicken Shack's daring approach coincided with the re-enlistment of Christine Perfect - for whom the prospect of finishing up half-a-century later as a retired department store manageress had lost its allure. Too hot for the Midlands to hold, the ensemble was signed in 1967 to Blue Horizon, a company founded by former Decca recording manager Mike Vernon.

To grab Vernon's attention was a feather in any aspiring R&B act's cap. For a start, he knew what he was talking about, having edited with his brother, *R&B Monthly*, perhaps the first fanzine of its kind in Britain. While still at Decca, Mike's first essay as a producer was an LP by Texas-born blues pianist Curtis Jones who - like another client, Champion Jack Dupree - had made this sceptr'd isle his home. As well as the bona fide US article, Mike searched out blues-derived domestic talent. Among his earlier discoveries were The Graham Bond Organisation, The Yardbirds, The Artwoods and The Spencer Davis Group - whose leader had recommended Chicken Shack to him.

After lending an intrigued ear to their demo tape, Vernon hastened to catch Chicken Shack in their natural habitat. Among principal factors that impressed him was that 'Stan struck me immediately as being a complete extrovert, a complete and utter lunatic with a very exciting visual appeal on stage. He had a good band, probably the most solid Stones-type Chicago blues band of them all'.

Robert Plant wouldn't have minded being in a group like Chicken Shack as he shook a frustrated fist in the direction of London, which was only maybe two to three hours away by rail, but might as well have been Alpha Centauri. The road he was on was obscure, a dusty and frequently wearisome road that didn't look as if it was leading anywhere important - but there was always a chance that it might. You only had to put yourself in the way of things. What happened next was up to others. They'd push you in whatever direction fate ordained, even if it was one that had never occurred to you before.

Whether he'd become internationally famous in later life or not, Robert Plant would have been remembered as more than a run-of-the-mill local pop star - certainly one who would have been profoundly disappointed if he hadn't Made It. By the time he filed out on his last day at the grammar school, he was entertaining regularly at the Seven Stars Blues Club whose clientele, like that of Richmond's Crawdaddy embraced both 'youths' and, half a class up, a greater number of 'young people' from families like Robert's, whose father had unbent sufficiently to drive him from Kidderminster to the weekly session, and collect him afterwards.

As it had been with Stan Webb and The Blue Four, Plant fell in with a pool of Seven Stars musicians who formed the nucleus of a more fixed set-up. The Delta Blues Band's stock-in-trade was mostly 'I Got My Mojo Working', 'Baby Please Don't Go', 'Route 66', 'Hoochie Coochie Man' and other set-works that were common property of groups you'd encounter in every other town in Britain. When he and an acoustic guitarist played floor spots in parochial folk clubs, Robert also remained true to the blues, giving 'em 'Corinna Corinna', 'In My Time Of Dying'[71] - to be resurrected on Led Zeppelin's *Physical Graffiti* - and further stumblings from this Blind Willie or that Cripple Clarence half a world away.

He'd spat out the plum and now had a singing style that was bashed about and lived in. By European *bel canto* standards, Robert Plant 'couldn't sing' - not 'real singing', as sonorous as Roy Orbison's cowboy operatic or Elvis when he tried hymns. While reminiscent of the clear tenor of The Zombies' Colin Blunstone, Plant's voice had little of that exquisite vowel purity and nicety of intonation, probably because he had been endeavouring consciously to sound like the bluesmen and classic rockers he admired while it was either still breaking or just freshly broken. As Gene Pitney's polished tenor had been warped to a dentist's drill-like whine - albeit an oddly appealing one - so Robert's uncertain treble had been corrupted for all time by, say, hot-potato-in-the-mouth Presley, the hollered arrogance of Muddy Waters, the nasalings of Bukka White and neo-hysterical Little Richard.

Plant's performance grew more strangled as his adolescent spots rose through the lacto-calomine lotion and turned red, and he started to exude the breathy sentience of a man who has been sprinting. He was probably a far lesser vocalist without a public address system, but when he became intense, every sound he dredged up was like a brushstroke on a painting. Backing off until the microphone was at arm's length, just a sandpapery quiver during a dragged-out note could be as loaded as a roar with it halfway down his throat.

This was the passport to his entry into the ranks of The New Memphis Bluesbreakers, The Black Snake Moan and The Banned, while enduring a home life that became so intolerable that his parents had come near to washing their hands of him. In reciprocation, he'd be driven sometimes to sleeping in one of his various group's vans rather than at Hayley Green with its incomprehension, lamentation and deprivation over issues like hair, the imposed shortness of which no backcombing, pulling or applications of a gel called Dippety-Do could disguise.

One day, Robert ceased fighting against fighting, and soon the Mod trim he'd sported at the Sonny Boy Williamson show at Birmingham Town Hall became but a recollection as, after a period with a *bouffant*, razor-cut back-combing, his blond tresses began touching his shoulders, and attracted comment that today's ponytailed navvy would find incredible. During the so-called Swinging Sixties, however, it wasn't generally acceptable for males to have long hair, and you'd be persecuted by heterosexual chauvinists. In an England where even quiffed Elvis was not yet a symbol of masculinity, the least of it was some Oscar Wilde bawling 'get yer 'air cut!' from a passing car while his grinning mates twisted round in the back seat to gauge the effect of this witticism on you. The worst of it was uproar and assault as epitomised by 'Peter's pride was his shoulder length hair,' the opening sentence of an amused write-up in the *Daily Express* about the scalping of a teenager by British soldiers garrisoned in Cyprus.[72]

On stage, Plant stoked up aggression with a studied radiance of effeminacy. More insidiously aggravating were the subtly narcissistic endeavours as he pretended that he couldn't care less about the cow-eyed efforts of the girls near the front, tits bouncing, to grab his attention, shivering with pleasure if the focus of one of his pseudo-bashful grins. Further back were lads whose coiffures were governed by work conditions, school and parental pressure. If bold with beer and bluster, they couldn't admit finding that Robert nancy boy guiltily transfixing as, by slightly overdoing the subliminal obnoxiousness, he wallowed in a repellent bewitchment.

He restyled that contentious hair as best he could for when, so the story goes, he was seen by day as a trainee chartered accountant after he completed his college course. If this was true, he didn't last long - not much more than a fortnight - owing to overall passive disinterest and an extra-mural objective with which those on other desks could have identified. They guessed correctly that Robert's leisure hours were not being spent with crosswords, watching television or membership of the Young Conservatives. At work, he may have been regarded as one of these quiet, shy blokes who keep themselves to themselves. They're the ones you need to watch, the ones most likely to go berserk and heave the managing director down a flight of stairs or machine-gun the queue for the photocopier.

It's possible to imagine columns of figures swimming before budgerigar eyes on the too many occasions when Plant had only got to bed as the graveyard hours chimed that morning. The candle was burning to the middle, and hardly able to think straight, he'd muddle through the day on automatic, perhaps greeting with a snarl colleagues of the same lowly rank who approached him as he turned pages, balanced books and swivelled on his chair to chuckle politely when a superior bantered about what the temps were like that week. Much of the time may have been spent glancing over his shoulder for nosier members of staff and doing something 'normal' whenever one or other of them hoved into view as he figured out a set-list or nagged in biro at fragments of scribbled lyrics and notation peculiar to himself. Otherwise, Robert let his mind go numb with the listlessness of one totally bored by convertible debenture and compound interest in pounds, shillings and pence, nauseated by the thought of it stretching ahead of him, day after day, until he received the gold watch that would tick away the time left to him before he trudged along that bourne from which no traveller returns.

By 1965, Robert had taken enough exasperated stock to pack in his soul-destroying job if it ever existed, and be a full-time musician, however much his mother wrung her hands. He was now cavorting on the boards as one of The Crawling King Snakes. Though their name had something to do with John Lee Hooker, riding roughshod over the blues was a repertory preference for soul and Jefferson Airplane, Buffalo Springfield, Moby Grape, Love and further psychedelic sounds wafting from California. This was to leave its mark most obviously on *Led Zeppelin III*'s 'Since I've Been Loving You', a track that owed much to 'Never' from a Moby Grape album.

Hedging his bets, Plant also accepted invitations to sing with The Good Egg - on whose behalf he complained bitterly to the Walsall Teacher Training College's social secretary when the group wasn't paid on the very evening of a booking there - and, more lucratively, The Tennessee Teens, a trio - guitarist John Crutchley, drummer Geoff Thompson and, on bass, Roger Beamer - who were, reckoned Robert, as loud as The Who. They were to mutate into Listen after obtaining a one-shot single deal in 1965 with CBS, then far from the global conglomerate that it was to become.

So began Robert Plant's commercial discography. Coupled with 'Everybody's Gotta Say', one of several self-penned efforts[73], the A-side was a xerox of 'You Better Run', a US Top

Twenty entry for The Young Rascals, four New Yorkers who had less to do with flower-power than soul, ploughing much the same furrow as label-mates The Vanilla Fudge, albeit more credibly with original material than overhauling black music.[74] By bilious coincidence, Listen's 'You Better Run' was also up against a simultaneous cover on a subsidiary of the more powerful EMI label by - of all people - The 'N Betweens, whose Noddy Holder had served briefly as Listen's driver.

THE YARDBIRD

'I want to contribute a great deal more to the group than just standing there looking glum' - Jimmy Page[75]

With internal sources of new material and their own publishing companies, a lot of these blasted beat groups had given the music business a nasty turn. The rules of *Ready Steady Win*, a *Search For Stars*-like spin-off from ITV's *Ready Steady Go* pop series, had even insisted on at least one original per entrant.

Composers have to start somewhere, but the possibility of a group developing songwriting to any great extent had been relatively unheard of before 1962. As far as the middle-aged publishing offices of Denmark Street - and now Tin Pan Alley - were concerned, the rot had set in when John Lennon and Paul McCartney, in creating the precedent of penning all of their Beatles' A-sides, had stepped over the demarcation between artiste and 'professional' songwriter.

This had set the others off. Stirred when Lennon and McCartney completed 'I Wanna Be Your Man' virtually to order when looking in at a Stones rehearsal in 1963, Mick Jagger and Keith Richards had made their first attempts at songwriting. Likewise, though another metropolitan rhythm-and-blues unit, The Kinks, had started with a Merseybeat-flavoured A-side, they caught the lightning in 1964 with 'You Really Got Me', the work of their Ray Davies.

It wasn't quite Sinatra, but a feather in Ray's cap was when Peggy Lee, international entertainer since before the war, had been first in the queue for his 'I Go To Sleep', a hit when revived by The Pretenders in 1981. He also mailed demos to Elvis Presley, though the King did not deign to use them - but so far there have been around three hundred recorded non-Kinks versions of Ray Davies songs.

To the further detriment of Denmark Street's worker ants, the albums, sheet music and, if lucky, demo tapes of other groups containing songwriting teams were scrutinised for potential smashes. The most obvious example, The Beatles' 'Yesterday', did the trick for both smooth balladeer Matt Monro and soul-shouter Ray Charles, and, decades later, Wet Wet Wet's revival of 'Love Is All Around' made Reg Presley of The Troggs a near-millionaire, but earnings in this direction were generally more modest for the likes of Pete Townshend of The Who, the Hollies 'L. Ransford' - an umbrella pseudonym for Allan Clarke, Graham Nash and Tony Hicks - Unit Four Plus Two's Tommy Moeller and Brian Parker, Phil May and Dick Taylor from The Pretty Things, Denny Laine and Mike Pinder of The Moody Blues, Steve Marriott and Ronnie Lane from The Small Faces - and The Yardbirds.

If lacking 'image' beyond a generalised 'arty' aura, The Yardbirds were to leave a lasting impression on pop, particularly after they began to find their feet as composers during a two-year golden age from 1964 when 'For Your Love' (by Graham Gouldman of Manchester's Mockingbirds) precipitated more international chartbusters for The Yardbirds in 'Heart Full Of Soul', 'Evil-Hearted You', 'Still I'm Sad' - their first self-penned A-side - 'Shapes Of Things' and 'Over Under Sideways Down', all hybrids of instant familiarity and unpretentious musical challenge.

As they ventured into areas far removed from their R&B core, among extraordinary musical visions realised were the pioneering of extended improvisation - 'rave-ups' - and the imposition of symphonic tempo changes, Gregorian chant and other eruditions onto their basic guitars-bass-drums-vocals musical grid. With The Kinks, The Yardbirds were also the first pop explorers of Indian sounds. Nevertheless, though, indeed, a sitarist had been hired for 'Heart Full Of Soul', such ostentation was disregarded after Jeff Beck's guitar tone exhaled what was in pop terms a more pungent breath of the Orient - more like the real thing than the real thing - albeit with a sub-flavouring of Jimmy Page's fuzz-box.

He also made a feature of what might have been an aggravating hazard to, perhaps, The Dave Clark Five or Herman's Hermits - with 'Shapes Of Things' and its 'You're A Better Man

Than I' coupling the most conspicuous examples of Jeff over-driving his Stratocaster through a Marshall amplifier to actively create feedback. For Beck as much as Jimmy Page (when a given session required it) and Pete Townshend - it was a deliberated contrivance for sustaining notes and reinforcing harmonics.

No question: Jeff Beck was an outstanding lead guitarist who displayed eclecticism and unpredictability in compatible amounts. Nonetheless, though posing no limelight-threatening challenge to the front line, drummer Jim McCarty, for example, co-wrote nearly all Yardbird originals, bearing out the argument of Richard MacKay, editor of the Y*ardbirds World* fanzine, that 'The Yardbirds made names for their successive guitarists and not the other way round - because the main ideas stemmed from the others, namely the late Keith Relf, Jim McCarty, Paul Samwell-Smith and Chris Dreja.'

'In The Yardbirds, everybody's contribution was recognised,' confirmed Dreja, 'Paul was the most musical member in the purest sense. Jim was a fair songwriter. Keith was an interesting lyricist (though I wrote the words, for example, to 'Lost Women'). We were the sum of the parts as opposed to one guy presenting, say, five numbers as a *fait accompli.*'

In 1966, a *New Musical Express* critic compared the all-original *Yardbirds* LP, generally known as 'Roger The Engineer' after its cover drawing by Dreja, favourably with *Revolver*, The Beatles' latest. Such praise was all the more deserved because, unlike The Beatles, The Yardbirds' studio time was always limited, but, though they were granted only five days off from a punishing booking schedule to record *Yardbirds*, any extension might have detracted from the proceedings' spontaneity and endearing imperfections. Certainly no cover - whether Al Stewart's 'Turn Into Earth' or, also with Jimmy Page to the fore, Paul and Barry Ryan's 'I Can't Make Your Way' - ever surpassed The Yardbirds' blueprint.

Yet it was in the heat of such syndication and the group's general world success that the scum of internal dissent was allowed to surface. As he'd been within earshot of the others for every working day for the past not-quite three years, Jeff Beck would awake sickened with the contemplation of further allocated hours shuttered in the studio with them or grinding up and down motorways. Amid the drip-drip of hovering off-stage aggravations too, Keith Relf's periods of pure enjoyment on the boards were marred more and more these days as he fought to be heard against the guitarists' gradually more powerful amplifiers - Beck's 'musical utopia as far as The Yardbirds go'.[76]

Furthermore, Beck - second only to Hank Marvin in that *Beat Instrumental* poll - was proving nearly as much a visual asset to The Yardbirds as he was a musical one. Within his archive of tricks were leaving the guitar howling like a banshee against the speaker as he prowled the stage, and turning round abruptly to play it on the back of his neck Joe Brown-style, above his head or in the small of his back. For a crowning bit of swagger, he might then use a microphone stand or edge of a speaker cabinet to simulate the careen of a bottleneck.

Paranoia split concentration as flare-ups grew in frequency, and the group's investors struggled to keep them from the public. Behind the intimacies of off-mike comments and momentary eye-contacts, there was territory impenetrable to outsiders. Matters became so inflammable that a tacit implication in a seemingly innocuous remark might spark off a hastily unplugged guitar and a slammed backstage firedoor.

A spirit of appeasement might prevail for a while after such an incident, but there remained temptations - particularly on tour - for any one of the five Yardbirds to take himself off to the nearest airport departure lounge or railway ticket office and slip smoothly out of a frequently near-insufferable existence in which a light-hearted mood might persist for a few fiery-eyed miles before souring to cynical discontent, cliff-hanging silences and slanging matches. Bickering helped pass the time, and certain personnel, looking after Number One, kept their ears to the ground for openings elsewhere.

Commercially too, fast was coming the hour when fades the fairest flower. It may be dated from the resignation of the gifted Samwell-Smith, the most active Yardbird in the studio, a month before the release of 'Roger The Engineer'. Emitting an almost palpable aura of self-loathing as he slouched on with a face like a Black Country winter, Samwell-Smith's last straw was on 18 June 1966 at an Oxford college ball - at which Jimmy Page was present as escort to Cass Elliot of The Mamas And The Papas - where Relf was roaring drunk at the microphone. 'He couldn't stand up,' gasped Paul, 'I actually had to sing some numbers just to try to keep the thing going. Jeff sang too. Under previous circumstances, we'd say, "Don't do that again, Keith, because it was awful", but I'd had enough of years and years of getting out of the van - and I was starting to snap at every-body.'

In its aftermath, Paul dared the speech that he'd been agonising over for months. 'We gigged virtually every night for three years,' confirmed Chris Dreja, 'and it all became a bit un-civilised for Paul. An advantage of him leaving then was that it freed us to explore other areas - music with more muscle.'

Within a week, an announcement was made to interested press that the other Yardbirds intended soldiering on without Paul, having persuaded Jimmy Page to step in at last, despite - or because of - his recall of the Oxford fiasco where 'Everyone was dressed up in dinner jackets, and Keith was rolling around the stage, shouting "Fuck!" at the audience, and eventually he collapsed back into the drum kit. It was great, just fantastically suitable for the occasion, I thought.'[1]

Samwell-Smith's subsequent departure coincided with a low point in Jimmy Page's session career. Of late, he'd been booked more and more to churn out 'musak' for supermarkets or something like that. The work was stifling. It was often like being a computer when you had no involvement with the artist. It should be stimulating to do sessions with other groups, but it wasn't working out that way. Another problem was that for a while, guitarists were becoming out of vogue on sessions. Peo-ple had this obsession with something new, using sax sections and things like that. 'I rarely had the chance to roar into some-thing. The sax players and violinists looked on me as some kind of joke with my feedback ideas. I played a lot of rhythm guitar, which was very dull. Most of the musicians I know think I did the right thing in joining The Yardbirds.'[75]

In the first instance, he'd stepped in simply to honour dates previously contracted, commencing with a two hour rehearsal prior to the first of these - at the Marquee on the Tuesday after Oxford. He didn't mind thrumming bass as long as it was understood that he was to revert to a more apt role as co-lead guitarist with Beck as soon as general factotum Dreja was able to take over. 'I had been becoming very stale,' confessed Jimmy, 'Once I was back on stage again, even though I was playing bass, I was thinking in terms of a guitar, and I found I was covering new ground. As soon as I got back on the six-stringer, I found I was doing new things.'[76]

It was during this period that Page tried an effect trailblazed by The Creation, one of the most striking of London's Mod outfits, but now on its last legs. They climaxed their act by splashing an action painting onto a canvas backdrop that was then set alight amid feedback lament from guitarist Eddie Phillips. What awed Page, however, was Eddie's scraping of a violin bow across a fretboard on the group's brace of 1966 Top Fifty entries - and a hasty LP, *We Are Paintermen*, issued only in Scandinavia and Germany, where 'Painter Man', the second of the minor hits at home, had gone to Number One.

Jimmy kept much quieter about his liking for The Creation than that for Kaleidoscope, a quintet of psychedelic bent from Pasadena, who also lacquered their music with bowed guitar. Covering his tracks, nevertheless, Page claimed to have been shown the technique by one of a string section during some session or other before lending an ear to either The Creation or Kaleidoscope.

Both groups had long disbanded - and most of Led Zeppelin's audience had heard of neither - when this gimmick figured most prominently in Page's index of possibilities. By the mid-1970s, his stylistic arsenal would also contain the shrieks and squeals of a theremin, most theatrically on 'Whole Lotta Love'. It was a device invented *circa* 1920 by Lev Termen (later,

Leon Theremin), a Russian physics professor. With tone and single-pitch note adjustable by the movement of one hand back and forth around a hypersensitive antenna and the twiddling of volume control with the other, the theremin's unearthly wails came into their own when used for incidental music in science-fiction movies and, for Jimmy Page, in The Beach Boys' 'Good Vibrations' - at Number One in Britain not long after he made the switch from bass to co-lead guitar in The Yardbirds.

With his low throb pulsating beneath the Page-Beck *maelstrom*, Chris Dreja was The Yardbirds' most hidden talent in that, however little you were aware of him on stage, you'd have missed him if he hadn't been there, principally on rhythm guitar in the pre-Page era. 'There've been occasions when I've been forced into playing lead through absences or walk-outs,' he would disclose, 'but it wasn't my natural field. Riffs, rhythm, jamming, energy: that's where I come from - and I've always been quite happy being behind the ideas without necessarily being the one performing them out front. When I switched to bass, I kept it fairly simple. A lot of the lines had been established already, but some were crazy when we started linking one number to the next.'

However, apart from a cameo in Antonioni's *Blow Up* movie and soundtrack, the only recordings credited to this edition of the group was the overtly psychedelic 'Happenings Ten Years Time Ago', a single that was The Yardbirds' farewell to the Top Fifty on both sides of the Atlantic. Its embrace of police siren-like oscillations and shreds of speech led the group to gild the stage show too with pre-recorded tapes of trains, Hitler in full Nuremberg rally rant and further examples of *musique concrete*. Headlining over The Yardbirds during a tour of Singapore and Australasia, Roy Orbison and his musicians were to shake baffled heads in the wings during the group's spell on the boards - and Jim McCarty's concentration wandered when the star in turn 'seemed to be doing all his old hits in chronological order.' The Yardbirds and Orbison, nonetheless, parted cordially, and Roy presented Jimmy with some Fender guitar accessories from Nashville.

In any case, neither faction appeared to be aware of underlying similarities. Orbison had already woven Ravel, flamenco and a balalaika onto his artistic tapestry, and, two years later, was to release 'Southbound Jericho Parkway', aswarm with jarring vignettes of music spiced together to coalesce his sung narrative. In retrospect, therefore, the chasm between 'Only The Lonely' and 'Happenings Ten Years Time Ago' is not unbreachable, but, by 1967, Roy Orbison was seen by *Rolling Stone, International Times* and similar 'underground' journals as an outmoded perpetrator of vulgar 'pop' while The Yardbirds were still playing 'rock' - which only the finest minds could grasp.

Among these was Richard MacKay, then a teenager living in Margate. One of the few engagements that featured Page transitionally on bass had taken place the previous summer in that Kent holiday resort's Dreamland ballroom where Richard vanished into the seafront night afterwards, lost in wonder: 'The whole night was magic, though the audience hardly moved (like the audience in The Yardbirds' scene in *Blow Up*). The band used to complain about the lack of response, but it was their own fault: they shouldn't have played like musical gods.'

During a harrowing trip to North America that followed, however, the erratic Beck was fired - though, however unknowingly, he had already commenced his career without the group several months previously via 'Bolero', an instrumental taped with a seemingly *ad hoc* crew that included Jimmy Page and The Who's madcap drummer, Keith Moon.

When the *NME*'s 'Alley Cat' tittle-tattler reported - without naming names - that two of The Yardbirds were leaving to form a group with two similarly malcontented members of The Who, it was, therefore, a distortion of old news. When breaks in both groups' itineraries coincided with a mid-week morning during 1966's rainy summer, Jeff Beck and Jimmy Page 'thought of cutting a track with Keith Moon just to see what would happen,' confided Jeff, 'so we rang him up, expecting to get the blank - but he said, "Yeah, I'll be there". Moon was pretty fed up with The Who at that time, but he still had to turn up at the studio so that nobody recognised him. He got out of the cab wearing dark glasses and a Russian cossack hat, so that no-one could see him being naughty with another session.

'We had to have something to play because Keith only had a limited time. He could only give us, like, three hours before his roadies would start looking for him. So I went over to Jimmy's house a few days before, and he was strumming away on his twelve-string Fender electric that had a really big sound. It was the sound of that that really inspired the melody. I invented that melody. We agreed that we would go in and get Moon to play a bolero rhythm with it.'[12]

There remains division about the authorship of this stubbornly chromatic but appealing instrumental with the working title, 'Bolero'. 'I wrote it, played on it, produced it,' insisted Jimmy, 'and I don't give a damn what he says. That's the truth.'[77] Finally, it was attributed to Page in the Performing Rights Society's files.

Nonetheless, just as Paul Samwell-Smith believed that, for their much-covered 'Shapes Of Things', 'Jeff should have got a composing credit for the way he developed it when the song was being formed', so Beck's playing brought 'Bolero' belligerently alive. As capable of severe dissonance as serene melody, he wound on slackened extra-light strings for unprecedented *legato* effect on a piece that, if a new group with the other participants wasn't to happen, he hoped would be issued by EMI as an A-side of a Beck solo 45. After all, even a 1966 single by Keith Relf alone had made the UK Top Fifty, and 'Bolero' could do the same.

During the winter after the hush-hush session that created 'Bolero', Jimi Hendrix was brought to Britain by Chas Chandler of the recently-disbanded Animals. Like every other British guitarist that counted, Beck - and Page - had been capitivated by Jimi, a psychedelic Wild Man of Borneo. Reportedly, Eric Clapton, Pete Townshend and The Rolling Stones' Brian Jones went so far as to attend every Jimi Hendrix Experience engagement in London prior to the trio's first assault on North America in 1967.

Nearly forty years after his sudden death in 1970, Hendrix remains the most omnipotent yardstick by which other electric guitarists judge themselves. While he did not owe his celebrity entirely to instrumental boldness, his way with a left-handed Fender Stratocaster transformed him from journeyman accompanist to such as The Isley Brothers and Little Richard to one of the truly innovative rock icons of the late 1960s. Nevertheless, at a Jimi Hendrix exhibition in 2004 at the Marquee, Jimmy Page strode on stage and admitted humbly that he never saw Hendrix perform owing to his commitments with The Yardbirds.

Tellingly, since Samwell-Smith's exit, the group's repertoire had begun to contain a higher percentage of non-originals other than the blues stand-bys that they'd always played. The Velvet Underground's 'I'm Waiting For The Man' had already joined Bob Dylan's 'Most Likely You'll Go Your Way' in the stage set when a certain Jake Holmes, backed by two acoustic guitarists, opened for The Yardbirds at New York's Village Theatre on 25 August 1967. He earned an encore with 'Dazed And Confused' from *The Underground Sound Of Jake Holmes* LP. Impressed, the headliners spent a free evening that same week at a Holmes recital at the nearby Cafe-A-Go-Go. It wasn't long before 'Dazed And Confused' closed The Yardbirds' performance with, first, the original lyrics and then an adaptation by Keith Relf - not that either were heard very clearly in the midst of the now-flat-out blast of the guitarists.

The interaction between Jimmy Page and Jeff Beck had been compulsively exquisite. From the outset, the concept of one cementing the other's runs with subordinate chord-fretting - *à la* Sullivan and Page on 'The Crying Game' - hadn't entered the equation as the two anticipated and attended to each other's idiosyncrasies and stylistic cliches - as instanced on the instrumental call-and-response on 'Psycho Daisies', B-side of 'Happenings Ten Years Time Ago'. Yet transcendental moments that would look impossible if transcribed were arousing a green-eyed monster in Jeff. 'Having two guitarists was no longer a great idea by the middle of 1967,' sighed Chris Dreja, 'It had become so undisciplined, and Jeff felt - justifiably - that his space was being invaded.'

The Yardbirds did not replace Beck, favouring instead the simpler expedient of carrying on as a quartet. Certainly, instrumental 'power trios' were fashionable then; most of them harking back to the *one* guitar-bass-drums test cases of such as Johnny Kidd and the Pirates, The Tony Sheridan Trio, The Big Three and, later, The Troggs - though any muted cleverness or restraint that The Jimi Hendrix Experience, Cream - Eric Clapton's new group - The Who, Rory Gallagher's Taste and even Black Sabbath might have displayed in the studio was lost to heads-down-no-nonsense rock. Now as gut-wrenching in their way as any of them - on stage at least - The Yardbirds could have as easily reached out to nascent headbangers via blues-plagiarised sound-pictures of Genghis Khan carnage.

En route, a few records were issued after the desperate enlistment - at Page's urging - of console whizz-kid Mickie Most, now one of Britain's most renowned manufacturers of hit parade fodder. Theoretically, he was just what The Yardbirds needed, but whispered misgivings - like diners becoming increasing unhappy about service in a restaurant - were to wax to bold complaint with the appearance of *Little Games*, an LP not thought worth foisting on Britain.

This final studio album was dashed off as a testament less to quality than to market pragmatism. Treasured by most only in retrospect, it wasn't, therefore, first-rate, but it was enjoyable enough and more rounded an entity than it might have been. Of course, it was to be lost in the shadow of 'Roger The Engineer', a hard yardstick for any group, particularly when the *Little Games* compositions *per se* were stripped of, say, Page's wah-wah on 'Smile On Me' and the electronically-warped voice and violin-bowed guitar of 'Glimpses'. Those that stood tallest were Page's 'White Summer' acoustic party-piece, 'Smile On Me' - fanning dull embers of the old fire - the subdued ghostliness of 'Only The Black Rose' and, after a flawed fashion, the remaindered 'Spanish Blood', an instrumental prefacing a hilariously bungled recitation by Jim McCarty, which anticipated his ventures during the 1980s into New Age, a musical form in which moods commensurate with relaxation and pursuits of the mind are investigated undynamically and at length in a manner akin to Indian ragas and Gregorian chant - for which McCarty's Yardbirds experience was to prove invaluable.

Dashed-off *Little Games* aside, with a still-necessary weather-eye on the singles chart, the group had been driven to go once more to outside composers for would-be hits - and on many of these, the presence of some Yardbirds personnel, now past caring, remains in doubt. Already, it had provoked no friction when, for instance, John Paul Jones had been on bass for 'Happenings Ten Years Time Ago'. Into the bargain, Mickie Most forbade much elaboration on the title track 45 of *Little Games*, a sly US-only cover of Manfred Mann's *Ha! Ha! Said The Clown* and other releases symptomatic of The Yardbirds' attempted mutation, however much certain devotees refuted the idea, into just as much of a hard-sell pop act as Herman's Hermits.

THE WAYFARER

'John Bonham - my best mate at the time - and I were the most feared musicians in Birmingham. In 1967, Ozzy Osbourne was in a bus queue, and this old Rover pulled up. I got out in a frock coat, skin-tight trousers and white hair. I was like a skeleton with sunken cheeks. I jumped into a Mini with Jen - my girlfriend, who had long blonde hair - and sped off. Ozzy was thinking, "What an image!" - and I became his idol' - Ace Kefford

Within a year, Ozzy Osbourne was fronting Black Sabbath during a residency at Hamburg's Star-Club that invested a 'progressive' blues style with a bleak but atmospheric intensity. Donning satanic fetishist adornments, they delivered mordant self-composed pieces that reflected the incorporeal dread that Ozzy had sensed emanating from Kefford and his less illustrious friend Bonham.

John, however, remained on civil terms with Mike Kellie, even after the more tractable drummer superceded him in Locomotive as he had in Pat Wayne and the Beachcombers. Containing ex-members of The Blueshounds, and led by trumpeter - and *Midland Beat* picture editor - Jim Simpson. Locomotive had been The Kansas City Seven prior to a transition from jazz via rhythm-and-blues to ritualised let-me-hear-you-say-yeah soul routines. During personnel upheavals over 1966's rainy summer, the tenor saxophonist/flautist was ousted in favour of Chris Wood, now a neighbour of Simpson's in Cradley, to be part of a sensational four-piece horn section. Wood's sister, a provincial Vivienne Westwood *de ses jours*, designed the Seven's stage costumes, charging only for materials.

It was decided too that, as a name, The Kansas City Seven was too Acker Bilk. More in keeping with the changed repertoire, *Midland Beat* announced that the septet would now be known as Locomotive and were 'full steam ahead for the charts'.[78] This statement of intent was amplified by the group's new singer, the talented Danny King: 'We like the crowd to really join in and feel they're actually participating. We try to create a happy party atmosphere.'[78] Bookings were flooding in, even from London by the time John Bonham left.

Throughout the Locomotive period, he had been moon-lighting in any number of competent-but-boring R&B groups trundling out twelve-bars until chucking out time in a pub near you, none of them reaching beyond the stylised limits of 'Hoochie Coochie Man', 'Route 66', 'Smokestack Lightning', 'Dust My Broom', 'Sweet Home Chicago' (hah!) and similar set-works that he'd hear now no more than a sailor hears the sea.

Sometimes, however, Bonham would jump at the chance to accompany the genuine articles such as John Lee Hooker, Jimmy Witherspoon, Jimmy Reed - who, according to Mike Cooper of Reading's Blues Committee was 'drunk for breakfast' - and further US blues potentates who visited Europe so often that a zealot in Solihull or Coventry would see more of the genre's Mississippi and Chicago practitioners in person than his counterpart in the USA. Perhaps the oddest public expression of this overseas surfacing was to be a *Birmingham Evening Post* 'Pop Special' printing full-colour pin-ups of the wizened troupe of an American Blues Legends package - which included heart-throbs like Homesick James, Washboard Willie and Boogie-Woogie Red.

With little time to rehearse, star and pick-up group would frequently entertain with mutually familiar standards during which pseudo-hip blues pedants, tainted by a sort of inverted colour prejudice, would blame musical errors on the white ac-companists rather than the jet-lagged dotard fronting them. He was the genuine article, wasn't he? What did the town oiks up there with him know about blues? Yet one such audience was to swerve from sufferance to delighted acclamation when the boys in the band were introduced towards the finish. It turned out that they were personnel from Fairport Convention, then at a com-mercial zenith.

This lay on a distant horizon for Dave Pegg when he was heard on The Ugly's (*sic*)1966 treatment of The Kinks' nonchalant 'End Of The Season', taped in three hours at Birmingham's Ladbrook Sound. After this A-side flopped, Dave joined singing drummer and vibraphonist Alan 'Bugsy' Eastwood in the Exception. CBS released two singles by the group: 'The Eagle Flies On Friday' and 'Gaberdined Saturday Night Streetwalker', a mordant narrative typical of composer Eastwood, a Winwood-esque Boy Wonder.

'The Eagle Flies On Friday' featured Listen's Robert Plant, still a CBS signing, on tambourine. A close friend of Dave Pegg - and with stronger connections in the record business - Plant introduced The Exception to Eddie Kassner, The Kinks' music publisher, who signed the group to his associated record label, President, for a 1969 album and a retinue of singles.

As none of these sold particularly well, Pegg, now married with a daughter, amalgamated with Cirencester drummer Cozy Powell to become the Tweedledum and Tweedledee of demo sessions at Ladbrook Sound. One day, the studio's house rhythm section encountered Ian Campbell, who Pegg - and Denny Laine - had known at Yardley Grammar School. Skiffle survivors and stalwarts of the West Midlands folk scene, The Ian Campbell Folk Group had supported Bob Dylan at the Town Hall in 1965, and had amassed an impressive booking schedule stretching across to continental Europe.

Dave entered the orbit of the Campbell unit when asked to plonk bass on 1968's *The Circle Game*, an album recorded in Decca's West Hampstead studio under the aegis of Gus Dudgeon, who would be at the console too for David Bowie's imminent 'Space Oddity' session over at Trident. Pegg's official inception into the Folk Group involved swapping his Fender for a double-bass, and a rapid mastery of the mandolin for particular numbers. 'I was still a long-haired rocker,' he grins, 'None of my clothes fitted their Arran sweater image, but they were great people, and it was through them that I developed an interest in and love for folk music.'

About as far from acoustic folkiness as it was possible to be, John Bonham, now beating a blue-grey perloid Ludwig kit like that of Ringo Starr[79], had been drifting from pillar to post, from group to unsatisfactory group since leaving Locomotive. None of them had been able to retain his services for long, even those for whom he seemed not only sincerely loud in not only praising, but also on whom he imposed himself.

After a Crawling King Snakes recital at Wolverhampton's Old Hill Plaza, he'd put himself forward as a more suitable drummer than the incumbent one, speaking first to Robert Plant, who'd taken over from the previous lead vocalist, despite a simultaneous commitment to Listen. Plant called over the others, and the subsequent conversation concluded with Bonham inviting himself to the next rehearsal. His faith in himself proved to be entirely justified both there and at consequent Snakes bookings. Certainly, he had, as Bill Ward noticed, 'a killer bass drum sound - and it got him thrown out of this club. The bouncers came up and said, "You can't play like that in here." The rest of The Crawling King Snakes hadn't even shown up.'[64]

Soon, he was vacillating between the Snakes and The Way Of Life in which he took a solo, putting his back into a truculent frenzy with cross-patterns on snare and tom-toms more prominent than any ringing silverware. This was similar to that which was to last up to thirty minutes on the boards in 'Moby Dick', the number that would frame a drum solo on *Led Zeppelin II*.

The Way Of Life had been the brain child of Ace Kefford's young uncles, singer Reg Jones and Chris, his guitarist brother. After The Chantelles, the latter had been in The Chucks who, like The Rockin' Berries, The Hellions and Shades Five, had served a professional apprenticeship in Germany. On returning, they'd taken stock, and tried again with The Way Of Life, recruiting guitarist 'Sprike' Hopkins (from Gerry Levene's Avengers) and, on bass, Tony Clarkson, who'd once backed Nicky James - who was willing to join The Way Of Life too (as a second vocalist).

On the very afternoon before the first booking - at Club Cedar on Constitution Hill - the group was trying out drummers in the darkened venue with its chilly essence of disinfectant and echo of the previous night's intake of alcohol and tobacco. 'John Bonham showed up and demanded the job,' exclaimed Reg Jones, 'and told all the other hopefuls to go home.'[66] Buoyed by John's uncompromising self-confidence, the group not only went the distance, but were booked regularly at Club Cedar, even though one member's bar tab one night swallowed up the agreed fee.

After Tony Clarkson was superceded by the versatile Danny King, The Way Of Life were taken on by Rik Gunnell, chart-topping Georgie Fame's manager, who had fingers in various showbusiness pies in London. He booked the Midlanders at the Bag O'Nails off Carnaby Street, one of about ten fashionable clubs from which a pop elite and their hangers-on - the 'in crowd' - could select an evening out: evening being defined as round midnight to dawn; fashionable meaning that the super-cool Ad-Lib near Leicester Square would be 'in' for a while before the inscrutable pack transferred allegiance to the Speakeasy or Great Newport Street's Pickwick before finishing up at the Cromwellian, the Scotch Of St. James, the Bag O'Nails and maybe four other hang-outs, attractive for their strict membership controls, tariffs too highly priced for the Average Joe, and no photographers admitted.

In the audience the night The Way Of Life appeared were, apparently, Tom Jones, Paul McCartney - and internationally-acclaimed flamenco guitarist Manitas de Plata. Within his limits, therefore, Bonham was on his best behaviour, slinging a stick at Danny King and shouting 'this *is* the Bag O'Nails, y'know!' when the singing bass player was lighting a cigarette between numbers.

King was replaced by Dave Pegg, who, was keen to revert to electric bass in the hard rock antithesis of Ian Campbell's Folk Group. After rehearsing at Yardley Wood's Warstock pub, Pegg made his Way Of Life debut at Perry Barr's Crown-and-

Cushion, opening with 'You Keep Me Hangin' On' in the 'heavy' manner of a recent hit arrangement by The Vanilla Fudge rather than that of the original by The Supremes.

Immediately, it became clear to Dave that the brute force of Bonham's drumming had increased to the extent that 'the promoter sent us home after the first spot.' During the post-mortem, the case for the defence was that the rest of the group was too quiet. To this end, Bonham employed carpentry skills gleaned from his father to build bigger speaker cabinets. They looked impressive too after a coffin-like fashion, albeit with lime-green cloths and shiny orange finish on the chipwood. He also lined his bass drum with aluminium to creat a booming, cannon-like effect. 'We were so loud then that we'd never get return bookings,' sighed Dave, 'At the Top Spot in Ross-on-Wye, John's bass drum alone sent their decibel meter into the red.'

With Rik Gunnell increasingly more distant since that night-of-nights at the Bag O'Nails, The Way Of Life's campaign for work had now confined them almost exclusively to the West Midlands, the trivial round of bookings - not all of them recurring, owing to the tinnitus-inducing volume - that Bonham had been doing since Pat Wayne and rthe Beachcombers. It was beyond him to show it in public, but there was private regret that, overwhelmed by the exciting news about the Bag O'Nails, he'd turned his nose up at that opportunity to join The Move.

During the planning stage, Ace Kefford and Trevor Burton had, revealed Ace, 'approached Roy Wood from Mike Sheridan's Nightriders on the quiet. Next, we wanted to get Jess Roden from The Shakedown Sound - which would evolve into Mott The Hoople - but he turned us down. By then, I'd told Carl Wayne I'd be leaving the Vikings. Next thing I knew, Carl was saying he wouldn't mind changing his image and joining us. He was in his twenties, and like an old man to us then - so was Bev Bevan - but Carl could get work, was a good front man, and it seemed logical to include him.

'We tried to get John Bonham, who was in The Way Of Life with my two uncles, but he didn't like Carl. Instead, as it had been with the Vikings, it was me that got Bev into The

Move. Initially, we played the same circuit we'd done with the Vikings, but we started getting a reaction from the young girls who pulled us off the stage.'

Principally through The Move's five year chart run - as creative as it was remunerative - the Midlands arrived belatedly at a genuine 'sound', even as its hitherto most renowned groups fell by the wayside. Indeed, after 1966's 'The Water Is Over My Head' peaked in the lower reaches of the Top Fifty, that was that for The Rockin' Berries as far as the charts were concerned. However, contingency plans had long been laid to ensure that they would recoup more than just golden memories; a panto season in Great Yarmouth being a reliable indicator of future direction. Decades later, they'd wind up as permanent fixtures on the 1960s nostalgia circuit with an act as much comical as musical.

By 1966 too, The Moody Blues had been sagging on the ropes - though the aftershock of 'Go Now' still enabled them to just about break even in an outer darkness of cabaret and the back-of-beyond dance hall orbit of northern Europe. After 'From The Bottom Of My Heart' clocked in at Number Twenty, later Moody Blues singles made less and less impact, and, with the departure of Denny Laine by 1967, the outfit all but threw in the towel. Nonetheless, they revived with a vengeance via an ambitious 'concept' LP, *Days Of Future Passed* and its spin-off 45, 'Nights In White Satin' after *Sgt. Pepper's Lonely Hearts Club Band* made it clear that the humble beat group was now progressing - if that is the word - from guitars and drums to sitars, backward-running tapes and further funny noises as record companies found themselves underwriting concept albums, rock operas and other 'works'.

As album followed similar platinum album, The Moody Blues refined a grandiose style so nebulous in scope that such diverse units as Yes, King Crimson and Roxy Music were all cited erroneously as variants of The Moody Blues prototype. However, though you could take the boys out of Birmingham, you couldn't take Birmingham out of the boys. In the midst of the most excessive magniloquence, poetic gems were declaimed in thick Brummie accents over a thicker orchestral backwash.

Back home, The Move had taken over as the city's flagship pop stars. Following a maiden engagement in Stourbridge's Belfry Hotel, they followed, initially, much the same path as The Moody Blues: formation from key members of leading Brumbeat ensembles; a season at the Marquee; a Decca contract (albeit on the Deram subsidiary), and acquiring the same manager (Tony Secunda) and record producer (Denny Cordell). The first indication that The Move were out of the ordinary came in March 1966 when *Midland Beat* in March 1966 frontpaged Roy Wood gripping a 'banjar', his own invention that combined properties of both sitar and banjo.

By the time The Move descended on London in a blaze of Secunda-inspired publicity stunts, the group was delivering an alarming stage act that climaxed with Wayne charging about, axe in hand, to hack up effigies of world statesmen before turning his attention to imploding televisions - and if that's not Art, then I don't know what is.

Beyond the gimmicks, they laced Roy Wood originals with sterling reworkings of contemporary 'progressive' items of similar hue to those incorporated into The Crawling King Snakes' repertoire - as well as hedging their bets with a novel 'Zing! Went The Strings Of My Heart', Eddie Cochran's 'Something Else' and other chestnuts that wouldn't have been out of place in a Valets, Nightriders, Avengers, Chantelles or Diplomats set a few years earlier.

'Night Of Fear' - with a riff from the *1812 Overture* - was the first hit, and 1968's chart-topping 'Blackberry Way', the biggest. Yet even before 1967 was out, the discords and intrigues that make pop groups what they are had started to overwhelm The Move. During a round-Britain package tour with The Jimi Hendrix Experience, Syd Barrett's Pink Floyd and Amen Corner, 'Ace and I were dropping acid every day,' sighed Trevor, 'and it tipped Ace over the edge.' So began Kefford's tragic odyssey of drug abuse, suicide attempts, incarceration in mental institutions, divorce and a correlated estrangement of his two children. A recurring sentence throughout my lengthy and frank discussion with him was 'my head had gone'.

On *Top Of The Pops* with the post-Kefford Move, Trevor Burton's constant scowl had become less an effusion of 'image' than the real thing. Unhappy with The Move, he had become a frequent visitor to the remote communal dwelling on the Berkshire Downs where Steve Winwood had become as far removed from his previous incarnation as front man of the Spencer Davis Group as anyone in 1964 could have imagined with Traffic, which also featured Locomotive's Chris Wood, and Jim Capaldi and Dave Mason, once of The Hellions. They'd combined gladly with the gifted Steve who was to have the full entrepreneurial support of Island Records.

Sometimes, Burton would mount the concrete platform built for Traffic rehearsals in the garden that, under a starry canopy, could be perceived miles away. Bleached in bleak midwinter, jam sessions beneath more leaden skies were still feasible if participants wore fingerless Old Steptoe mittens. On warmer evenings, with the eight-windowed front of Winwood's cottage for back projection, they'd set up a light show and, bathed in swirling colour, lose themselves in music 'til dawn.

Among other callers were Eric Burdon, Pete Townshend and, undermining Capaldi's confidence, Ginger Baker and John Bonham. Joining Winwood in the absence of the other members of Traffic one evening were Baker, Burton, Eric Clapton and the bass guitarist from Family. Just for a few moments - subtracting Burton - the four who'd constitute the short-lived Blind Faith 'supergroup' had found each other.

As the clouds thus parted on the rock gods at play, 'the seeds were sewn for my leaving The Move,' affirmed Trevor, 'I wanted to get away from mainstream pop and that side of the industry.' Socialising with The Ugly's too, particularly their gifted lead vocalist, Burton not only joined them, but procured the group a new manager in Tony Secunda - who suggested a change of name. 'We all wrote a few down and put them on the floor,' said Trevor, 'I wrote "Balls" and put it in the middle, and it stood out.' Secunda's next directive was to relocate to a bungalow in the New Forest.

Yet 'getting it together in the country' Traffic-style wasn't without problems for Balls. 'A lot of madness went down,' growled Trevor, 'a lot of drugs too.' However, a lucrative record company advance was promised after the recruitment of Denny Laine on his apparent understanding that 'we were going to swap instruments around, and bring different people in for different things.'

Naturally, a name that cropped up in related conversations was that of John Bonham, still the most powerful drummer in the West Midlands. Louder than ever, he'd seemed to have come to terms with toiling behind his kit, a barrage of perpetual and pounding motion, in The Way Of Life, as much a lead instrumentalist as the guitarist. However, Trevor had heard that John had slipped his cable on the evening the group were to play the Majestic, a ballroom in West Heath. The others arrived to pick him up at his parents' house, but John Bonham was already at the Majestic, soundchecking quite unashamedly with something called The Band Of Joy.

THE TIME SERVER

*'You would do The Rolling Stones, The Everly Brothers,
French rock 'n' roll sessions, German ones, Engelbert, Tom
Jones - and all in the same day quite often'* - John Paul Jones[9]

'Sunshine Superman' had been one of Jimmy Page's last
sessions before he threw in his lot with The Yardbirds and the
consequent power struggle with Jeff Beck. There was, however,
still concord between Beck and Page - on an electric twelve-
string - when they'd convened at IBC studios to try that instrumental with the working title 'Bolero' - and, if time permitted,
a vocal item - because Keith Moon had recommended John Entwistle, feeling similarly discontented about being in The Who,
as both bass player and singer. It was only when Entwistle failed
to show up that the three wheeled in John Paul Jones as well as
twenty-two-year-old pianist Nicky Hopkins, who, since working his notice with Lord Sutch's Savages, had been heard on
discs by such as The Who and The Kinks (who immortalised
Hopkins in the 1966 LP track, 'Session Man').

Simon Napier-Ball, The Yardbirds' then-manager, was
the nominal producer of 'Bolero', but the *de facto* one was
Page, who 'wanted to see a band come out of there, cemented
with that one record - but Keith obviously couldn't do it because
of The Who, although he led us to believe he was leaving them,
probably just to make The Who jealous - and John Paul Jones
was a fabulous bass player. It was the obvious solution, going
with that band, but it never happened.'[12]

They had, however, already given it a name: Led Zeppelin. As it was with the very composition of 'Bolero', there was
dispute over who had originated this. Beck calculated that Moon
and Entwistle between them had coined it. Nevertheless, to his
dying day, John Entwistle would maintain that it was he who
had first commented that the line-up was 'so heavy it should go
down like a lead *(led)* zeppelin' to Richard Cole, a Who aide

who was to work with The Yardbirds. Yet Page ascribed it to Keith, adding 'Cole asked Moon for his permission when we decided to use the name.'[8]

Though the trail was going cold by 1967, Jeff and Jimmy continued as if 'Led Zeppelin' or whatever they decided to call it was still a possibility, although John Paul Jones wasn't prepared yet to forgo the financial safety net of session work, and, when they discovered what Moon had been up to, The Who chose to treat his cloak-and-dagger hand in the project as a registered protest rather than boat-burning.

'After some discussion, we decided to use another singer,' continued Page, 'The first choice was Steve Winwood, but he was too heavily committed to Traffic. Next, we thought of Steve Marriott of The Small Faces. He was approached and seemed full of glee about it. A message came through from the business side of Marriott, though, which said, "How would you like to play guitar with broken fingers? You will be if you don't stay away from Steve."

'After that, the idea just sort of fell apart. Instead of being more positive about it, and looking for another singer, we just let it slip by. The Who began a tour. The Yardbirds began a tour and that was it.'[8]

Perhaps this 'Led Zeppelin' would have disintegrated sooner rather than later anyway. Another writer might tack on a phrase like "- which was a great pity", except maybe it wasn't. Perhaps Jones, Moon, Beck, Page and Hopkins were meant to make just this one grand gesture, and then do no more. In parenthesis, the appealing 'Bolero', the only track that they completed - was to appear on vinyl - as 'Beck's Bolero' - with a contractually mandated production credit to Mickie Most when it B-sided Jeff's debut single as an ex-Yardbird, 1967's singalong 'Hi Ho Silver Lining'. With John Paul Jones on bass too, it made Number Fourteen in the domestic Top Twenty, totally eclipsing a rival version by The Attack.

With Beck's triumph putting paid to any reawakening of the 'Led Zeppelin' idea, disinclined releases continued to punctuate The Yardbirds' downfall - paradoxically, at a point where many pop acts had stopped thinking of themselves as just enter-tainers. By 1967, the notion of pop as an egghead activity had intensified. More and more 'bands' began demanding more and more public attention for 'concept' albums and similar epics that couldn't be crammed into a ten minute spot on a scream-rent package tour as the mere day needed to tape an entire LP in 1964 was no longer considered adequate for one *track* now.

Output, therefore, betrayed a conscious musical progres-sion for what had once been called beat groups. When still in The Moody Blues, for example, Denny Laine - anticipating the policy of Brian Wilson in The Beach Boys - had chosen to con-centrate on composition and production in London while the other personnel continued a touring schedule with Justin Hay-wood from Marty Wilde's Wilde Three. Yet, with Decca's pa-tience snapping as yet another Moody Blues single missed the charts, Denny couldn't be worse off solo, but 'I was adrift for a bit. I went to Spain for two years to study flamenco. I came back with the idea of doing a folky, acoustic-style thing, but with strings - and those on my first single like this were scored by John Paul Jones.'

For a few months, he was backed by The Electric String Band, an amplified string quartet from the Royal Academy - 'technicians', he called them - plus former Pretty Things drum-mer Viv Prince and, on bass, Andy Leigh of Spooky Tooth. 'It was a bit of a nightmare actually,' Denny admits now, 'because the technicians were all so busy doing other things. It was fun for them, but they didn't find it easy. They were, nevertheless, all really good players. A lot of good ideas came from them.'

If lyrics to 'Too Much In Love', Laine's second 45 un-der this regime, were a throwback to the Bobby era, whereas once the average pop musician may have entreated God as a sort of divine pimp, some had already become pseudo-mystics, whose songs required repeated listening to comprehend what might be veiled but oracular messages. Taking their cue from The Beatles and The Rolling Stones, real or imagined extremes of drug experience beyond simple pills and reefers were impli-cated in self-conciously 'weird' discs by the likes of The Pretty

Things, Family, The Pink Floyd and The Small Faces, and, on 'Happenings Ten Years Time Ago', which was the last Yardbirds single before Mickie Most's death touch.

Instead of screaming hysteria, there was now knotted-brow 'appreciation' as a working band's appeal became reliant on not so much cheeky grins and tight trousers as stamina to sustain lengthy extrapolations of items from both its last album and the unfamiliar successor being 'laid down' during a studio block-booking of weeks and months; much of it impossible to reproduce on stage using conventional beat group instrumentation. Though gadgetry and constant retakes disguised faults while impinging on grit, there surfaced an even deeper respect for instrumental proficiency as outlines dissolved between rock and jazz, and bands like Soft Machine and The Nice thrived on 'meaningful' interplay as artists became more aware of - even concerned about - the formal do's and don'ts that traditionally affect creative flow.

This was all very well, but, in 1967, you were still only as big as your last 45. 'If you didn't have a hit single,' elucidated Jim McCarty, 'you were a fading band.' In Britain certainly, his Yardbirds were no longer contenders, and they'd become too indolent, weary and out-of-touch to do much about it when, for instance, Chris Dreja was replaced once more on an A-side - 'Ten Little Indians' - by a John Paul Jones growing tired of groundhog days amid the tape spools and blinking dials.

Over at Decca, while he received absorbing commissions such as one to arrange orchestral strings for 'She's A Rainbow' on *Their Satanic Majesties Request*, the Stones' most nakedly psychedelic LP, this was marred by him 'waiting for them forever. I just thought they were unprofessional and boring.'[31] Possibly, however, this was not as boring as a more well-concealed ledger in Jones' artistic account when, on two days in February 1968, he reported in at EMI's Abbey Road studio, along with The Mike Sammes Singers and a full orchestra under the baton of bespectacled, middle-aged Norrie Paramor, to play bass and, allegedly, arrange two of six possibilities for Cliff

Richard to perform in that spring's Eurovision Song Contest. One of these was a masterpiece of song entitled 'Shoom Lamma Boom Boom'.

John Paul was coming to know by sight individual sweet wrappers, and note their day-to-day journeyings up and down a ledge, where an empty can of orangeade might also remain for weeks next to a discarded swap-stick made grubby from cleaning tape-heads. Though old Dick Rowe had continued to strike lucky with outfits like The Tremeloes - now *sans* Brian Poole, Love Affair and Marmalade, he was more at home with 'real singers' like some of his pre-Beatles finds had been - and so it was that Tom Jones and Engelbert Humperdinck, when contracted by the late Rowe in the mid-1960s, were the figureheads of a counter revolution on behalf of 'decent' music on the basis that whatever the prevailing trend, the opposite is always represented to some degree in the charts - though, paradoxically, 1967 was a high-tide mark for both psychedelia and old-tyme balladeering. Petula Clark, Harry Secombe, Des O'Connor and - you'd better believe it - Donald Peers, the post-war Light Programme's 'Cavalier Of Song', all groped into the charts during this period before Dick Rowe's calculated withdrawal from a business in which his critical prejudices - like those of EMI opposite number Norrie Paramor - no longer fitted.

Rowe was aided and abetted by persons of like aesthetic persuasion and vocational background such as Ken Woodman, whose Ken Woodman Sound provisioned arrangements and accompaniment to hits by Adam Faith, Sandie Shaw, Chris Andrews (notably, the remarkable 'Yesterday Man') - and Neil Christian, amongst many others, and whose two albums of his own were brass-laden, middle-of-the-road affairs embracing his smashes with Sandie, Adam *et al* and further then-current favourites, rather similar to those of The Andrew Oldham Orchestra.

Woodman's music was appreciated by Les Reed, who, from a Royal College of Music scholarship and National Service in the Royal East Kent Regiment, had, on demobilisation in 1956, become a freelance session player before an active dislike of touring did not prevent his joining The John Barry Seven who, as well as concerts and records in their own right, backed other artists - notably those appearing on *Oh Boy!* and, later, Adam Faith for whom Reed dashed off a B-side.

In the mid-60s, it was unusual for a British singles chart not to list a Les Reed song. Among numerous Top 30 acts indebted to Reed as writer *and* arranger were The Applejacks ('Tell Me When'), Herman's Hermits, Tom Jones, P.J. Proby, Mirielle Mathieu, Engelbert Humperdinck ('The Last Waltz'), Des O'Connor ('I Pretend') and the Dave Clark Five (1967's 'Everybody Knows'). His biggest smashes were mostly with rather schmaltzy ballads - and a similar easy-listening criteria pervaded Reed's own steady-selling light orchestral outings and occasional novelty singles.

No records by Les for Tom or Engelbert, even (or especially) the ones he was on, were on John Paul Jones'recreational play-list - though, under pressure, he'd concede that for guts and conviction layered onto the unlikeliest items, Tom Jones was the more bearable of the two balladeers, albeit in a rather one-dimensional fashion. Tom's old backing group had faded away soon after he scented success with 1965's chart-topping 'It's Not Unusual'. What *was* unusual was that he was not effeminate or subversive like a Jagger, a Lennon or, later, a Robert Plant. A working-class *boyo* from mid-Glamorgan, he'd been married with a baby on the way at sixteen. However, with more hope than he could possibly justify, he'd announced his intention to make a go of it as a full-time entertainer.

In 1964, he was billed quaintly as 'the Twisting Vocalist from Pontypridd', and, though a solo performer singer in an age of groups, impressed Dick Rowe for a picaresque charm as much as his being the proverbial 'pop singer who can really sing'. Certainly, Tom had a piledriving but flexible vocal command and a steady consistency - 'squareness', some would say. The magnificence of his voice so smothered some of the piffle he was persuaded to record that he was second only to Joe Cocker in 1969's *Beat Instrumental* readers' poll, even though he had found an apparent niche by then as a tuxedo-ed Las Vegas cabaret performer, and could no longer take Top Forty placings for granted, even if his vocal endowment had guaranteed such prestigious commissions as singing over the credits of the James Bond thriller, *Thunderball*.

During the interminable re-running of each taped mile of Tom and, particularly, Engelbert, ennui manifested itself in John Paul Jones just hovering around during some interminable fiddle-about at the desk. It was now a job just like any other, and much of the time nowadays, his work corresponded with conventional Home Counties office hours - and if he had to keep them, maybe he'd sooner do so in an air-conditioned high-rise than in breathing stale air in some grubby isolation booth with his headphoned ears like braised chops. A lot of the music he was helping to create wasn't exactly extending the limits of the avant-garde either. Sometimes, it was positively mind-stultifying. He could play it in his sleep.

While always delivering what was required, John Paul Jones thrummed into the tedium and, if not making a mental note to collect the eiderdowns from the dry-cleaners, wondered whether this would be all he'd ever do. Somehow, it was all too pat, too dovetailed, too sensible, this eager-to-please sham of being happy with the situation because all the other participants seemed to be. Some of those with whom John Paul was rubbing shoulders truly believed that, even when providing backing for, say, Pinky and Perky or Ken Dodd's Diddymen, they were involved with the creation of quality goods. The Mike Sammes Singers, for example, were among the most ubiquitous vocal ensembles in London studios from the mid-1950s until the early 1980s. More a choir than a group, their more renowned clients included Ronnie Hilton, The Beverley Sisters, Tommy Steele, Cliff Richard, Anthony Newley, Matt Munro, Helen Shapiro, Tom Jones, Engelbert Humperdinck - and the latter-day Beatles. Like John Paul Jones would have been, the Singers were equally at ease with psychedelic 'I Am The Walrus' as 'Goodnight', the lullaby that closed 1968's *White Album*.

When the Marine Offences Act had become law the previous August, The Ken Woodman Sound's 'Town Talk' was the opening and closing theme to *The Jimmy Young Show* on one of the BBC's two new national pop stations. Ken and the lads also went in one ear and out the other when maintaining Radios One and Two's ordained quota of 'live' music that was, so grimaced the discerning Ringo Starr, 'what seems like half a dozen terrible bands playing for most of the day.'[80]

A combination of the demise of pirate radio and BBC radio's cautious programming had rendered the charts generally shallower and less adventurous in content, brushing a 1960s nadir one week in 1968 when the only group - and the wildest act - featured on *Top Of The Pops* was The Tremeloes who, with Marmalade and Love Affair, were a prong of a grinning triumvirate who ruled this silver age of British beat.

Herbie Flowers rather than Jones had been on bass when an orchestra, backing singers and all the customary participants had been assembled to ghost Love Affair's first hit, 'Everlasting Love', produced by Mike Smith, Dick Rowe's second-in-command, who'd also overseen 'The Crying Game'. Like other recording managers, Smith was finding John Paul Jones less available these days. Nevertheless, with his fingers on automatic too, John Paul would be spotted by the sharp-eyed, reading the dots alongside Jimmy Page, Nicky Hopkins and Clem Cattini on television and in prestigious auditoriums for Cliff Richard, Roy Orbison, The Everly Brothers and Engelbert Humperdinck among others.

One morning after one of these stints, John Paul, Clem, Nicky and Jimmy - plus Albert Lee, Big Jim Sullivan and saxophonist Chris Hugues - pitched in on a pot-boiling - and now highly collectable album - issued eventually just weeks before the formation of Led Zeppelin. It was supposed to both catch an aspect of late 1960s pop via its embrace of rock 'n' roll revival, and serve as a vehicle to launch Keith David de Groot, a vocalist who vanished straightaway from the pages of history.

Yet, looking him up and down, former Pye recording manager Alan A. Freeman and producer Reg Tracey had decided that it might be worth taking trouble over lean and handsome Keith - whose pop star potential was supplemented by a lithe if tight-throated singing style much in vogue just then. With Spark Records, albeit a label of no great merit, sparing no expense, an artiste of Keith David de Groot's calibre deserved nothing less than the finest available session crew that could be assembled in Olympic Studios in Barnes with Glyn Johns, now engineer for both The Beatles and Stones, at the console.

To allow the boy the best possible chance too, his investors looked round for a handy bandwagon onto which he could jump. One bright spark noticed that Bill Haley and Buddy Holly reissues were hovering round the middle of the Top Forty during 1968's cold April, and that medleys of classic rock closed the show of 'nice little bands' whose names - Tea-and-Symphony, Warm Dust, Puce-Exploding Butterfly - implied artistic insights that weren't instantly graspable.

Entertaining a truer underground than these denizens of Students Union stages were provincial outfits led by extant Teddy Boys like Crazy Cavan, Shakin' Stevens and others - like Sha Na Na, Flash Cadillac and Cat Mother, across the Atlantic - who carried a torch for the 1950s. Though not so obviously regressive, 'Fire Brigade', the latest smash from The Move, had been freighted with an antique Duane Eddy twang - while The Beatles' new 'Lady Madonna' was reminiscent of Fats Domino.

So it was, therefore, that the selections were chosen from crowd-pleasers that had got the assorted ex-Pirates, Savages, Innocents, Crusaders *et al* through rough nights in provincial dance halls way back when. Apart from two Hopkins originals for good measure, every number was an amble down memory lane to an era when boys were spotty and girls untouchable - and when Jerry Lee Lewis and his child bride were hounded from a prudish Britain's shores.

The Killer was represented with 'Lovin' Up A Storm' plus 'Down The Line' - composed by an adolescent Roy Orbison - 'Livin' Lovin' Wreck' and the 1958 million-seller, 'Breathless' - while Buddy Holly weighed in almost as heavily via 'Everyday', 'Think It Over' and - the one that had recently returned him to the charts - 'Rave On'. Respects too were paid to Eddie Cochran ('Boll Weevil Song'), Charlie Rich ('Everything I Do Is Wrong', 'Lonely Weekend'), Carl Perkins ('Dixie Fried') and Charlie Gracie ('Fabulous') in what Spark saw as a worthwhile exercise, even if the the record-buying public didn't until the LP named *No Introduction Necessary* acquired historical importance through the global renown of Led Zeppelin, and was reissued many times, notably by Thunderbolt in 1984, and by Armoury in 2000 (retitled *Lovin' Up A Storm*) - and always with Page and Jones - and even Hopkins, Sullivan, Cattini and Hugues - more prominent on the sleeve than poor old Keith David de Groot - whose precise identity and biographical details had sunk deep in backwaters of the collective memory of his illustrious helpmates.

With the possible exception of the vanished Keith David, none of *No Introduction Necessary*'s participants had much time to reminisce about a session that still sounds as if it was a lot of fun to make - and remains far less objectionable in its overall aim of harmless amusement than any more feted 'supersession'. Fresh from the sundering of Traffic, Steve Winwood explained to *Melody Maker* that 'today's scene is moving very away from permanent groups, and more towards recognition for individual musicians. The trend is going more in the direction of jazz where musicians just jam together as they please.'

In tacit endorsement in December 1968 came A.N. Other, an *ad hoc* quintet that materialised when John Lennon, Yoko Ono, Eric Clapton, Keith Richards (on bass) and Jimi Hendrix's drummer, Mitch Mitchell appeared on *The Rolling Stones Rock 'N' Roll Circus*. A month prior to this spectacular, Clapton had been invited to a less glamorous all-day function in a Staines warehouse where some of the ablest musical technicians of two continents merged the contents of rock and jazz. Among those captured on seldom-seen film were Steve Stills, Buddy Miles, veteran multi-instrumentalist Roland Kirk and Jack Bruce - who, with two other participants, saxophonist Dick Heckstall-Smith and drummer Jon Hiseman, would record a one-shot jazz album the following year. The three had as close knowledge of each others skills and particular musical style as any crew of battle-hardened London session players - Jones, Cattini, Hopkins, all the usual shower.

On aggregate, these received a bigger wage than a young business executive did in those days. Nevertheless, just the re-motest hint of a more glamorous alternative would be sufficient excuse for John Paul Jones to up and quit this roundabout of principally harmless 'decent' music on which he depended for a living. 'After years of non-stop sessions, it getting too much,' John Paul sighed to anyone listening when they took a break, 'I'm making money, but I'm not enjoying it anymore.'[76]

THE BANDSMAN OF JOY

'I'd meet him for lunch when he was working with the Irishmen, digging up West Bromwich High Street' - Austin Griffith (The Stringbeats)[66]

Though 'You Better Run' had been a 'turntable hit' during the dying days of pirate Radio London, CBS did not take up its option with Listen. Nevertheless, Robert Plant kept his foot in the company's door, mailing demos by his new group, The Band Of Joy, whose founder, Vernon Perara was related to Maureen, Robert's fiancée from Walsall. Perara also played with The Stringbeats, a long-established mixed-race aggregation from Stourbridge, with whom Plant was moonlighting.[81] Spotted at either the Brumbeat Cavern and a restaurant in Digbeth, they had once backed Millie - of 'My Boy Lollipop' fame - throughout a club residency somewhere in the Midlands.

More like The Crawling King Snakes than The Stringbeats, Plant's main concern, The Band Of Joy, were picked to click in 1967 by *Midland Beat* on the strength of the group affording a lighting rig - courtesy of an Abdul Benson, who Plant knew from college - and, crucially, enthusiastic response to re-bookings at such as the Casa Fiesta in Stourbridge and, in Kidderminster, the Grotto cellar bar - and Frank Freeman's Dancing Club, whose new policy of engaging rock groups had given the elderly promoter's profit graph a sharper upward turn than his strict-tempo evenings.

Nevertheless, the discord and intrigues that make pop groups what they are, forced Plant's departure at one point, but he bounced back with another Band Of Joy whose painted Red Indian faces owed something to The Crazy World of Arthur Brown, while pre-empting those of Adam and the Ants by at least twelve years, and creating such a stir at the Rainbow Suite in Birmingham city centre that when Plant jumped into the crowd, frightened onlookers fled into the corridors beyond the auditorium. The Band Of Joy also managed side-trips over the edge of the world to Middle Earth and elsewhere on London's 'underground' circuit where in-house light shows were also among audio-visual aids meant to simulate psychedelic experience as 'bands' played on and on and on and on for hippies in a cross-legged trance and whirling dancers with eyes like catherine-wheels.

This was not, however, a springboard to chart penetration or even a record deal for The Band Of Joy, who, by 1968, consisted of Plant, organist Chris Brown (ex-Stringbeats), guitarist Kevyn Gammond (from The Shakedown Sound), John Bonham and, on bass, Paul Lockey. It wasn't for lack of trying, most conspicuously when they assembled at expensive Regent Sound Studios in London to tape two originals - 'Memory Lane' and 'Adriatic Seaview' plus overhauls of Buffalo Springfield's 'For What It's Worth' and 'Hey Joe', a murder ballad from time immemorial that was a fixture in the repertoires of The Byrds, The Shadows Of Knight, Marmalade and countless other outfits. Though the intention was to make it *not* sound like any other act's version, The Jimi Hendrix Experience's 'Hey Joe', the 1966 smash that set Hendrix on the road to glory, was the blueprint for The Band Of Joy, just as US singer-songwriter Tim Rose's arrangement had been for the Experience.[82]

These demos proved useful in gaining support spots to the disparate likes of Fairport Convention, Ten Years After, Peter Jay and the Jaywalkers, Mick Farren and his Social Deviants - and Tim Rose, who was to offer Bonham a post in his backing combo. Nevertheless, on the afternoon following such performances, you might have noticed Plant and one or two of the others mooching about the town centre, calculating what the one-and-sixpence they had between them could do. A plate of beans-on-toast washed down with a cup of liquid smoke? It was as if Robert had never made a record with Listen, invoked - possibly ironic - screams from girls for a particularly bravura crack at 'For What It's Worth' or got drunk with Trevor Burton, his pal in the hitmaking Move as Ace Kefford was Bonham's.

The rats started leaving the sinking ship, and penury obliged Plant to take up employment as a labourer, laying asphalt on roads in West Bromich, as, newly wed, he became more and more embroiled in cash-flow problems, talking more and more about the lack of bookings. It was nothing very tangible, just a steady whittling away with little peaks and troughs - sometimes both at once.

As 1966 drew to a close, CBS, if considering this Robert person a little bit *femme*, decided to stick with him for two solo singles, 'Our Song' - a translation of a Italian ballad of Tom Jones-like persuasion - and, drawing a favourable review in the *NME*, 'Long Time Coming'. Neither were to Plant's taste in that boom time for such as 'Release Me' and 'The Last Waltz' by Engelbert Humperdinck, remembered in Midlands music circles as Gerry Dorsey, a palais crooner from Leicester - which kept the latest from The Beatles and Traffic from Number One.

More palatable to Plant than going so smooth had been running for metaphorical office when New York producer Jimmy Miller arrived in London with the backing track of feverish 'Incense', his own composition. He was seeking advice about a suitably fiery singer to ice the cake for a single he intended to attribute to The Anglos, signifying breadwinning English connections. Certainly, Miller furrowed his brow over Plant prior to giving the task to a pseudonymous Steve Winwood.

Miller was, however, present at London's fashionable Speakeasy in 1967, grooving to a Band Of Joy no longer up-and-coming, and containing former members of Danny King's Mayfair Set and The Ace Kefford Stand at a loose end. Recognising the star quality of the vocalist in the desperate group too, Alexis Korner poked his head into the bandroom afterwards. He and Robert began talking blues, partly because they both remembered Plant as a Crawling King Snake once volunteering, nay, insisting, on blowing harmonica during Korner's second set at Kidderminster's Cannon Hill Arts Centre a while back.

Had Robert ever enjoyed a more interesting conversation? The feeling seemed to be reciprocal, and it wasn't long before Plant and Korner started working together, on and off, as a duo of the same kidney as those with whom Robert had performed in the folk clubs. With pianist Steve Miller, they also attempted to tape an album that was aborted after two tracks, 'Operator' - and 'Steal Away', a fragment of which was to be quoted in Led Zeppelin's 'How Many More Times'.

Thus the middle-aged Korner became the despairing young minstrel's careers advisor, father confessor and a major catalyst in the recovery of his artistic confidence, 'Alexis absorbed me into his large family of musicians and friends in London,' beamed Plant, 'He aided my schooling for what was about to come, and is still coming.'[83]

Yet it was fanciful for Robert, tired of waiting for something to happen - and with CBS's patience snapping - to look to future victories then. Unknowingly, The Band Of Joy had completed its final booking - on the back of a lorry at an open-air event in the Malvern Hills. They threw in the towel when, according to Paul Lockey, 'We were driving up to a gig in York one summer's day, and the engine dropped out of the van onto the road. I phoned my dad, and he towed us back. He said, "It's going to cost you five hundred pounds for this, that and the other." We didn't have that amount, and there were things happening at the time. Robert was married to Maureen, and John had just had a son, Jason, so he was under pressure to get money, not go out playing. Kevyn had had enough, and I was the only one enthusiastic about carrying on.'[84]

A miracle had occurred too late when Tony Secunda and Denny Cordell alighted on a package labelled 'Band Of Joy' among a backlog of demos that had accumulated around their in-tray. Cordell wasn't keen, but, instead of yawning and clicking it off halfway through the first chorus, Secunda at least became 'interested' in Robert - of whom they been made aware by Trevor Burton - to the degree of auditioning him at the Marquee Studios with a view to signing him to Regal-Zonophone, The Move's new label.

Plant's ears had been burning too when the nascent 'N Betweens were thinking about the recruitment of a second lead vocalist. 'The others didn't know him, but I did,' recalled Noddy Holder, 'Personally, I didn't mind if we got another singer or not. I knew that I could front the band by myself, and I preferred being in a four-piece.'[85] Though Noddy got his way, perhaps in a parallel dimension, it is Plant with a similar cement-mixer tenor and a guitar round his neck - rather than Holder who became the rabble-rouser-in-chief with Slade, co-writing their six year UK chart run of unremitting ravers with misspelt titles, though it is debatable whether he'd have conceded to planing his crinkly golden hair when their manager recommended a 'skinhead' image as a means to get up onto that next level.

Long before Slade's time came, however, a world pop scene had flowered after the United Kingdom's battle for exports had been won in the mid-1960s through the 'British Invasion' of North America. Indeed, a common complaint throughout the continent was that of Frank Zappa, then of Los Angeles' Soul Giants: 'If you didn't sound like The Beatles or the Stones, you didn't get hired.'[86] Crawling from the sub-cultural woodwork, therefore, were legion Anglophile 'garage bands' who'd grown out their crew-cuts - in defiance of Bible Belt old timers quoting *I Corinthians xi 14* ('If a man have long hair, it is a shame unto him') - and seized upon whatever easy-to-play aspects of the new Limey idioms they felt most comfortable. The bigger names were The Shadows Of Knight, The Sonics, The Seeds, The Thirteenth Floor Elevators and ? and the Mysterions - who captivated Robert Plant nearly as much (and possibly for much the same reasons) as The Orieles, The Fideltones, The Pelicans *et al*.

On the surface, US garage rock never had much going for it. One of its virtues for Robert, maybe, was that he was never sure how he was meant to take it - because if it was actually *meant* to be crap, it was neither overtly laughable nor so-bad-it's-good. Form was determined by the phonographic equivalent of bottling lightning in youthful (or not-so-youthful) adrenalin with thrilling margins of error pumped onto a spool of tape - while content mingled overhauls of genre artefacts with riff-based (and often derivative) originals, executed with a home-made verve. With the benefit of hindsight, it may be seen as on par with Stuckism, the antithesis of Brit Art - and that among those who emerged from this background of 'punk' by original definition were Lou Reed, Iggy Pop and Alice Cooper, all blips on the test-card of a post-Woodstock era as devoid as it could be of whatever makes pop fun.

Earlier, it had connected too with The Doors, whose Jim Morrison may be viewed now as the Wagner to Robert Plant's Gilbert-and-Sullivan. As he's been the posthumous subject of both a best-selling biography and a cinema film, the myth has snowballed that Morrison *was* The Doors. Whilst his ritualised cavortings on the boards brought the Los Angeles group much publicity - and notoriety - their recorded compositions were mostly either team efforts or by personnel other than Morrison, a singing poet whose lines were, nevertheless, the lyrical of many numbers - such as 1967's 'Light My Fire', the US Number One that created demand for its album, *The Doors*, and the *Strange Days* follow-up. Further high placings in both the singles and album lists peaked in 1968 with chart-topping 'Hello I Love You' - which plagiarised a Kinks riff - and *Waiting For The Sun*. The turning of the tide may be dated from a 1969 concert in Miami where Morrison was alleged to have exposed himself. During a long wait for the 'guilty' verdict with its expected custodial sentence and appeal, he exiled himself to Paris where he passed away in 1971. His long shadow proved such a hindrance that The Doors broke up a year later - reuniting only to provide backing on *An American Prayer*, a 1978 album of Morrison reciting his deathless verse.

If not to the same degree as he had Elvis Presley, Robert Plant might have practiced being Jim Morrison before his bedroom mirror - and even on the boards. Such a display could have been sinister without the subtle merriment in Plant's eyes.

In the real world, however, he was trying to ignore parental mitherings that it wasn't too late for him to resume chartered accountancy, and marking time with an entity called Hobbstweedle, who added vaguely pixified gingerbread-castle lyrical imagery to the cauldron he'd boiled with The Band Of Joy. With John Trickett, Bonham's successor in The Band Of Joy, on drums, the use of Noddy Holder's window-cleaning father's van and Mr. Holder himself as road manager, the group had been working in a Wolverhampton pub where Plant had turned up, not really by chance. He wasn't convinced that Hobbstweedle had what it took, but, before the evening was out, he told them he'd be their lead vocalist.

On a local par outfits sporting names like Custard Tree and Deaf Cuckoo, Hobbstweedle were hastening towards the same downward spiral as all Plant's other groups, Yet out would pour stretchers about how close they were to a major recording contract and how they were a sure-fire certainty to share the bill with Screaming Lord Sutch when his journey along an endless highway next reached the Midlands. They carried on as if these possibilities were still on the cards long after the trails went cold, if they had ever existed in the first place.

The old vexing question resurfaced: how did you rise to the next level? Arbitrary isolations - a mislaid telephone number, Mickie Most's extended lunch break, a bass player's hangover, a flat tyre - all these unrelated trivialities can trigger changes affecting the entire course of a musician's career, even that of a musician with the tenacity of a Robert Plant.

A Radio London chart entry, a one-shot record contract, even an encore was still sufficient to feed hope. Without vanity, mere awareness of worth in the teeth of ill luck was enough, though with every passing week you were less likely to become Elvis Presley. You had the right haircut, clothes and haircut at the wrong time. The drummer takes up Tim Rose's offer. If only there hadn't been a power cut when Larry Page was there; if only I hadn't had a sore throat at that audition; if only the organist hadn't written off the van the day before that string of one-nighters with The Yardbirds; if only I hadn't lost my way...

It was most disenchanting when somone who'd cadged a cigarette off you the previous month would be pictured in *Record Mirror* with his group, posing round a fire escape, cramming themselves into a telephone booth or copying that mid-air leap patented long ago by either The Rockin' Berries or The Beatles. Entering his twenties, Robert Plant was becoming venerable, a Grand Old Man of the West Midlands music scene who was or was not revered by younger performers as certain as his former self had been that they were about to soar to the very pinnacle of pop.

It was so unfair. All Robert needed was to catch the lightning just once, and then it'd be onwards and upwards. Like that cliched movie sequence of dates being ripped off a calendar to a background of clips, a slow dazzle would preface the final local dates, then package tours with big names... sessions on *Saturday Club* and *Top Gear*... Number Ones... *Sunday Night At The London Palladium*... America!

It's always more difficult when you're in the middle, isn't it? A blending of modest achievements and lingering hip sensibility guarantees that, regardless of passing fads, a loyal following keeps your head above water financially for at least some of the time. Perhaps the right to represent yourself as, say, 'CBS Recording Artists' - which Robert, if not the rest of the group, was or had been - precipitates a fractional rise in booking fees before a foreseeable slide back to waiting like Mr. Micawber until another such peak comes your way. There's always just sufficient cheese-paring incentive to carry on.

THE NEW YARDBIRD

'The band will be reformed under the same name by Page and Dreja, who seek two new members' - EMI press release, 8 July 1968

While The Yardbirds were deteriorating too on the live circuit - as immortalised on a doctored *Live Yardbirds* album - Keith Relf improvised clever lyrics in the middle of an 'I'm A Man' that bore as much resemblance to 1964's *Five Live Yardbirds* arrangement as dairy butter to low-fat margarine, and the Led Zeppelin future was telegraphed conspicuously in a subsequently bootlegged arrangement of 'Dazed And Confused' for French television. Otherwise, The Yardbirds' virtue was all but gone. What mattered most as 1968 loomed, was raking in as much loot with the least effort by accommodating thousands in one go in the US baseball parks and exposition centres with which no European venue could yet compare.

After completing such remaining commitments, the aeroplane back to London was an opportunity for continuous thought as individual Yardbirds wrestled with professional and personal stock-taking. Because North American collegiate youth seemed fair game to buy anything British labelled 'heavy', 'progressive' or - surely taking coals to Newcastle - 'blues', Dreja, Relf, Page and McCarty could have had if not a walkover, then a smoother regaining of lost ground during this late 1960s 'blues boom' that would turn the likes of Fleetwood Mac, Ten Years After, Jethro Tull and Black Sabbath into pop stars by letting them retain artistic individuality whilst absorbing many other musical idioms.

Moreover, with Jimmy Page, Jeff Beck, Eric Clapton, Jimi Hendrix, Steve Winwood and The Who's Pete Townshend, Fleetwood Mac's Peter Green had been among the 'Magnificent Seven' guitar heroes designated in a *Melody Maker* feature in autumn 1967. After scuffling about in various curate's egg groups since his East London schooldays, Peter Green's musical career had left the runway in 1967 when he replaced Clapton in John Mayall's Bluesbreakers, in which lead guitar was coming to be as important as vocals. 'God' was a hard act to follow. Also, though all good men and true, not every Mayall axeman became a superstar. For every Clapton, there'd been a Jeff Kribbett, a Roger Dean, a Bernie Watson...

Yet, more enterprising than the over-valued Eric, twenty-one-year-old Peter proved as equal to the task as Jeff Beck had as a new Yardbird. Indeed, Green achieved the same level of qualified recognition as Clapton had in the employ of the exacting Mayall, a adherent to the leadership principle and firm enforcer of his own order. As the suspensions of bass player John McVie testified, he wouldn't tolerate heavy drinkers - and Christ help you if you were caught with drugs.

However, it was mainly the artistic restrictions of being a Bluesbreaker that led to the formation of Peter Green's Fleetwood Mac with McVie and Mayall's drummer Mick Fleetwood after enlisting Jeremy Spencer, an Elmore James-style bottleneck player. Later, a third guitarist, Danny Kirwan, was added. Next, the group began moving away from the blues with 'Albatross', 'Man Of The World' and others in a fast run of hit singles penned by Green - just as those by Jethro Tull were by Ian Anderson, conspicuous for his vagrant attire, matted hair and antics with a flute on *Top Of The Pops*. This exposure came after the group's third 45, 1969's 'Living In The Past' proved that as well as being a moderately popular album act since 1968's *This Was* debut, they were Top Ten singles merchants too. Crucially, North America was beckoning.

Also up-and-coming was Love Sculpture, a Cardiff three-piece for whom enthusiastic reaction to a maiden LP, 1967's *Blues Helping* and, much moreso, a high-velocity arrangement of Khachaturian's 'Sabre Dance' during a 1968 spot on John Peel's 'progressive' *Top Gear* series on Radio One led to its climb into the domestic Top Ten. Their guitarist, Dave Edmunds - later signed to Led Zeppelin's Swansong label - might have caused the likes of Page, Beck, Green and Clapton nervous backwards glances had he not lacked 'image'.

Food for thought too was the development of Free who - like Robert Plant - were protéges of Alexis Korner. Already, this guitar-bass-drums-vocalist quartet had accrued enough support in British and European colleges for their first blues-derived albums - musically unambitious but punchy - to be a worthwhile exercise financially, and prompted one one music journal to cite them as 'the New Stones'.

The Yardbirds weren't the New anything. Now incapable of major commercial recovery, they downed tools as a working band - a much-mooted decision - on 7 July 1968, two years after 'Over Under Sideways Down', the final UK Top 30 strike, in the inauspicious setting of Luton Technical College. On a drizzling Sunday, they ran through this final evensong any old how; Keith forgetting words and Chris fluffing one or two bass runs as Jimmy endeavoured to make a show of it.[87]

'By then, The Yardbirds had split into factions,' explained Chris Dreja, 'Jim and Keith had got more aethereal and delicate. There was a thread between that and the New Age music Jim did later, but it lacked excitement for me and Jimmy - though I helped Jim and Keith start Renaissance.'

During this interregnum that followed The Yardbirds' valedictory flight at Luton, Jimmy Page occupied himself constructively too. While instigating animated debate with Dreja and Peter Grant, The Yardbirds' last manager, about what could be salvaged from the group, he nodded towards John Renbourn by picking 'White Summer' very prettily on a BBC2 series hosted by folk *chanteuse* Julie Felix. One gushing television reviewer compared him to Manitas de Plata.

Page was, therefore, well-placed, had he wished, to side with Keith Relf and Jim McCarty, who'd pooled their resources more immediately in the short-lived Together. From sessions at Abbey Road under the eye of Paul Samwell-Smith, this amalgam's stylistic determination was to hinge on heavy acoustic overspill, most obviously in the fingering of Jon Mark, a Renbourn-esque guitarist who had previously shared stages with Marianne Faithfull, and, when he wasn't available, Alun Davies, later Cat Stevens' right hand man.

Had a 1968 A-side, 'Henry's Coming Home', sold sufficient for Keith and Jim to hold on hoping, Together might have had greater potential to win a non-headbanging following like that of The Incredible String Band, Lindisfarne, Renbourn and Bert Jansch's Pentangle and other leading turn-of-the-decade outfits in the same bag. In the death, Together's career didn't plummet, simply because it never got off the ground.

Meanwhile, Chris Dreja, while procrastinating about what to do next, was rehearsing with a casual combo intended only to work at weekends. 'Chris's band contained a guy called B.J. Cole on slide guitar and John Hawken on keyboards,' remembered Jim McCarty, 'Chris knew we were forming Renaissance, and suggested them.'

Cole wasn't to be a Renaissance man, but Jim, Keith and John Hawken teamed up with Louis Cennamo of The Herd on bass, and Relf's sister, Jane - whose clear soprano was worthy of a Maddy Prior, Sonja Kristina or Jacqui McShee. Praised mainly for its stunning vocal harmonies, a promising debut album in 1969 was to cover waterfronts from folk to *musique concrete*, leaving a vaguely 'classical music' aftertaste. However, though McCarty co-wrote much of 1972's *Prologue,* he (like the Relfs) had moved on by then. On vocals and keyboards, Jim led Shoot through the promising *On The Frontier* LP while Relf emerged as grey eminence behind Medicine Head, returning to 'live' performance as the duo's bass guitarist.

He stepped further into the limelight with Armaggedon, an unenduring heavy metal outfit of mystical bent - for, scheduled to cross the Atlantic for a proposed series of worthwhile tour supports, the question of whether Armaggedon could have reached at least the middle league of the 'adult-orientated' rock hierarchy there became purely academic after Keith absorbed more than enough high voltage to kill him, when on 14 May 1976, he touched a guitar fed through an unearthed amplifier.

Following Cream's more calculated disbandment in November 1968, Eric Clapton and drummer Ginger Baker had been stampeded into Blind Faith with Steve Winwood and Rick Grech, the bloke from Family who'd been on the periphery of

Traffic's cottage circle. This 'supergroup' threw in the towel after a free concert in Hyde Park, one patchy album and a troubled US tour. However, a bigger stadium attraction had emerged already, led by one whose name was to be honoured to almost the same degree as to Clapton's with Cream. On 14 June 1968, The Jeff Beck Group made an extraordinary US concert debut, creating much the same effect throughout six weeks of further engagements.

Guided in the first instance by Mickie Most, Beck had already entered the UK Top 40 thrice - with 'Hi Ho Silver Lining', 'Tallyman' and 'Love Is Blue'. The lead vocal on 'Tallyman' was shared with Rod Stewart who Beck, a hesitant singer, had enlisted into his Group for the North American tour and a debut LP, *Truth* - which, like *Little Games*, was to be a repertory template for what was mutating into Jimmy Page's New Yardbirds.

Truth was a diverting mixture of workmanlike originals, casseroled blues and 1950s classic rock, plus oddities like 'Greensleeves'. That *Truth* rose with almost mathematical precision to Number Fifteen in the *Billboard* list was especially gratifying for Nicky Hopkins as he'd chosen Beck rather than the higher wages that Jimmy Page reckoned could be proffered after his formation of another outfit from what remained of The Yardbirds - namely himself and Chris Dreja, who attended a few half-hearted rehearsals with Page and singing guitarist Terry Reid before losing interest. He chose instead to commence what turned out to be a successful second career as a freelance photographer.

'After The Yardbirds came to a natural end in 1968,' Dreja ruminated, 'I was in on the discussion stage of Led Zeppelin, even going up to Birmingham to audition Robert Plant and John Bonham, but I wasn't interested in becoming a jobbing musician with strangers, and had made a conscious decision to go into freelance photography. 'Friends in photography who used to come and watch The Yardbirds advised me to go to New York - where I was based for three years. There was no private angst about what might have been.'

Back in late 1968, when the new group was smouldering into form with seemingly majestic slowness, Page contemplated whether or not it needed a second guitarist, going so far as to see if Big Jim Sullivan could be convinced not to take up an offer to join Tom Jones'touring band. While coming to the conclusion that such an idea might lead to the same problems as it had when there were two lead players in The Yardbirds, Jimmy kept the wolf from the door as a hired hand for such as Joe Cocker, a gas fitter by day, but, after work, almost as much a local pop star in his native Sheffield as Dave Berry had been. He'd called himself Vance Arnold then, and his debut 45, a routine race through The Beatles' 'I'll Cry Instead' had had Jimmy on guitar, just as he'd be on Cocker's 'With A Little Help From My Friends'. This funereal-paced waltz through another Beatles number was set to wrench Mary Hopkin's 'Those Were The Days' from Number One in November 1968. Page was to be evident too on the associated long-player, as were Nicky Hopkins, Clem Cattini - and John Paul Jones.

'PRINCE MARIO'

'I was seventeen, and earning thirty pounds a week with Jet and Tony, which was enormous. That's when I first met Peter Grant. He was tour-managing Gene Vincent for Don Arden' - John Paul Jones[31]

Overall, The New Yardbirds - soon to be rechristened Led Zeppelin - had in Peter Grant the manager they deserved. He was not one to emphasise the importance of making themselves pleasant to reporters and fans or pull the stroke that everyone from Elvis Presley to Bestial Vomit (of Death Metal combo Sore Throat) had or would do: that the most depraved rock 'n' roller could be A Nice Lad When You Got To Know Him. If a stranger came up to Jimmy Page and said, 'Hello, Jimmy. How is your brother Larry?', Grant didn't mind if, rather than a courteous lie along the lines of 'Fine, thanks. He's keeping well', Jimmy asked the enquirer why he didn't bugger off.

Peter Grant, see, was all for expletives, gesturing with cigarettes and beer-bottles, frankness about drugs and sex, and a general winding up of Authority's rage and derision to ensure that Led Zeppelin would be as rabidly worshipped by both the young and the 'adult-orientated' rock market, especially in North America. Furthermore, if educated in the traditions and lodged conventions of British pop management, he'd never been a stereotype from a monochrome Ealing movie like 1959's *Idle On Parade* with Anthony Newley as a conscripted rock 'n' roller. Unlike Sid James, Newley's on-screen handler, Grant did not seem as if all he liked about his clients was the money he could amass, selling them like cans of beans - with no money back if they tasted funny.

Once - like Larry Page and Jimmy Miller - he'd aspired to stardom himself. Then he accepted that his time in the spotlight was up, and that solid cash was preferable to public acclamation. Since the late 1950s, he'd accrued enough connections in the business to make a living behind the scenes. Eventually, he founded his own organisation, a company concerned more than others with the long term development of its artists' careers. Attempting to instil into them what he perceived as 'professionalism', he succeeded sometimes in only diverting them with his name-dropping and endless anecdotes about the old days. Nevertheless, Grant's relationship with Led Zeppelin at least was to be based always on as much friendship as profit.

With an almost paternal pride in them - and some of his earlier clients - he was able to visualise himself as a qualified hybrid of four role-models. The oldest of these was Colonel Tom Parker, a cigar-gnawing huckster prone to Goldwyn-esque homilies, spectacular amorality - epitomised by his disgusting practice of trapping sparrows, staining them yellow and selling them as canaries - and an icy ruthlessness formidable to those accustomed to Tin Pan Alley's glibber bonhomie. Film producer Hal Wallis grew to 'rather try and close a deal with the Devil' than Parker.[88]

Yet, as country-and-western entertainer Eddy Arnold noted, 'When Tom's your manager, he's all you. He lives and breathes his artist.' By far. the Colonel's biggest coup was in March 1955 when twenty-one-year-old Elvis Presley melted into his managerial caress for life - and beyond. From that month, reckoned Parker, 'Elvis required ever minute of my time, and I think he would have suffered had I signed anyone else. I always knew he had a million dollars' worth of talent. Now he has a million dollars.'[88] This fortune - and those that followed - were made through the single-minded - some might say 'bloody-minded' - dedication that Eddy Arnold had observed, combined with Parker's hard-nosed certainty about everything he did and said.

Closer to home, Peter Grant had also learnt much from close observation of far-sighted and bombastic Andrew Loog Oldham - and, moreso, Tony Secunda who, if a Londoner, will be remembered always for guiding later famous Black Country outfits - most conspicuously, The Moody Blues and The Move - signed to Straight Ahead, an all-purpose pop industry firm established by himself and Denny Cordell.[89]

The Move would be on the way up when Peter Grant entered The Yardbirds' orbit after Simon Napier-Bell had surrendered without fuss their management to him. With the group's sundering in 1968, he'd stay on as Jimmy Page struck while the iron was lukewarm by attempting to put together a New Yardbirds.

Previously, Peter, following a tough upbringing, had been a welder in a sheet metal factory (for five weeks); a corporal in an airforce catering corps when on National Service; recreations manager for both a holiday camp and a Channel Islands hotel; a cabaret club's security officer; an all-in wrestler under the *nom de guerre*, 'Prince Mario' - and a bit-part actor, notably in *Dixon Of Dock Green, Hancock's Half-Hour* and in the 1961 war epic, *Guns Of Navarone*, when he was twenty-five. He was also a stunt double for portly Robert Morley. While these were minor roles that needed little preparation, Peter found onerous all the hanging about during the demanding schedules with their early morning starts.

He had been nearing his thirties when, somewhere along the line, he first dipped his toe into the music industry as a bouncer in the final days of Soho's celebrated 2 I's skiffle cellar, where Harry Webb and Terry Nelhams used to sing before gaining national renown as, respectively, 'Cliff Richard' and 'Adam Faith', and Mickie Most was a waiter, plotting his next move now that his time as South Africa's Elvis was up .

Not long after that, Grant was hired as a booking agent by his fourth role model, the fearsome Don Arden, known, not with amusement, as 'the Al Capone of pop'. In the first instance, he flew Grant to the States to sort out the nuts-and-bolts of Chuck Berry's first UK tour. Mostly, however, Arden had Peter hurtling round the kingdom as general runaround for Berry, Gene Vincent, The Everly Brothers, Little Eva and other visiting North Americans.

Like an army batman without the uniform, Peter would attend to his charges' food, sleep and general health requirements. In a wider sense, this meant checking security, prising unwanted company from dressing rooms, buttonholing promoters, signing chits and bills, and, now and then, squaring up to opponents of greater strength and mobility. With the M1 only half-completed, Grant was also on hand to cope with the tactical problems of moving each operation from A to B. Flat batteries, snapped towropes, overcharging alternators and lengthy waits for Automobile Association patrolmen were very much part of a day's work.

The aftermath of the Merseybeat craze in 1963 found Peter looking after the day-to-day trials and tribulations of The Animals - who he'd sampled in their native Tyneside when they were The Alan Price Rhythm-and-blues Combo - and The Nashville Teens before being sucked into the vortex of The Yardbirds. Though Don Arden's overview of a man 'hugely overweight, unable to walk any great distance'[90] tended to contradict this, Peter's reckless physical resource was among hard-won qualifications for the eventual job of managing the latter group. Beneath the blubber was solid muscle, and he had a knack of glaring out of countenance the most intransigent ditherers over agreed percentages - 'dreadful misunderstanding, Mister Grant, sir... never forgive myself' - causing them to concede some kind of intangible defeat before he'd uttered a syllable. Dictating terms to Peter Grant was simply something that you did not do.

There is a showbusiness legend that, during a US tour with The Animals, he outfaced a support group's thuggish road manager - all bloodshot eyes, cauliflower ears and neanderthal forehead - at a venue in Arizona, who was not only barking orders and spraying spittle on Peter's face but also pointing a shotgun. Very deliberately, Grant raised his arm, all the while keeping his eyes on the man, and whacked him across the face, the momentum loosening the firearm from his grasp and sending him sprawling across the room. Slurring his words through blood, he began to see the Englishman's point of view.

Such combative skills, whether backed by concrete proof or not, were reassuring when Peter - essentially a decent fellow in a savage business - hardened a resolve to strike out on his own. 'I just kind of came around to it,' he shrugged, 'With all the odd jobs I'd done, it just gravitated that way. You don't just wake up in the morning, having been a salesman or a dentist and say, "Hey, I'm going to manage groups." You've got to move around the showbusiness scene, and that, I think, is what I've done.'[1]

'BOB PLANTE'

'He was open-mouthed. "The Yardbirds want me," was all he could manage to say' - Austin Griffiths[66]

As things turned out, Robert Plant's crestfallen headway as a pop singer was a springboard for a brighter future that was to commence with Peter Grant, Jimmy Page and, stringing along for the time being, Chris Dreja following up recommendations by Alexis Korner, Tony Secunda and Terry Reid, and rubbing their chins over him during a Hobbstweedle engagement at the West Midlands College of Higher Education in Walsall - where there'd been that unpleasantness over The Good Egg's money. Soundtracking the trainee teachers' drinking and pursuit of romance, the group, admitted Robert, 'weren't very good. There was a lot of rubbish and flash, but no real content.'[91] He may have been under-rating himself for, after having a brief word afterwards, Jimmy Page rang to summon Plant to his riverside abode in Pangbourne, Berkshire a few days later.

As he hitch-hiked back to the Midlands afterwards, Robert Plant was in a daze. The hidden agendas at school; the scowling disapproval about a concept of self-advancement so alien to his parents that it nearly always cadenced in a spat; the yearnings and daydreams; the slow hand-clapping and howls of derision; the insulting payments in loose change; the Snakes, Listen, Hobbstweedle and all the rest of them, the bitter disappointments...the wheels of the universe were coming together at last.

While it was by no means over, the battle every inch of the way - literally, as far as the length of his hair was concerned - seemed to be turning in Robert's favour. It was just like the Aesop's fable of the frog who'd fallen into a bowl of cream. The frenzied efforts to keep himself afloat churned up the liquid so much that, just as he was on the point of giving up and drowning, he found himself sitting safely on a pat of butter. 'The next thing I know,' gasped Paul Lockey, 'Robert's turned up at our watering hole in West Bromwich, the Tudor Bar, and said, "I've joined Jimmy Page's new band for forty pounds a week" - which was a lot of money then.'[84] A telegram from Peter Grant confirming this had arrived at another boozer, the Three Men In A Boat in Walsall, where he was rehearsing with Hobbstweedle.

After the 17 September, 1968 edition of the *New Musical Express* had listed him as 'Bob Plante' in the line-up of Jimmy Page's New Yardbirds too, there was some kind of future with no more hint of tragedy or farce. Among the most minor of his later celebrations was, apparently, scribbling 'Robert Plant of Led Zeppelin' at eye-level on the plaster wall of a pub urinal in rural Worcestershire. Certainly, the licensee believed it was genuine, and was to have it sellotaped over for posterity.

When history was rewritten by a press agent, Plant became the group's chosen one, its *beau ideal*. Prior to enlisting him, however, Page, Dreja and Grant had approached Terry Reid, who had also been considered by Spencer Davis as a replacement for Steve Winwood after that clever young man formed Traffic. Once in Great Yarmouth's Peter Jay and the Jaywalkers - who had supported on a Yardbirds tour of Britain with The Rolling Stones - Terry was now something of a cult celebrity, whose rise to stardom was seen as a foregone conclusion by factions of the music press. While unable to take up the invitation to join this New Yardbirds, Reed suggested that Jimmy, Chris and Peter ought to seek out this Robert fellow who, when The Band Of Joy had supported the Jaywalkers at Boston Gilderdrome, he'd heard giving 'the best rendition of "Stormy Monday" this side of the Atlantic'.[92]

Whilst making further enquiries about Plant, another possibility may have been Chris Farlowe, who often sounded as if he needed to clear his throat when embroidering his shout-singing with strangled gasps and frantic howls. Before chart-topping 'Out Of Time', he'd released a lengthy reading of the pervasive 'Stormy Monday Blues', T Bone Walker's signature tune - and it was a tribute to Farlowe's soulful delivery that, under the guise of 'Little Joe Cook' on the disc's label, he fooled most of the people into thinking he was an obscure black blues shouter from the Deep South. All he ever lacked was the right song. Who cared if he wasn't much of a composer or even - in a Roy Orbison sense - much of a vocalist either? If nothing else, Chris Farlowe always sounded like Chris Farlowe.[93]

However, the final fingers pointed at Robert with his Viking good looks, tight-trousered gyrations, and avalanche of blond tresses that ensured an ever-increasing cluster of females, stage front, round the central microphone. He also had a voice of such lived-in passion that, as much as Chris Farlowe's or Steve Winwood's, could go from *sotto-voce* intimacy to full-blooded screech or mountainous roar in the space of a few bars. Slipping easily from lazy insinuation to raucous lust to beseeching heartbreak, Plant - on a good night - could convey such exquisite detail of enunciation and inflection that a fractional widening of vibrato could be as loaded as his most anguished wail. Indeed, if you half-closed your eyes, you could - with delicate suspension of logic - truly believe that he'd got the blues from the chain gang or the ghettoes of southside Chicago; that he was world-weary, cynical and knowing beyond his twenty-one years.

THE THUNDERBIRD

'I noticed a couple of hairy blokes at the bar, watching the drummer intently. A member of my staff told me that one of them was a local artiste, Robert Plant, and the other was none other than Jimmy Page. Something was cooking' - Martin Hone, proprietor of the Factory[66]

Robert Plant hadn't been able to help liking John Bonham, despite his over-the-top drumming, his professional perfidy, his frequent lack of transport - which would necessitate time- and petrol-consuming diversions in the van to pick him up in Redditch - and a disconcerting incident when Bonham hurled his dismantled kit down a flight of stairs rather than pack and carry it, case by case, to the van. Yet, as Denny Laine had discovered, Bonham was capable of surprising gentleness and sensitivity, sometimes being moved to tears by pieces of music of specific sentimental resonance.

Plant had, therefore, invited Bonham to join The Band Of Joy. Dave Pegg had also attended rehearsals, but preferred to take his chances in Beast, a trio with drummer Cozy Powell and Clem Clempson, former guitarist with Bakerloo. After Clempson and Powell accepted respective posts in Colosseum and The Ace Kefford Stand, Pegg auditioned for The Foundations, a London outfit fresh from a Number One, and, via Dave Swarbrick, Fairport Convention - whom he'd seen at Birmingham's 'progressive' Mothers club.

He had also remained involved - albeit more and more distantly - with the faltering Way Of Life. John Bonham turned out for them too sometimes. While he couldn't be trusted not to stray again, The Way Of Life were willing to put up with him vacillating between them and Robert Plant's latest shot at the Big Time.

While he wielded reversed sticks in The Way Of Life so that the heavier ends battered the skins, what Bonham may have found burdensome in The Band Of Joy was the lighter touch required to accentuate the vocal harmonies inherent in their repertory choices from the 'underground' pop wafting from California that would climax with 1967's Summer Of Love.

Partly because their music aligned exactly with what made the cats all groove then, a local agency made efforts to find work for The Band Of Joy all over the country, particularly Scotland, though sometimes the bookers seemed to imagine that a couple of hundred miles was just a few inches on a map. Sooner rather than later, therefore, the spurious thrill of thus 'going professional' gave way to stoic cynicism as each man's small fee for a given string of engagements dwindled.

Rumbustious repartee when shoulder-to-shoulder in the van became desultory and, on occasion, suddenly nasty. In transit from Exeter to somewhere north of the border, a violent quarrel broke out between John Bonham and Kevyn Gammond, who demanded to be dropped off at a lay-by within walking distance of his Kidderminster home, thus obliging the others to struggle through the immediate contracted bookings one musician short.

The Band Of Joy was dying on its feet when Bonham resisted inducements from Denny Cordell to join an outfit - the Grease Band - being assembled to back Joe Cocker, whose fleeting Top Fifty entry with 1968's self-penned 'Marjorine' was then presaging his sweaty belly-aching of chart-busting 'With A Little Help From My Friends'.

Rather than enlist as a Grease Bandsman, Bonham ticked over in combo accompanying US singer-songwriter Tim Rose - whose version of 'Hey Joe' had been lifted by The Jimi Hendrix Experience.[94] In the set too was Rose's equally famous 'Mountain Dew' - and 'Foggy Mountain Breakdown', the main title theme for the 1967 film about 1930s bank robbers- *cum*-murderers, *Bonnie And Clyde*. This bluegrass instrumental by banjo-pickin' Lester Flatt and Earl Scruggs had been re-arranged to accommodate a Bonham drum solo. 'I was a big fan of Tim,' gasped Ace Kefford, 'and had all his albums. He was supposed to have written 'Hey Joe' - and John was in the backing band when I saw Tim one night in Birmingham. I was over the moon! There, on stage, my best mate was drumming for Tim Rose! I couldn't believe it!'

At a Rose recital at the newly-opened Factory, once a warehouse, in the middle of Birmingham, Robert Plant brought Jimmy Page along to check out John Bonham. Then, in late July 1968 at the West Hampstead Country Club in north London, Page listened again to Bonham, this time with Peter Grant, prior to offering him what worked out as an initial twenty pounds a week over the fifty he received from Rose.

Though he was delighted by this wage, Bonham was sceptical about joining what was still the has-been Yardbirds, and kept that most noxious of human phenomena - a decision - at arm's length by taking on a short stint with the like orni-thologically-named Thunderbirds, backing group to Chris Far-lowe, who he admired for being comparable in style to Jimmy Powell, and for his Robert Plant-like determination to succeed, even in the teeth of no less than ten flop singles. Among these were the forgettable 'I Remember', 'Itty Bitty Pieces' - which competed against another flop version by The Rockin' Berries - and 1964's loping 'The Blue Beat', which, despite Radio Lux-embourg airplay, rode that particular craze far less lucratively than The Migil Five, an act from the same part of *norf* Lon-don. 1965 had brought unprofitable notoriety when EMI's be-lated executive appreciation of the drug-related hipster slang on 'Buzz With The Fuzz' necessitated its deletion. Nonetheless, not quite a year later, he'd hit the Big Time at last when 'Out Of Time' dragged Georgie Fame from Number One during 1966's rainy summer - though it didn't take long for the going to get rough again.

Even before Bonham began weighing up the options on the road with Farlowe, Grant and Page had made contingency plans by sounding out an unenthusiastic B.J. Wilson of Pro-col Harum.[95] He'd been in the studio with Jimmy on Cocker's 'With A Little Help From My Friends'. Another possibility was Mitch Mitchell, a seasoned session player whose *resumé* includ-ed servitude under Lord Sutch, Johnny Kidd and Georgie Fame.

He'd also been in The Riot Squad, The Tornados and The Pretty Things prior to a successful try-out for The Jimi Hendrix Experience, who were embroiled in 'musical differences' by mid-1968.

Less likely a candidate, but a candidate all the same, was Bobby Graham, who, in a recent autobiography,[39] answered the oft-asked question about who actually beat the drums on The Dave Clark Five's first hits. Graham's working life had taken him from local groups to a holiday camp season and then tenures with Joe Meek's house band, and the likes of Joe Brown and the Bruvvers and The John Barry Seven before coming safely into harbour as one of the London studio scene's most respected figures.

Peter Grant also twice invited Clem Cattini to a business lunch 'to discuss a new project'. Like Bobby Graham, Clem was more in demand than ever by artists from every trackway of pop. He was on at least as many hits as Bobby, Jimmy Page and John Paul Jones. Among a vast number were those by Twinkle ('Terry'), Sandie Shaw ('Long Live Love'), Ken Dodd ('Tears'), Dusty Springfield ('You Don't Have To Say You Love Me'), Tom Jones ('Green Green Grass Of Home'), Gene Pitney ('Something's Gotten Hold Of My Heart'), Jeff Beck ('Love Is Blue') and Scaffold ('Lily The Pink').

A session that resulted in P.J. Proby's idiosyncratic reading in 1964 of 'Somewhere' from *West Side Story* was, according to Clem, 'hilarious. He sang laying on the floor, absolutely blotto. That's how "Somewhere" came out the way it did. He had a terrific voice, mind. I worked for him again about a year ago, and he's completely off the bottle now.' More recent acts that had benefitted from Cattini's ministrations were Marmalade and Love Affair - whose admitted non-participation in the instrumental recording of their first two hits brought them much unwelcome media coverage.

Too preoccupied with session work, Cattini had cancelled Peter Grant's lunch date on both occasions. 'I now had a family, and I thought - wrongly - that I'd found my niche as a session drummer,' explained Clem, 'As I was working three sessions a week, I hadn't a lot of time for that meeting with Peter, so I left it. Two years later, Zeppelin had really made it big, and I said to Peter, "That lunch date, was it to do with...?" He just nodded.'[96]

THE WISHFUL THINKER

'John simply wanted to be part of a group of musicians who could lay down some good things' - Jimmy Page[1]

While Mickie Most was head-to-head with an engineer in the control booth at a Donovan record date, John Paul Jones asked Jimmy Page who he had in mind for this New Yardbirds of his.

As the new decade loomed, it appeared a more dignified means of extricating himself from session work than that of Roger Cook and Tony Burrows. A two-man escape committee of sorts, they would have no qualms about fronting the clownish Pipkins, who were to record and promote 'Gimme Dat Ding!', an infuriatingly insidious ditty composed for the children's television series, *Oliver And The Overlord*. A polished production, it was to jostle to Number Six in the domestic hit parade following several trouser-dropping plugs on *Top Of The Pops*. While this was the last the world saw of The Pipkins, their triumph would be but one in a golden year for Burrows who, in his capacity as a studio vocalist, would attend also to 1970 hits by Edison Lighthouse, White Plains and Brotherhood Of Man.

Being part of such yuck-for-a-buck projects had never appealed to John Paul Jones. As unappetising was following the Alan Caddy route to carbon-copies of then-current hits. Only the occasional misjudged timbre of the lead vocals - illustrated by an Embassy reading of The Dave Clark Five's 'Bits And Pieces' in which the singer spat out every word - made such efforts so-bad-they're-good. 'Can you tell the difference between these and the original sounds?' read the tacky sleeve of one such vinyl album. Indeed, you could. While these perky, workmanlike efforts are as much a cultural summary of the late 1960s as the actual smashes the anonymous participants ghosted, certain now world-famous acts were once so desperate that they were willing to record on such second-rate terms; among them Rod Stewart and, before he mutated into a cross between Liberace and a male Edna Everage, Elton John. Indeed, if you've the inclination, there might be sport in listening out for Elton and Rod, and speculating on other guilty secrets within the grooves of long-players that sounds like a resident band on *Radio One Club*, removed to the sterile surroundings of a studio with a pound-sign hanging over every note.

While there was easy money to be made here, John Paul Jones was more inclined to drink in travellers' tales about touring countries that would always be outlandish and unreachable to a behind-the-scenes bass player, however prosperous. Look at Jack Bruce, Eric Clapton and Ginger Baker, all members of diverse jazz, R&B and pop outfits around London before their merger as the Cream 'supergroup'. Bruce wasn't the most extrovert of performers, and had only agreed to undertake the bulk of the singing only after other possibilities had been investigated. Baker, for example, gave first refusal to Ray Phillips of The Nashville Teens. A similar invitation was made by Clapton to Steve Winwood.

From rehearsals in a Willesden scout hut, the initial humble intention had been simply to work the clubs. During early one nighters and then in the retractable sphere of the studio, Cream's output contained piquancies of blues, experiment and humour - with Bruce adding harmonica, 'cello and other acoustic subtleties. However, a double-album, *Wheels Of Fire*, went gold across the Atlantic where in concrete colosseums, all the sensitivities of old were lost to drugs, groupies, easy money, maximum volume and numbers like Willie Dixon's two-chord 'Spoonful' cut, dried and dissected for up to twenty po-faced minutes to snowblinded applause.

Well, John Paul could equal that if he too was in an outfit that broke US box-office records, even if clever irony was corrupted by high-decibels and 'endless, meaningless solos,' sighed Clapton, 'We were not indulging ourselves so much as our audiences - because that's what they wanted. Then we got our first bad review, which said how boring and repetitious our performance had been - and it was true. We'd been flying high with blinkers for so long, we weren't aware of the changes that had been taking place musically. New people were coming up and growing, and we were repeating ourselves.'[97]

Among the 'new people' - some of them, not so 'new' - were The Climax Chicago Blues Band, connected genealogically to Emile Ford's Checkmates - pre-Merseybeat hitmakers - and two Staffordshire beat groups, Hipster Image and The Gospel Truth. During the present 'blues boom', they were building up a huge following in Europe and making a small beginning in North America where Canned Heat had long been ploughing a similar furrow.

Balancing humour and scholarly application, much of this inspired good-time blues group's appeal lay in the dissimilar natures of its front men: corpulent, jocular ex-supermarket charge hand Bob 'Bear' Hite and intense Alan 'Blind Owl' Wilson with his master's degree. After the unit's well-received spot during the Monterey International Pop Music Festival in 1967, a second album, *Boogie With Canned Heat* and its attendant 'On The Road Again' hit established them as an internationally viable act.

After longer years of struggle under other nomclatures, London's Status Quo had finally hit pay-dirt too - with 1968's psychedelic 'Pictures Of Matchstick Men' in both the home and US Top Twenties. Yet apart from another UK smash with 'Ice In The Sun', a series of flops over the next two years indicated that the group was on the way out - but, abandoning both 'progressive' pretentions and attempts to become cabaret entertainers, they were about to re-emerge with immense and lasting success as denim-clad blues-boogie merchants.

Yet, while noting these random success stories, John Paul Jones kept returning to the test-case of Cream, whose premeditated disbandment was marked by the aptly-titled *Goodbye* album, and a long-telegraphed farewell concert at London's Royal Albert Hall in November 1968. Just as an estate agent might speculate who would be doing the probate assessment following a Queen Mother-sized death, Jones wondered who would fill the market void left by Cream.

Once Eric Clapton's flatmate, Chris Welch had access to privileged information and the co-operation of the principals. Moreover, as a *Melody Maker* journalist esteemed for a droll wit, he was in a position to prod nerves pertaining to his old friend's career. As the press debated Cream's fragmented future almost before the announcement of the trio's split had been uttered completely, it occurred to Welch that, as Steve Winwood's Traffic was on hold then, next week's *Melody Maker* could lend tidy credence to his printed comments the previous month about 'a strong possibility that they (Eric and Steve) may get a group together.'[98] So Clapton and Winwood, soon to be lynchpins of Blind Faith, the lesser 'supergroup', were being set up to welcome vehicles bearing illustrious callers and their instruments, and exchanging telephone calls about rehearsals that were to sustain them for just one tour of North America where Cream too had stagnated artistically.[99]

In the air then too, Mountain was another 'new Cream' in construction. A guitar-bass-drums trio, they were being born from sessions for a solo album by Leslie West, a highly-regarded - if tubby - New York guitarist in artistic debt to Eric Clapton. This was supervised by Felix Pappalardi, Cream's producer, who proposed himself as Mountain's bass player for stage sets that would consist of triple-forte work-outs of tracks from their studio albums; one item, 'Nantucket Sleighride', extrapolated Cream-style for over seventy minutes on a Japan-only double-LP.

Meanwhile, a different type of 'supergroup' was emerging, containing Graham Nash of The Hollies, former Byrd Dave Crosby and Steve Stills from Buffalo Springfield. John Paul Jones had had his ear to the ground when this new combine had entered the lists, starting rehearsals in a Kensington flat for an eponymous album notable for tricky vocal harmonies, hippy lyricism and - all the work of Stills - neo-acoustic backing tracks. Its 45, Nash's 'Marrakesh Express', was to be a worldwide smash, and, if the trio's warblings weren't to everyone's taste, he ended up a lot richer than if he'd stayed a Holly.

Regardless of musical content, Blind Faith, Crosby-Stills-and-Nash and Mountain were gearing themselves up in 1968 to make fortunes in North America. They were all fighting the same battle, the battle for profits, the battle for money. Perhaps something that was less overtly motivated by avarice and not such a blatantly calculated 'supergroup' - that most smug and fascist of all pop cliques - could steal a march on these fiddlers before they got in tune, and likewise take the USA for every cent they could get.

John Paul Jones was, therefore, intrigued when his wife pointed out a news item in *Disc & Music Echo* about Jimmy Page putting together a new group. Why didn't John Paul ring him? After all, what with his assistance on most of The Yard-birds' latter-day singles, Jones was an obvious candidate for Jimmy Page's New Yardbirds - or, as far as I'm concerned, a sort of *ur*-Yardbirds - and Peter Grant's big plans for them. Who else was there? John Entwistle? Herbie Flowers?

After Chris Dreja lost interest, another possibility might have been Jack Bruce - who, if a recent biographer[100] is to be believed, was also asked to join, respectively, Crosby-Stills-and-Nash and The Shadows (!) - or Ace Kefford, late of The Move and now grappling with The Ace Kefford Stand, who'd been approached via drummer Cozy Powell to pitch in with The Jeff Beck Group. 'Jeff wanted me as the singer,' qualified Kefford, 'I said OK, but I didn't have much confidence. I went to a couple of London rehearsals with a bloke from Van Der Graaf Generator on bass. Afterwards, when Jeff dropped me off at the station, he said, "After you left The Move, I came looking for you all over Birmingham - not as a singer but a bass player".'

Kefford might have crossed Page's mind fleetingly - just as John Paul Jones, who was to play organ on 'Ol' Man Riv-er' on *Truth*, might have crossed Beck's - but all Led Zeppelin signposts pointed finally at John Paul, who Jimmy telephoned on 19th July 1968 with a firm offer for the use of talents that weren't as conspicuous as those of the other selected *dramatis personnae*. One of nature's sidemen - like Chris Dreja - Jones would be solidly at the heart of the music, ministering to over-all effect on bass and keyboards, and possessing a voice reliable enough for harmonies.

THE NEGOTIATOR

'I don't want to name the people who put us down and thought we were wasting our time, but there were plenty of them' - Peter Grant[1]

Via Mickie Most, Peter Grant had come to manage The Animals, The New Vaudeville Band - who thrived during a craze in 1966 for olde-tyme whimsy - Jeff Beck and, ultimately, The Yardbirds. Only the brave incurred his wrath. In every kind of unpleasantness at the most unrefined engagements, he kept his cool, striking a bellicose stance when necessary, even when surrounded by a Mafia-connected promoter and his hulking, shirt-sleeved hitmen - who'd be bludgeoning him in vain with shouting and swearing that the contract wasn't worth the paper it was written on, and The Yardbirds were in breach of it anyway.

If a verbal connivance akin to that of - take your pick - Sergeant Bilko, Del Boy, Bradley Hardacre of *Brass* or *Dad's Army*'s spivvy Private Walker didn't achieve the desired result, his mouth could, at a moment's notice, spew out dizzying facts and figures for affable if persevering bouts of discussions only half-understood by protagonists already wondering if the effort of fighting him was worth it. With subjugation came an odd feeling of relief - because, if nothing else worked, Grant had no qualms about bringing into play the naked threat, no, the open promise that, in so many more polite words, if his wishes weren't met, then a degree of correction might be in order. Cowed by the way he said it - gritted in an unexpectedly soft husk - and the fathomless eyes, a show of defiance, then hesitation and final agreement would chase across the face of anyone who hadn't heard that Peter Grant didn't argue and expected the same from you.

His strengths were to be tested more throughly and not found wanting when he took the reins of The New Yardbirds - i.e. what was to metamorphose into Led Zeppelin - with a strategy that seemed so well-thought out that hearsay about this fantastic new group was created virtually by word-of-mouth throughout the industry. As confirmed by Ace Kefford, this was similar to how Tony Secunda launched The Move: 'Tony's idea was not to sign us to a record company until we'd built up a reputation, and got the name in the newspapers. It was just like Peter Grant and Led Zeppelin. The band sounded good, but he brought this publicity in to create a buzz. Tony was the brains behind Carl Wayne chopping up televisions on stage, and the road crew letting off thunderflashes. It'd be Tony who'd ring the police and the fire brigade who'd steam in with hoses, and he'd be there with photographers and a story for the press. It made for a wild, violent image, and we finished our Marquee season with queues round the block.'

If nowhere as hard-sell as Secunda, Grant was to make sure that Led Zeppelin's was to be a smart name to drop before, brushing aside obstacles like demos and auditions, he so much as commenced painstaking, energetic and blunt negotiations with Atlantic, the chosen record label. By the time he was through, Led Zeppelin had been granted a mind-boggling advance and more freedom - artistic and otherwise - than any other act, extending to lease control over master tapes and a pronounced say in album artwork and marketing procedures for both vinyl and non-vinyl goods. Nothing was left to chance - or to Atlantic - in order to ensure that record-store windows everywhere bloomed with Led Zeppelin's splendour.

THE OCCULTIST

'I'm not saying it's a system for anybody to follow. I don't agree with everything, but I find a lot of it relevant' - Jimmy Page[1]

A certain type of reader may have been looking forward to this chapter - because, before proceeding any further, it is necessary to address hitherto unexplored issues, some of which may seem far-fetched - often for their triteness - but are at least trace elements in the artistic melting pot of what became Led Zeppelin.

As *omerta* is to the Mafia, a vow of silence among roving minstrels and their employees has always persisted concerning hard drugs as well as illicit sex - and, in Led Zeppelin's case, dabblings in sorcery. Inklings of this leaked to John Citizen through the underground press, the most persistent of which was that, like bluesman Robert Johnson, tormented by an inferno of demons and ectoplasmic monsters, three of the group had been driven a hard bargain by Lucifer to achieve success.

As to which musician had advocated the pact, there was never any lingering doubt. Jimmy Page's fascination with the black arts was to extend to the ownership of a London bookshop devoted to the genre; the purchase of Boleskine, magician Aleister Crowley's Scottish mansion, and being the brains behind the etching of the so-called Great Beast's 'DO WHAT THOU WILT' maxim into the playout grooves of US pressings of *Led Zeppelin III*.

During the formation of the group, Page was also commissioned to compose and record the soundtrack to *Lucifer Rising*, a film directed by Kenneth Anger, who, then in middle life, styled himself 'The Most Monstrous Movie Maker In The Underground'. He and Page had met at a London auction of Crowley memorabilia. Much more than Page, Anger, a former Hollywood child star, modelled both his private life and public persona on that of the Great Beast, and his livelihood and reputation depended on bleak cult flicks such as 1963's apocalyptic *Scorpio Rising* - which betrayed as deep an absorption of the netherworldly novels of Dennis Wheatley as that of Black Sabbath's Terry 'Geezer' Butler.

That Anger's *Invocation Of My Demon Brother* contained footage from The Rolling Stones' Hyde Park concert in 1969 indicated that, as well as the likes of Anais Nin - whose prose poem-*cum*-novel provided the libretto to post-serialist composer Edgard Varese's murkiest work, *Nocturnal* - his social circle extended to what Marianne Faithfull described as 'a veritable witches' coven of decadent illuminati, rock princelings and hip nobility'.[101] Indeed, during pre-production of *Lucifer Rising*, he visualised as 'Beelzebub' Rolling Stone Keith Richards, also volunteering to officiate, after suggesting in vain that Keith and girlfriend Anita Pallenberg wed in a pagan ceremony at dawn on Hampstead Heath.

Though Jimmy Page's involvement in the *Lucifer Rising* project was abandoned after he produced less than half-an-hour of music, his name was to be as synonymous with the occult as George Harrison's was already with Krishna Consciousness, and Reg Presley's would be with crop circles - though that of the front man of The Troggs wasn't one that tripped immediately off the tongue when discussing rock's mystics, even if *FAB 208* magazine reported Presley's outing to a Hampshire hill to look for UFOs late one night during 1967's psychedelic summer. Nevertheless, his findings since might be regarded as dangerous knowledge if put forward by a head of state rather than a former bricklayer from Andover - or a London session guitarist.

Among precedents for such explorations known personally to Page was Graham Bond, whose pop pedigree was most cultivated. Quite at ease playing alto sax and organ simultaneously, he'd worked with Blues Incorporated and then with Jack Bruce, Ginger Baker and saxophonist Dick Heckstall-Smith in a modern jazz octet before the four of them constituted the first

Graham Bond Organisation. They came to be appreciated by a hip metropolitan coterie as a 'group's group' for their stylistic tenacity and exacting musical standards.

Next came various unrewarding outfits whose overall ethos reflected Bond's fascination with incorporeal practices. This got so out of hand that he started professing that his father was actually Aleister Crowley - though, as it was with the myth of Jimmy Page playing on Beatles sessions, this could be refuted by evidence that the much-misunderstood black magician need-ed to have been in two places at once to be so. Prone to bouts of drug addiction too, Bond was to be at a personal and profes-sional low when, on 8th May 1974, either slipping or overcome by a sudden urge to end it all, he finished under the wheels of a tube train. The police took two days to identify the body.

In 1999, David, Screaming Lord Sutch's apparent sui-cide put a tragic full-stop to what was also, on its own terms, a triumphant professional career. A familiar of Jimmy Page since the Neil Christian era, he may be seen superficially as a cartoon version of Graham Bond, what with the blood-curdling routines on the boards and much of the content of his records suggested he too was in league with some kind of devil. Yet, even cumu-latively, the likes of 1963's 'Monster In Black Tights' - with its 'wrinkled-up chin where the worms have been' - 1964's 'She's Fallen In Love With The Monster Man', 'Dracula's Daughter', the self-composed 'All Black And Hairy', 'Wailing Sounds', nine-minute 'Hands Of Jack The Ripper', 'Monster Ball' and 'Murder In The Graveyard' were no more harmful than a ride on a fairground ghost train.

The comedian to Neil Christian's straight man, Sutch too was accompanied by many nascent stars. As it was with John Mayall, the number of musicians who can also claim a tenure with Sutch to their credit runs into three figures. Among such helpmates were Jimmy Page (on 'She's Fallen In Love With The Monster Man' and its 'Bye Bye Baby' B-side), Jeff Beck ('Drac-ula's Daughter') and Ritchie Blackmore - though Sutch would stress that 'Roger Mingay, the one before Ritchie, was as good a guitarist as him, Jimmy Page, Jeff Beck, you name 'em. He was nicked by Joe Meek, who put him with The Outlaws. Then he emigrated to Australia, and we never heard of him again.'

Enlisted too, often in pick-up groups with little or no time to rehearse or even soundcheck, were drummers like John Bonham, Viv Prince of The Pretty Things and The Who's Keith Moon - while the diverse worlds of music, drama and literature have been represented by keyboard players Nicky Hopkins, Paul Nicholas - and, yes, Alan Clayson.

'Two of Led Zeppelin, two of Jimi Hendrix's Experience and two of Deep Purple passed through the Savages,' noted Lord David, not differentiating between stage and studio, 'I was an idiot not to have made albums with the line-ups we had, but there's not much time to record when you're working seven nights a week, sometimes afternoons too. We never gave records a thought. We were more of a visual experience.'

Bandleaders such as Page, Johnny Kidd, Spencer Davis and Jimi Hendrix as well as the likes of Procol Harum and Deep Purple all sought His Lordship's advice when vacancies arose - and a small army of famous ex-Savages were the 'Heavy Friends' who turned out for their old boss after he landed a profitable two-album deal with Atlantic Records in 1970, following a season at Los Angeles' Thee Experience.

While the first 'Heavy Friends' offering was cited in a recent poll amongst the nation's more unimaginative radio presenters as the worst rock album ever made, Sutch's repellant public allure diverted attention from the quality of his music during this period when a controlled, melodic vein of heavy metal underlined a witty if gruesome lyricism.

Borrowing more insidiously from Sutch, The Crazy World of Arthur Brown captured Robert Plant's imagination after they had come into being in the watershed year of 1967 when philosophy graduate and cosmic ham Arthur teamed up with organist Vincent Crane and a drummer with the technicolour name of Drachen Theaker. The toast of London's psychedelic dungeons, the act was as good as it would ever get when the Crazy World 'went public' on gaining a recording contract. Robed and wearing a helmet spouting flames (originally a candlestick attached to a sieve), the self-styled 'God of Hellfire' had a quasi-operatic vocal arsenal at his behest as he cavorted and stared psychotically.

The group nodded to prevailing trends on their first single with droll 'Give Him A Flower' but its A-side, 'Devil's Grip', was a truer reflection of the Brown dialectic. After this created a stir, The Crazy World of Arthur Brown went for the jugular with 'Fire' - how the 'God of Hellfire' will 'destroy all you've done' - a *tour de force* that was their only hit - a Number One, mind, and still the commercial zenith of horror-rock.

Brown left his mark on both Robert Plant's singing style and, more fleetingly, The Band Of Joy's phase of slapping on the warpaint. From the Midlands too came the fiery furnace's overlords in the later 1960s.

At least a tributary of the flow chart of Led Zeppelin's influences, Black Sabbath's climb to fame was possibly more interesting than what occurred afterwards. They were connected genealogically to The Rest, the Erdington beat group who mixed socially with John Bonham and Robert Plant. However, the in-dividuals who'd be Black Sabbath found each other in Mythol-ogy, a 'progressive' unit who switched policy and name with the advent of the blues boom. They were first known by proprietor Jim Simpson as just four of many - including Bonham and Plant - who coughed up the one shilling membership fee for Henry's Blueshouse which functioned once a week ('Tuesday Is Blues-day') in central Birmingham's Crown Hotel. As desperate for work as The Band Of Joy and Hobbstweadle, Earth - formerly Mythology - offered their services as an interval band for the price of a Henry's t-shirt each. In this capacity, they acquitted themselves well enough for Jim Simpson - that same function-ary of *Midland Beat* and Locomotive - to firstly procure them paid bookings and, eventually agree to manage them.

When Earth graduated from supporting the likes of Colosseum, Birmingham's own Tea-and-Symphony and even The
Band Of Joy, to packing out Henry's on their own, the idea of
seeking a record deal was no longer a laughable afterthought.
With the strongest possible Midlands reputation, guitarist Tony
Iommi had already been head-hunted by Jethro Tull whose
chart-topping second LP, *Stand Up*, was to mark the apogee of
the British wing of the blues boom.

Its passing obliged artistes and manager to find a new
direction. Day upon day was spent round Jim's house listening
closely to selections from his enormous record collection. Especially reassuring to Earth's self-doubting singer John 'Ozzy'
Osbourne were the gravelly nuances of Joe Turner, Wynonie
Harris and other post-war blues singers who, as Robert Plant
knew already, capitalised on, rather than shrank from, inabili-
ties to reach beyond their vocal compasses without cracking.
Through Simpson too, Bill Ward, was re-introduced to rhythm
aesthete Pete York (now *ex*-Spencer Davis Group) with whom
he formed an experimental percussion ensemble.

Having ministered to Earth's musical education, Jim sent
them to win their spurs at Hamburg's Star-Club where the need
to *mak schau* for hours on end toughened the unit - now renamed Black Sabbath - for less demanding but more reputable
tasks back home.

When they returned from the Reeperbahn, Black Sabbath's blues had mutated into a musical and visual presentation
that affected a bleak but atmospheric intensity. Sporting inverted crucifixes and similar satanic fetishist gear, they were smash-
ing out self-penned pieces like 'Hand Of Doom', 'Behind The
Walls Of Sleep', 'Children Of The Grave', 'Paranoid', 'Electric
Funeral', 'Into The Void' and so on. As to the tunes - 'most of
the numbers are based on a certain riff', explained Terry 'Geezer' Butler with quiet pride, 'We don't use a melody, just a raw
type of riff'. Simpson described his clients' recitals as 'basic,
dirty and bad. It is an honest interpretation of their environment' - meaning that it was a product of England's industrial

hub where, fouling the air and waterways, the thick black fumes and chemical waste percolating from the connurbation's blast furnaces and factories caked employees' poky dwellings with soot and grime as indelibly as Lady Macbeth's damned spot.

Nobody could deny the impact on the crowd when Black Sabbath performed at Bletchley Youth Centre or faraway Dunstable Civic, but few A & R representatives time-serving in the capital's record companies considered then that it would come across on vinyl.

The Who's John Entwistle, earmarked to sing and play bass with the 'Bolero' Led Zeppelin, had been a musical master of the macabre for longer than either Black Sabbath or Arthur Brown - though, in the midst of the group's 'Anyway Anywhere Anyhow' finale of smashed amplifiers, smoke bombs, flares and feedback lament, he'd be almost stock-still whilst extrapolating the song's principal riff. A revered bass guitarist, John was also The Who's second-string composer - and if you can't be first, be peculiar. A minority of listeners, including myself, found his macabre, cynical creations the most attractive aspect of The Who. Indeed, Jimi Hendrix's favourite Who track was Entwistle's 'Boris The Spider', squashed against the wall it was climbing. On the group's *A Quick One* LP, in which the hallucinating alcoholic of John's 'Whiskey Man' was condemned to a padded cell. Other areas covered might not have been everyone's bag either but you cannot dismiss easily a man who wrote pop ditties about miserliness ('Silas Stingy'), childhood bullying ('Cousin Kevin') and paedophilia ('Fiddle About'). Entwistle was also prone to wearing garb apposite to his emotional vocabulary on stage and in publicity shots.

This did not impinge seriously on his private life - though there was some substance to the moonshine about what 'insiders' claimed they knew about Brian Jones of The Rolling Stones. Straight up. A mate of mine told me. Sado-masochism, coprophagy, Crowley-esque meddling with the black arts, and capsizing of assumptions that humans could only be gratified sexually without mechanical appliances and only with other humans were the least of it after Brian and Anita Pallenberg (his girlfriend before she ran off with Keith Richards) had purchased in 1966 an upmarket studio flat in South Kensington, which after they'd settled in, emitted a dimly-lit aura of either cartoon scariness or fascinating depravity, depending on the credulity of a given visitor, a frequent one of which was Jimmy Page, to whom it became clear that, if Brian wasn't the most dominant Stone anymore, he was going to be the most 'mystical' one. Like Dean Moriarty in Jack Kerouac's *On The Road*, he'd be oddly fascinating for his mastery of an instinctive and crazed pagan Zen, radiated by the incongruous juxtaposition of Moroccan tapestries and a poster advertising Seven-Up on the walls of the new apartment.

The Ancient Greeks had a word for it: *hubris*, which defies succinct translation, but alludes to a heroically foolish defiance rooted in a feeling that you are beyond the reaches of convention and authority. Brian had been trying to reach that plateau all his life. Now, in an adolescence extended by adulation, his *hubris* was one learnt not through asceticism and self-denial but via the dynamics of careless sex, psychedelics, the sub-criminality of his adolescence, and making it up as he went along.

In Brian and Anita's apartment, the mood of the hour might dictate a seance; a cosmic safari to some midnight tor in Cornwall to look for UFOs; 'Satanic spells to dispel thunder and lightning', as Winona, a mutual friend, reported to Jim McCarty; an excursion up west to the hip Indica Gallery and Bookstore for merchandise of occult and modishly aerie-faerie nature - and fireside palavers that swung from otherworldly matters to Brian's shy-making soliloquys about his life, his soul, his agony.

After Anita, an aspiring film star, had landed a leading role in a German film, *Mort Und Totschlag* ('A Degree Of Murder'), late in 1966, Brian - motivated perhaps by jealous imaginings - had materialised whenever possible on set in Munich, watching her act on a monitor screen, and monopolising her during the lengthy intervals as cumbersome movie-cameras were repositioned. His omnipresence entered discussions by the flick's backers, aware of both its budget and the publicity value of a Rolling Stone's involvement.

Volker Schlondorff, the twenty-seven-year-old director, was elected to sound out Jones about composing the soundtrack. If flattered, Brian confessed that he hadn't a clue how to go about it, but rather than baulk at the task like a gymkhana pony refusing a fence, he decided to muddle on with it, getting a clearer picture from the confusion, learning what he could *in situ* and unwittingly dismissing many ingrained preconceptions and introducing new ones. As if it was the most natural thing in the world, he was 'spotting' each sequence with a stop-watch, and returning to London to routine it in South Kensington before repairing to Olympic Studios to supervise the taping of music that was impressive in its own right, regardless of imagined visuals. Within its tight strictures, it was to testify to the presence of more intrinsic virtues than had been expected of one in an industry where sales figures are arbiters of success.

In Olympic Studios Brian himself attended to sitar, organ, dulcimer, banjo, harmonica and autoharp, but he also called the shots to a small ensemble hand-picked by himself and engineer Glyn Johns, among them Jimmy Page - on the point of joining The Yardbirds - and now former Lord Sutch Savage,Nicky Hopkins.

Compared to the Stones sessions that nearly always left him in a foul mood, nowadays Jones found his new studio companions' blithe dedication to the job in hand refreshing. Furthermore, they enjoyed being under Brian's surprisingly straightforward baton as, rather than sinking morbidly surreal teeth into *Mort Und Totschlag* and exploring an abstract unknown that needed to be explained rather than scored, he delved into country-and-western, blues, soul and what might be described as country-and-eastern - though the lightweight main title theme was reprised in wracked, menacing fashion in keeping with the illicit burial of a corpse on the construction site of an auto-bahn.

Elsewhere, a serene if subdued ghostliness vied with severe dissonance, but little was designed to divert attention from the action - which was precisely what Volker Schlondorff required, 'It wasn't just that his music was special. It was that the score was so spontaneous and vital. Only Brian could have done it. He had a tremendous feeling for the lyrical parts, and knew perfectly the recording and mixing. techniques to achieve the best sound.'[104]

To Brian's chagrin, this, the closest he'd ever come to a solo LP, wasn't to be released on vinyl anywhere. Nor was the *Mort Und Totschlag* movie to be sub-titled or dubbed and put on general circulation in Britain. Instead, it was the stuff of occasional showings in arts centres and film clubs.

Few common-or-garden pop consumers, therefore, were aware of *Mort Und Totschlag* - though they were all too cognisant of Brian's most jaw-dropping fashion statement, the black jack-booted uniform of a World War II stormtrooper in which he was frontpaged - with evil grin and stamping on a doll too - for *Stern* a glossy magazine published in West Germany, a territory in which Jones was, debatably, more idolised than Mick Jagger. This was particularly inflammable in the light of a recent election triumph by the 'new Nazis' in Bavaria. There had also been a recent chronicled incident of Keith Moon, Vivian Stanshall of The Bonzo Dog Doo-Dah Band and Screaming Lord Sutch parading round London clubs in Nazi attire, though after morning came, Sutch cried off when Moon sought further exhibitionist fun in one of the city's most Jewish quarters.

An *NME* interviewer noted a swastika flag draped over one of Jones'armchairs, but believed his protestations that the *Stern* picture was 'a put-down. Really, I mean with all that long hair in a Nazi uniform, couldn't people see it was a satirical thing?'[105]

Brian was out of earshot of a hastening conspiracy. Soon, nearly all the cards would be on the table. Becoming quite accustomed to life without him, The Rolling Stones wouldn't be able to accommodate one who was present at sessions - like the one for 'She's A Rainbow' with John Paul Jones - only if his rising from a bed of dreams induced by prescribed tranquillisers coincided with a remembered record date. In reciprocation, Brian, now referring to the Stones as 'they' rather than 'we', was bracing himself for a leap into the unknown - in absolute terms as it turned out.

Soon to die, Brian Jones' departure from the group in June 1968 was worthy of an item on BBC television's *Six O'Clock News*, and there followed heated discussion about who would replace him. Among those under consideration were Dave Mason of Traffic, Mick Taylor - John Mayall's latest lead guitarist - and Eric Clapton, now that the last note of Cream (until a brief reformation in 2005) was about to resound at the Royal Albert Hall that November. Another name that cropped up was that of Jimmy Page. He was also among the callers at his friend Brian's home in the Sussex Weald, where Jones had at least talked about forming a new group. However, despite the impending break-up of The Yardbirds, Page was not to be at the loose end that the former Rolling Stone first imagined.[106]

THE GROUP

'People have associated a type of sound with the name. It's a heavy beat sound, and I want to keep that' - Jimmy Page[107]

On 12 September 1968, the US trade periodical *Amusement Business* was to ratify officially that 'London session bassist John Paul Jones and vocalist Robert Plante (*sic*) have been asked by Jimmy Page to join his New Yardbirds'. Yet, throughout 1968's rainy summer, Jones, Page and Plant with John Bonham had been rehearsing together in a cramped rehearsal studio in central London, readying themselves for ten immediate summer dates in Scandinavia that had long been scheduled for the old Yardbirds - as were some in North America, beginning on Boxing Day. A set was cobbled together from exploratory - and rather hurried - arrangements of items drawn from a common unconscious. These included The Nashville Teens' 'Tobacco Road', 'Something Else' from Eddie Cochran (which had been the title track of an EP by The Move earlier that year), 'As Long As I Have You' by US soulman Garnett Mimms - from The Band Of Joy's repertoire - Chuck Berry's 'No Money Down', and 'Chest Fever' from *Music From Big Pink*, a debut album of insidious impact by Bob Dylan's backing Band, that, like *John Wesley Harding*, Dylan's own austere, understated new beginning, was helping to steer pop away from the backwards-running tapes and further clutter that disguised many essentially banal artistic perceptions.

The New Yardbirds even tried a couple of numbers associated with The Beatles - 'I Saw Her Standing There' and 'Long Tall Sally'. Some were re-worked in a melodramatic, sloweddown style vaguely reminiscent of the waning Vanilla Fudge, described in a recent edition of *International Times* as 'molten lead on vinyl'.[108]

Back from Scandinavia - where they'd seemed too eager to please with what would be a cautious politeness by later standards - the four functioned as a session team - with Plant on mouth-organ - at London's Lansdowne complex on a P. J. Proby album, *Three Week Hero*, produced by Steve Rowland, who'd been in the control room for previous offerings by The Pretty Things and Dave Dee-Dozy-Beaky-Mick and-Tich. 'They admired P.J.'s talent,' remembered Rowland, 'and agreed to do it for Musicians Union scale. John Bonham couldn't make some of the sessions so I asked Clem Cattini to fill in.'[109]

With John Paul Jones in charge of most of the arrangements, *Three Week Hero* spawned a Dutch chart-topper in 'Today I Killed A Man' - with Proby imitating Johnny Cash - and a remaindered medley with the umbrella title 'Jim's Blues', which was the first studio item to feature all four members of the group that were about to commence trading as 'Led Zeppelin', begging the question about whether a rechristening as, say, 'The Jimmy Page Four' would have had the same subliminal lure.

'I drove John and Robert to their first engagement as Led Zeppelin in my Jaguar,' recollected Reg Jones, then still hanging on in The Way Of Life, 'It was at Surrey University in Guilford. There was a huge banner outside that read, "Tonight! The Ex-Yardbirds". Underneath in smaller lettering, it said "Led Zeppelin". After the gig, I couldn't start the Jaguar, and we all came home on the train.'[66]

It wouldn't be long before 'formerly The Yardbirds' became the footnote on posters advertising Led Zeppelin bookings in London clubland that had started with an appearance as The New Yardbirds at the Marquee on an October Friday. Indeed, *Melody Maker* referred to them as 'the regrouped Yardbirds' in one associated critique, adding that they were 'very much a heavy group, with singer Robert Plant leading and ably holding his own against a powerful backing trio. Generally, there seems to be a need for Led Zeppelin to cut down on volume a bit.'[110] However, they hadn't heeded this advice - very much the opposite - for another appearance at the place in December - when they were billed defiantly as Led Zeppelin with no apologetic references to the previous incarnation to be seen.

Peter Grant had been busy too. Looking for a record company for his clients was as chancy as looking for a girlfriend. Any representations from EMI and Epic, The Yardbirds' respective British and US outlets, were dismissed on the grounds that they hadn't bothered to issue the *Little Games* LP for the home market, and Atlantic were persuaded that the then-unheard of fortune required to secure world rights to Plant, Page, Jones and Bonham's output for the next five years would be money well spent. The name sounded similar to - and just as heavy as - Iron Butterfly, didn't it? Atlantic couldn't ship enough of that group's *In-A-Gadda-Da-Vida*, could they? Two million since it came out in spring! Well, Led Zeppelin could equal that, just like The Beatles had shut down The Beach Boys, their Capitol label-mates, back in '64. Furthermore, the group wouldn't need a staff producer either. They'd take care of that themselves. Had Jimmy Page deduced nothing from his comprehensive shadowing of the methodology of just about every professional console technician in London?

As an immediate consequence, a debut album, *Led Zeppelin*, was recorded in thirty hours, more or less like the lads did the numbers on stage, and plugged with a performance of 'Communications Breakdown' - the first song Page and Plant ever wrote together - late one autumn evening on *How It Is*, a BBC television magazine programme.

A decision not to issue this breakneck opus - or any of its companion tracks - as a British single resulted in only sporadic exposure on national radio. Virtually the only presenter who aired Led Zeppelin then was BBC Radio One's John Peel, whose *Top Gear* series tended to concentrate not on chart-directed singles but albums and in-person showcases by acts described as 'progressive' - though, with the passing of the Golden Age of British beat and then pop's fleeting 'classical' period', it had become easier to get by on instrumental proficiency rather than songwriting talent. It's rather a sweeping generalisation, but standards of composition often fell in favour of improvisation, constant retakes and blinded-by-science technology.

Furthermore, though determined to like it, *Top Gear* listeners - not to mention John Peel himself and other pundits - noticed more than a touch of The Jeff Beck Group's *Truth*, issued earlier that year, to the degree that both this and Led Zeppelin's album would contain the same song. 'You've got to understand that Beck and I came from the same sort of roots,' explained Jimmy Page, 'If you've got things you enjoy, then you want to do them - to the horrifying point where we'd done our first LP with "You Shook Me", and then I heard he'd done "You Shook Me" on *Truth*. I was terrified because I thought they'd be the same, but I hadn't even known he'd done it, and he hadn't known we had.'[12]

Just as The Pretty Things' *SF Sorrow* was lost in the shadow of The Who's lesser but more well-known 'rock opera' *Tommy*, so The Jeff Beck Group was to swallow dust behind Led Zeppelin. 'They had a better looking lead singer,' shrugged Beck, 'They also had Bonham on drums creating all sorts of pandemonium. It was a much better package than I had, so obviously they did better.'[12]

He noted too that *Little Games*, The Yardbirds' valedictory album, prevailed on Led Zeppelin's album debut - though it has to be said that *Little Games* too consumed grooves with such as 'Drinking Muddy Water', which was essentially its namesake's 'Rollin' And Tumblin'', just as 'Stealing Stealing' was precisely that - a theft of a jugband blues from the 1920s.

For the stage, The Yardbirds and Led Zeppelin had each rehearsed 'Flames' by Elmer Gantry's Velvet Opera, a fixture on Britain's 'underground' circuit in the late 1960s with a reputation enhanced - like Led Zeppelin's would be - by regular appearances on *Top Gear* and the championship of another BBC disc-jockey, Stuart Henry. In 1967, they recorded an eponymous debut LP, an amalgam of psychedelia with a brake applied, and the soul band they once were. Self-penned material included uptempo 'Flames', remembered not so much as an edited spin-off 45 so much as a highlight of CBS's *The Rock Machine Turns You On*, the first cheap sampler album.[111]

From The Yardbirds' act, Led Zeppelin also inherited 'The Train Kept A-Rollin'' and showstopping 'Dazed And Confused', which mesmerised the *Melody Maker* reviewer with its 'interesting interplay of Plant's voice and Jimmy Page's guitar on which he used a violin bow, creating an unusual effect.'[112]

'For Your Love', revived, incidentally, in 1969 as The Ace Kefford Stand's only single, was an early encore - and 'Howlin' Wolf's 'How Many More Years' - rewritten as 'How Many More Times' for the *Led Zeppelin* album - had also been in The Yardbirds' show.

As Chris Dreja confirmed, 'Jimmy took many ideas that we'd been working on in the last eighteen months of The Yardbirds for what became Led Zeppelin.' Page agreed that 'The Yardbirds allowed me to improvise a lot in live performance, and I started building a textbook of ideas that I eventually used in Led Zeppelin.'[76]

The Band Of Joy had played 'How Many More Years/ Times' too - with the insertion of a fragment of 'The Hunter' from Albert King or, if your prefer, Booker T and the MGs. Just as sturdy and just as derivative as Led Zeppelin, Free had bagged 'The Hunter' too just as The Jeff Beck Group had wrung the life out of Willie Dixon's 'You Shook Me', and, also appropriated by Led Zeppelin, Otis Rush's 'I Can't Quit You'. So much of the first LP was borrowed - a muttered Jim Morrison mannerism here, a drum fill from a Little Richard hit there, a B.B. King riff, a Phil May screech - that some tracks were almost like medleys.

Derived from Robert Johnson's 'Travelling Riverside Blues' from Plant and Bonham's Brumbeat days, 'The Lemon Song' was impregnated with 'Killing Floor' in which Howlin' Wolf in 1965 had attacked armed discord between nations. A few months before the release of *Led Zeppelin*, this had been unearthed already by Electric Flag, a US rock equivalent of a brass band - who had had the good grace (or legal advice) to credit it to Wolf.

Five years after the *Led Zeppelin* LP, did sixty-six-year-old Howlin' Wolf receive receive any royalties for its inclusion of 'Killing Floor' or, more pointedly, 'How Many More Years/ Times' - like Chris Dreja did his fee for snapping the album's back cover photograph? Where did Jake Holmes stand when Led Zeppelin altered the lyrics of 'Dazed And Confused'? There was even a pinch of Keith David de Groot's *No Introduction Necessary* in there as well, most conspicuously in the grafting of the *ostinato* from Eddie Cochran's 'Nervous Breakdown' onto 'Communications Breakdown'.

Moreover, 'White Summer' - though credited to Jimmy Page - was, of course, 'She Moved Through The Fair', though he'd put 'arr.' in front of his name for traditional 'Babe I'm Gonna Leave You', which both he and Plant had first heard on a Joan Baez album. While 'White Summer' had been a highlight of The Yardbirds' final *Top Gear* session in March 1968, so it was in Led Zeppelin's fifteen months later - and Page was also sliding a violin bow across the strings like Eddie Phillips, and lubricating his solos with feedback like old friend and rival Jeff Beck.

Yet it was recognised that Jimmy was as likely to be deified as a British guitar god as Beck, Clapton, Ritchie Blackmore (now with Deep Purple), Ten Years After's Alvin Lee, Tony Iommi of Black Sabbath and like rock icons of the decade's end. Certainly, he was technically as adroit as Beck, as fast as Lee - and much more daring than Clapton.

To Led Zeppelin's further advantage, 'power trios' were still the thing then too, following the examples of Cream and The Jimi Hendrix Experience, who had each harked back in any case to Tony Sheridan, Johnny Kidd and the Pirates and The Big Three. As gut-wrenching in their way as any of them - on stage at least - Led Zeppelin reached out to nascent headbangers rather than the introverted adolescent diarist who might have preferred becoming pleasantly melancholy to James Taylor, Melanie and like bedsit singer-singwriters who'd catch on after rain-soaked Woodstock, The Rolling Stones' disasterous free concert at Altamont and the sunset on The Beatles saw out the Swinging Sixties.

In the week each were released, The Beatles' *Abbey Road* and, issued out of sequence, *Let It Be*, barged their respective ways to a gold disc, outstripping current albums by pretenders like Fleetwood Mac, Creedence Clearwater Revival, the defunct Blind Faith, Ten Years After - and Led Zeppelin. After the latter's first eponymous effort crept to Number Six in the domestic LP list - in the year when Neil Armstrong took his giant step for mankind - it scratched the surface of that all-important US sales territory, as they took third place on the bill in Boston, Massachusetts to Vanilla Fudge and The MC5. Then came tour supports to Country Joe and the Fish and Iron Butterfly.

On eclipsing these *de jure* bill-toppers and placing their album in the US Top Ten, the English invaders clambered swiftly from the middle league of the adult-orientated rock hierarchy that had lately sprung up its head - to headlining at twenty-thousand seaters and beyond. While they didn't forget their British fans - as shown by a run of club and ballroom bookings in 1971 for 1968 fees and ticket prices - Led Zeppelin continued to storm North America during a hectic succession of tours over the next two to three years with Peter Grant demanding and receiving ninety per cent of gross receipts for every show.

A stabilising second album, *Led Zeppelin II*, appeared before 1969 was out. It ploughed a similar blues-derived hard rock furrow as its predecessor, and spawned a spin-off single, 'Whole Lotta Love', which sliced to Number Four in the United States as a wire through cheese. If unavailable on 45 in Britain, it was covered by CCS - Collective Consciousness Society - fronted by Plant's old mentor, Alexis Korner - which after lingering in the singles charts thoughout autumn 1970, became the theme tune to BBC 1's *Top Of The Pops*.

That September, John, John Paul, Jimmy and Robert were voted winners of the Best Group category by *Melody Maker* readers in the annual popularity poll, two months before the release of *Led Zeppelin III*, which walked a tightrope between the expected heavy business and a stronger element of introspection. This was epitomised by the contrast between hard-hitting, all-electric 'Immigrant Song' - another US singles chart strike - and an overhaul of the folk song, 'Gallows Pole' among predominantly acoustic numbers with 'laid-back' tempos and the gifted Page proving adept on banjo, mandolin and bottleneck acoustic guitar.

Such gentility was at odds with hearsay about Led Zeppelin's behaviour on their travels. Even so, dressing room scenes were sometimes how susceptible fans may have imagined:

a board game on the middle table; Robert shampooing at the wash-basin perhaps, and Jimmy tuning his new twin-necked Gibson.

That's as maybe, but mention of Led Zeppelin on tour still brings out strange tales of what people claim they saw and heard. Many of the antics later attributed to the band had taken place under the alibi of the stage act, were improved with age or were originated by others. Yet, though admirable young men in many ways, Bonham, Jones, Page and Plant had their quota of young men's vices, and time that hung heavy between soundcheck and show wasn't necessarily killed with chess tournaments or tea-and-biscuits.

According to Keith Relf, the latter-day Yardbirds' stage act had hinged ideally on an abstraction of sexual congress, riddled with musical foreplay, *carezza*, orgasm and all that. The basic premise affected Led Zeppelin's set-list too. It also slopped over onto behaviour off-stage. I realise that it's distasteful to mention such things but, alas it's true: with libidinous admirers aspiring to an climax at the thrust of the principals, members of the Led Zeppelin entourage took advantage of the casual and unchallenging sexual gratification procurable from young ladies practiced at evading the most stringent security barricades to impose themselves on illustrious musicians. Plant was cited in one US journal as 'a self-satisfied sexual gourmet'. This may have been as much of a slur on his good name as whispers that Jimmy Page, though a 'perfect gentleman' to super-groupie, Bebe Buell, was even more of a lothario on the road than Plant - for as well as requests for autographs, he received more invitations than most to partake in dalliances in the romantic seclusion of, say, a backstage broom cupboard.

During one otherwise debauched US tour, there came that plea for professional help from Screaming Lord Sutch after he landed a profitable two-album deal with Atlantic Records in 1970, following a season at Thee Experience, a Los Angeles club. Worming his way backstage at a Led Zeppelin spectacular in Los Angeles, his Lordship was astounded when Jimmy Page and John Bonham volunteered their services in the studio, for the resulting *Lord Sutch And His Heavy Friends* - produced by Page.

As Jimmy had stayed in the picture about David Sutch's activities since the bygone days of traipsing round Britain on the same circuit as a Crusader, so John Bonham had remained in touch with the less stable Ace Kefford, who, following a near-fatal drug overdose, had still been in hospital when 'I got a 'phone call from Dennis Ball, the Mayfair Set's bass player. His brother Dave played guitar, and later joined Procol Harum. They wanted to form a band with me as lead singer. At the first rehearsal in their mum's back room, they introduced me to Cozy Powell, a kid from a Cirencester group called The Youngbloods containing Dave and another brother on keyboards. Cozy had heard that *the* Ace Kefford was free to form a band. He also admired John Bonham, still my best mate at the time. Cozy was thrilled to be mixing with us socially, and the whole new band - The Ace Kefford Stand - moving into the cottages to 'get it together in the country'. The Stand was a covers band really - 'Born To Be Wild', 'Spoonful', that sort of stuff. Cozy used to do a solo. He was incredible even then. Later, we did 'Communication Breakdown'.

'I was taken to London by John Parsons who used to run the Belfry - where The Move did their first gig. He introduced me to the head of Atlantic Records. I was to be the second white act to be signed after Led Zeppelin. It was such a thrill to be on the same label that Otis Redding had been on that I signed the contracts without reading them - same as I did with The Move. I split the advance - not a vast amount but OK - between the guys, and that was the money gone.

'However, my head had gone again. I didn't know whether they expected Ace the Face, Ace the Bass, a has-been or something special. John Bonham was leaving Zeppelin a few times before he died, and wanted me and him to form a new band, but I hadn't got the bottle.'

Diversions such as this and the Lord Sutch episode, plausible or not, were incidental to Led Zeppelin's main purpose. As they had for *Led Zeppelin III*, Page and Plant, the group's most prolific songwriters, retreated to a cottage deep in the heart of rural Wales, grew a beard apiece and started work on the next album.

Just as 1966's *Yardbirds* LP came to be called *Roger The Engineer*, so the new Led Zeppelin product - with just four runic symbols the only indication of any title - is usually referred to as either *The Symbols Album* or, more commonly, *Led Zeppelin IV*. The only lyric printed on the sleeve was that to 'Stairway To Heaven'. While it is also the name of a series of twenty-one locks that elevate a West Midlands section of the Grand Union Canal, the Page-Plant opus was an anthem of mystical bent that progressed from murmured trepidation to strident intensity, and became a yardstick for later 'power ballads' such as 1975's 'Silver Tightrope' by Armageddon - the outfit led by Keith Relf - Whitesnake's 'Here I Go Again' and 'My Oh My', the opus that brought Slade back to a qualified contemporary prominence in 1983 after long 'wilderness years'.

Based structurally on 'Tangerine', a Page composition on *Led Zeppelin III*, 'Stairway To Heaven', nonetheless, did not overshadow the rest of *Led Zeppelin IV*, which ranged from 'Black Dog' - which lived largely in a careering riff stumbled upon by Jones - and Plant's engaging duet with Fairport Convention's Sandy Denny on the openly folky 'Battle Of Evermore'.

Yet if audience conduct - especially in the US - was anything to go by, 'The Battle Of Evermore', 'White Summer' and so forth - and even the subtleties within the more uptempo pieces - were regarded as aberrations rather than breaths of fresh air during four-hour Zeppelin extravaganzas. The 'festival seating' at many venues often meant 'no seating' - so when the stadium doors were flung open, everyone with the same-priced tickets grappled for a clear vantage point. With the universal surge towards the protective cordon of hired police, onstage silences and *pianissimos* tended to be undercut by a ceaseless barrage of stamping, whistling, discomforted snarls and, worst of all, bawled requests for the good old good ones like 'Communications Breakdown', 'Whole Lotta Love', anything loud from the first three albums.

By now, loud had become louder and then loudest at seventy thousand watts. Present at New York's capacious Madison Square Garden in 1971 for a Zeppelin *blitzkrieg*, Chris Dreja remembered the volume from the mega-watt PA system and flat-out amplifiers 'literarily moving the concrete in front of fifty thousand people. Having not been to many such events since The Yardbirds, it completely freaked me out.'

As for the band itself, while these uproarious tribal gatherings could still be enjoyable - and the cash accrued from them remained astronomical - often the highlight of the day wasn't the concert but the building-up and the winding-down. Moreover, a riot by thousands waiting for the box office to open at the Gardens in Boston finished with a bill for damages so hefty that the show was cancelled. Therefore, it may have been expected that Peter Grant would prune down his clients' touring schedules. This strategy served also to both re-awaken their enthusiasm for the stage, and mitigate over-exposure - though a string of dates in Japan was on the cards when the next Zeppelin album, *Houses Of The Holy* reached the shops in April 1973.

If nothing else, *Houses Of The Holy* was a display of versatility. As well as customary Led Zeppelin fare in menacing 'No Quarter', reggae in 'D'Yer Maker' and semi-acoustic 'Over The Hills And Far Away' represented the extremes of this latest stylistic spectrum. True to precedent, *Houses Of The Holy* went triple platinum in the US with 'D'Yer Maker' as its single nudging the Top Twenty. In Britain, however, while the album shot straight in at Number One, its slide downwards was a lot faster than expected, and it spent a mere thirteen weeks on the list as opposed to *Led Zeppelin IV*'s sojourn of over a year.

Perhaps the artists' long absences abroad may be one explanation for this comparatively modest showing - though Led Zeppelin were still ahead of all other contenders for the crown of Britain's top group. Amassing five million dollars in the first fiscal year alone, according to the *Financial Times*, another factor was that Led Zeppelin's vast wealth might have prodded a raw nerve or two in Britain's dole queues. Had they chosen, Page, Plant, Jones and Bonham - all still under thirty - could have lived quite comfortably into old age on far more than golden memories if they'd chosen to retire after *Houses Of The Holy*.

Led Zeppelin did, indeed, ease up on recording and stage commitments. Nevertheless, they diversified into other branches of entertainment. While they were among sponsors of the feature film *Monty Python And The Holy Grail*, the group were far more directly involved in the founding with Peter Grant of their own record label - named after an unissued Page instrumental - in May 1974, just as the Atlantic contract expired, although Led Zeppelin would remain connected to Atlantic as a parent company, as the dispersed Beatles' Apple Corps enterprise still was to EMI.

Though Led Zeppelin were to add themselves to Swansong's roster, the only other signing to have a pronounced measure of chart longevity was Bad Company, traceable directly to Free, whose 'All Right Now' had been *the* hit single of 1970. Both of Bad Company's Swansong albums of 1975 were in a profit position within weeks. After US Number Ones with both the first of these and 'Can't Get Enough', its single, the group achieved a megastardom that endured into the 1980s.

The same could not be said of Maggie Bell, a hard-faced Glaswegian contralto of gutbucket persuasion, who Swansong visualised as a sort of Hibernian Janis Joplin, but minus the on-stage histrionics. Prospects looked rosy. Maggie had finished 1972 as Top Female Singer in *Melody Maker*'s poll; her group, Stone The Crows, had disbanded with the full honours of war after gaining a respectable reputation as a 'live' attraction, and Jimmy Page had played on her first solo LP, *Suicide Sal*, but still Maggie Bell failed to set a larger world alight.

A sounder investment, the most venerable Swansong artists were The Pretty Things, even if they'd all but split up after 1969's *Parachute* had been *Rolling Stone* magazine's

'Album Of The Year'. Yet, Swansong's budget would stretch to expensive publicity photographs and the hiring of Norman Smith, sound engineer for their *S.F. Sorrow* rock opera, to reconjure the old magic. Directed at the United States, these outlays and the ensemble's relentless touring paid off with both their Swan Song albums, *Silk Torpedo* and 1976's *Savage Eye*, in the US chart - just about. 'It was the first time we got some attention,' gasped Phil May, 'Led Zeppelin would fly in under assumed names to wherever we were and sit in the front row.'

At the same time as lending practical encouragement to The Pretty Things and other of their Swansong label-mates, Page and Plant - with hair splayed halfway down their backs - insinuated their way into Elvis Presley's inner sanctum afterwards for that encounter in Las Vegas that was, by most accounts, cordial.

As it was in Vegas for Presley, there were round-the-block queues when Led Zeppelin slotted in a British recital at London's Earl's Court in May 1975, the first 'home game' since a bash at Wembley's Empire Pool four years earlier.

For those who paid touts up to one hundred pounds for a ticket, this was more than mere entertainment by a pop group. Veiled in flesh, the Local Boys Made Good were re-appearing before their people like Moses from the clouded summit of Mount Sinai to the Israelites. Adoration had been years a-dwindling, if at all. While none expected the waters of the Thames to part, the show was on the scale of a Cup Final , and the onlookers would surely mill into the streets afterwards, having participated, however passively, in the proverbial 'something to tell your grandchildren about'.

There was hardly a newspaper editor in the country who wouldn't promise a king's ransom for an exclusive interview with one or other of Led Zeppelin or a candid snapshot, but journalists needed to spin an impossibly likely tale to gain admittance to a backstage area as protected as Fort Knox.

Only a miracle could have rescued the show from anticlimax. Yet in retrospect, it was actually more atmospheric than any dished out in 1973 when footage was being collated for

The Song Remains The Same, a Peter Grant-produced celluloid documentary hinged mostly on Led Zeppelin in action at Madison Square Garden. Certainly, the majority at Earl's Court worried when the band showed signs of strain, glowed when they got second wind, and gave vent to an ear-stinging bedlam of applause when, inevitably, Led Zeppelin went down well. As if the audience had all sat on tin-tacks, the noise had risen momentarily to its loudest when the group kicked off 'Stairway To Heaven'. Nothing could have followed that, and, after Led Zeppelin waved into the baying blackness and vanished into the wings, the buzzing crowd filed out, blood pressure dropping in the cool twilight

Three months after the triumph at Earl's Court, Robert Plant and his tired wife Maureen were seriously hurt in a road accident whilst on holiday in the Greek Islands. Flown in plaster casts for treatment in London, the Plants were transported next to the Channel Islands and then to Switzerland where Led Zeppelin and Peter Grant had been obliged to spend a year in tax exile.

Owing to Robert's infirmities, there was no hope of any return to public life for nearly two years. Professionally, this was regrettable, but not disasterous as *The Song Remains The Same* soundtrack - named after a *Houses Of The Holy* item - functioned as a holding operation between two albums, *Physical Graffiti* and 1976's *Presence*, that couldn't now be publicised by in-person appearances.

The first of these was the band's only double set. It nestled in the US chart where each of Led Zeppelin's five previous albums were still holding their own. It was another strong reconciliation between thunderclap aggression and a homespun, acoustic pulse, running a gauntlet from 'Trampled Underfoot' - the US spin-off single - to 'Kashmir', which, with its breath of the Orient, proved to be almost as much of a US radio evergreen as 'Stairway To Heaven', though the same could not be said of a relatively unadorned crack at the traditional blues, 'In My Time Of Dying', from Plant's Midlands folk club repertoire.

Commercially, *Physical Graffiti* lasted longer in the charts than *Houses Of The Holy*, but *Presence* - like *Houses Of The Holy* - fell rapidly from an automatic Number One in Britain, a victim - if that is the word - of faint praise in the more radical quarters of a music press that had categorised Led Zeppelin as a 'dinosaur' band, out of step with the inspired amateurism of rising New Wave acts as diverse as Television, The Sex Pistols and Wreckless Eric. For only a fraction of the cost and discomfort, you could catch an act playing with more thought for the paying customer than any millionaire superstar forever in America and throwing a wobbler at the Hollywood Bowl because of a misconstruing of a dressing room amenities rider about *still* rather than *fizzy* mineral water.

Against this reaction to the distancing of the humble pop group from its grassroots, Plant and Page conducted themselves with observed good humour when they went to a London punk hangout to experience for themselves this 'street level' sub-culture that everyone was talking about. There, Johnny Rotten of The Sex Pistols and his cronies spoke in low voices and exchanged knowing smirks as Robert and Jimmy settled at a table with their drinks.

Years later, the calculatedly iconoclastic Rotten telephoned Plant to ask for the lyrics of 'Kashmir' as he was considering reviving it. By then, the grubbing music industry had stolen punk's most viable ideas and got its more palatable brand-leaders to go smooth. In the short term too, the impact of The Sex Pistols and their sort inflicted no appreciable wound on Led Zeppelin, whose next album, *In Through The Out Door* - recorded at Abba's Polar complex in Stockholm - was to tramp a well-trodden path to the top of the charts at home and - for seven weeks - in the USA.

It wasn't to be any external danger that would finish Led Zeppelin, but a combination of their own inner natures and desires, and further personal tragedies. Bonham sustained three broken ribs in a car crash in 1977, and, in the midst of a US expedition that summer, he, Peter Grant and one of the band's minders were arrested and later given a suspended sentence for assault after a fracas involving backstage staff at San Francisco's Oakland Coliseum. Within days of the incident, the rest of the tour was cancelled when news reached Plant that his infant son Karac had been taken ill with a respiratory complaint, and was on the point of death.

In any case, as it had been with Keith Relf in the latter-day Yardbirds, the old sweetness that Robert had invested into the slow numbers deferred more and more to stone-cold technique. While a show at the Silverdrome in Pontiac, Michigan before a seventy-six thousand-plus crowd broke Led Zeppelin's own record of nearly sixty thousand in 1973 in Tampa, Florida, Plant shared with the other three the exasperating realisation that, while the band was able to fill any given US stadium designed originally for championship sport, the audience went as ape over straggling lines of bum notes as it did over Page most startling solos.

On that ill-starred trek, John Bonham had loitered for several hours after a concert at an outdoor venue somewhere in the mid-West. Alone, he ambled round the arena, deserted but for a bulldozer scooping residual tons of broken whiskey bottles, cigarette packets, discarded garments and other litter left by the rabble. For many so-called fans nowadays, a Led Zeppelin show was an excuse for a social gathering, an opportunity to purchase soft drugs in the toilets, and get smashed out of their brains together while the matchstick figures on stage half-a-mile away became a gradually more distant noise, and more oblivious to the squalor before them. During his pensive stroll round the abused amphitheatre, John Bonham wondered what Ace Kefford was up to these days.

Amid rumours that the group was no more - prompted by the lay-off while Plant convalesced from his physical and emotional injuries - Bonham, purportedly, rang Kefford for one of those 'what if' discussions. Nevertheless, it was business as normal when, in the wake of *In Through The Out Door*, Led Zeppelin wowed 'em at the Knebworth Festival in England, and undertook a long-awaited tour of Europe in June 1979 that concluded at an ice-rink in Berlin. No time was better for another trip to North America, scheduled to begin in Montreal on October the 17th, but as dollar signs danced before Peter Grant's eyes, there occurred an insurmountable problem.

A heavy drinker, John Bonham had collapsed with 'exhaustion' during one of the concerts *sur le continent*, confirming Rod Stewart's sneaking feeling about Bonham - that he was 'pushing it just a bit too much and not being fit enough it carry it off.'[113] Nonetheless, to show what a hell of a fellow he was, the drummer had held down sixteen vodkas during a pub luncheon on 24 September 1980. At a rehearsal-*cum*-social gathering round Jimmy Page's house in Windsor that afternoon, he carried on imbibing until he was poured onto a bed to sleep it off. By the next morning, he'd turned blue, and before that creepy day was done, Led Zeppelin had given up the ghost too - though a formal announcement of the split wouldn't be made for three months after the funeral in the church local to John's home in Worchestershire.

EPILOGUE: THE NOW AND ZEN MEN

'The loss of our dear friend, and the deep sense of harmony felt by ourselves and our manager, have led us to decide that we could not continue as we were' - press release, 4 December 1980

Because record contracts frequently last longer than groups, it was necessary for Jimmy Page to cobble together *Coda* from left-over items for release two years after John Bonham's passing. While it struggled to get there, its peaking at Number Four in Britain and Six in the US wasn't a bad result for an act that no longer existed - though a full-time regrouping of Plant, Jones, Page and a new drummer was still seen then as probable by even the most marginally hopeful outsider for whom the concept of collecting every record members of Led Zeppelin ever made, together and apart, was not yet economically unsound.

Robert Plant had been quickest off the mark with a maiden solo album, *Pictures At Eleven*, after market-researching its content with unpublicised performances at small venues like the Golden Eagle, where he and Noddy Holder had been awestruck by The Spencer Davis Group back in nineteen-sixty-forget-about-it. *Pictures At Eleven*, all but topped the domestic chart, and two more efforts, *The Principal Of Moments* and 1985's *Shaken 'N' Stirred*, were lesser hits - but hits all the same. There was also a smattering of entries in the lower reaches of the singles lists - though 'Big Log', aided by a remarkable video, sneaked into the British Top Twenty in the middle of 1983.

'Big Log' was on its way down when Jimmy Page, Jeff Beck and Eric Clapton - The Yardbirds' three most illustrious guitarists - were persuaded by ex-Small Face Ronnie Lane to appear together on a bill with other musical philanthropists in aid of Action for Muscular Sclerosis (ARMS) on 20 September 1983 at the Royal Albert Hall.

Jimmy also took part in consequent ARMS galas in North America - where the wildest ovations were saved for 'Stairway To Heaven' with vocals by Paul Rodgers of Bad Company. Until then, Jimmy had been sighted less often than the Loch Ness Monster. Interest in him had been sustained, however, via the unstoppable Led Zeppelin bootleg industry, his 1982 soundtrack to Michael Winner's *Death Wish II*, and reissues of such as *No Introduction Necessary* and further items that had acquired at least documentary interest through his old group's fame.

Neither was there any escape from Led Zeppelin for John Paul Jones who had been haunting the backstairs of pop as a producer and arranger, notably for 'shriek-opera' diva, Diamanda Galas. He caved in too when, in 1984, the surviving personnel of Led Zeppelin were pressured to regroup in Philadephia for *Live Aid* with Phil Collins on drums.

When Phil's moment of *Live Aid* glory was over, Jimmy Page formed The Firm, again with Paul Rodgers. This venture was subject to reviews as mixed as those for a 1988 Page solo outing, the predominantly instrumental *Outrider*, and, next, his teaming-up with David Coverdale, front man with Deep Purple off-shoot, Whitesnake. He also contributed solos and *obligatos* to album tracks by The Rolling Stones - and A Box Of Frogs, a short-lived group centred on sometime Yardbirds Jim McCarty, Chris Dreja and Paul Samwell-Smith. He lent a hand too on an album by Roy Harper, subject of 'Hats Off To Harper' on *Led Zeppelin III*

Page also assisted on the only album - pressed on ten-inch vinyl - by Plant's new outfit, The Honeydrippers. Consisting of re-workings of ancient rhythm-and-blues classics and obscurities, it was greeted with near-indifference at home, but spawned a huge US smash in 'Sea Of Love', first recorded by Phil Phillips and his Twilights in 1959.

Resuming his solo career, Plant did his bit during *Heartbeat '86*, a all-star show organised mainly by Bev Bevan at Birmingham's National Exhibition Centre to raise money for a local children's hospital. As well as standing stage-centre with George Harrison, Ace Kefford, and Denny Laine during the finale of Chuck Berry's 'Johnny B. Goode', Robert completed a set in his own right with his young backing combo, ignoring demands for any numbers in his portfolio before *Pictures At Eleven*.

On disc, however, he and the new recruits nodded to the past by sampling Led Zeppelin on tracks from *Now And Zen* and *Manic Nirvana*. Nevertheless, by incorporating aspects of world music in 1993's *Fate Of Nations*, he pre-empted what was to come in 1995 when he and Jimmy Page began working together again on a semi-permanent basis, but on the understanding that either participant could pursue extra-mural projects with the other's blessing.

On the 21st of November that year, Peter Grant died of a heart attack in the backseat of a car on its way to his home in Eastbourne, Sussex. Rather a recluse after the demise of Led Zeppelin, one of his last services on the band's behalf was to reach a quiet out-of-court financial settlement with Jones, Page, Plant and the family of John Bonham. All future royalty payments were settled in complicated but fixed channels whereby the assorted and incoming monies could be divided and sent to the parties concerned.

After facilitating his boys' captivation of a global 'youth market', Grant's single-minded - some might say bloody-minded - willingness to not only make himself and Led Zeppelin rich, but also to make himself prouder of them and them of him, and his subsequently recognised instinct for the commercial and economic machinations of the record industry had obliged Atlantic to accede to his every desire, regardless of positioning research. Thus a ghastly corporate smile had been fixed as Grant took an intense and often unwelcome interest in every link of the chain from pressing plant to market place, hovering over the operation with an omnipotence as absolute as that of a Grand Vizier over the palace of four sultans.

Nonetheless, while his manipulation on Led Zeppelin's behalf of a label he had in a metaphorical half-nelson granted Peter a dotage rich in material comforts, it did not parallel the situation of Colonel Parker with Elvis Presley at RCA where monetary killings and unrealised artistic potential were not secondary to fair dealing and sound commodities - assets more valuable to Peter Grant, one with a greater capacity for selfless action, than driving a hard and unrelenting bargain for Elvis to star in another terrible movie. Besides, unlike the King - according to a common perspective anyway - Led Zeppelin were not relatively devoid of independent opinion - to the extent that, by the late 1970s, there were rumours of internal ructions with their manager.

Since his death, there's been talk - but, so far, only talk - about a Peter Grant bio-pic. Barrie Keefe - who also took care of the 1980 gangster flick, *The Long Good Friday* - was supposed to be preparing a script, and Malcolm McLaren, The Sex Pistols former manager, seeking finance, but those approached have been long-faced about the task, having failed to formulate in simple terms just what they were taking on. However, in the light of recent market triumphs like *Backbeat* - concerning so-called 'Fifth Beatle' Stuart Sutcliffe - and 2005's flawed *Stoned* (about Brian Jones), perhaps Grant's time will come, maybe as some kind of feature-length cross between a heavy docu-drama and a funny-peculiar situation comedy.

Maybe it was the way Peter would have wanted it, but there were further stage get-togethers of the surviving Led Zeppelin personnel at Madison Square Garden for Atlantic Records' Fortieth Anniversary celebration and a final brief reunion at Knebworth in 1990. Wielding the drum sticks on both occasions was Jason Bonham, John's son and very much a chip off the old block.

Such events fuelled evidence that the repercussions of Led Zeppelin's 1970s output resounded still, having gouged so deep a wound in pop that whatever its makers had got up to in the time since had been barely relevant. Indeed, there was no need for any former musician with the band to bother tilting for hit records - or, to be blunt, to do a stroke of any kind of work ever again. All he had to do was sit back and let the royalties that others were earning for him roll in.

As well as fruitful repackagings like *Remasters* and a four-CD boxed set in 1990, there were unsolicited overhauls of Zeppelin items like 'Communications Breakdown' from The British Invasion All-Stars - an amalgam of personnel from The Yardbirds, Downliners Sect, Nashville Teens and other old beat groups - and overhauls of 'Stairway To Heaven' by The Far Corporation in the States and, most jaw-dropping of all, in Britain by Rolf Harris - whose singalong rendition returned him in 1993 to the UK Top Ten after an absence of nigh on a quarter of a century. Not so lucrative, but as intriguing was 1990's *Unledded*,a something-for-everybody interpretation of early Led Zeppelin favourites over an entire album by Dread Zeppelin, garishly-attired Londoners who married reggae to an Elvis Presley-styled singer's renditions of 'Whole Lotta Love', 'Immigrant Song', 'Moby Dick' and all the rest of them.

Unledded was also the blanket title given to the renewal of Robert Plant and Jimmy Page's creative partnership. At first it was to be simply a televised concert and an associated album of them delivering 'unplugged' ambles down Memory Lane. However, though a lot of Led Zeppelin songs were used, the arrangements of these and four Plant-Page originals fresh off the production line, were startling - principally for the incorporation of exotic instrumentation that evoked visions of both Arabia and the ancient Celts.

Issued on 1994's *No Quarter*, complete with a loss-leader single of 'Gallows Pole' - and promoted on a Zeppelin-sized world tour, *Unledded* was a healthy balance between the invigorated oldies and the promise of the new material by two artists in their prime. While the expected ravages of middle age were evident, Jimmy, Robert and their accompanists brought much of the aura of a new sensation to those young enough never to have heard much of Led Zeppelin.

Walking away from the past has been easier for John Paul Jones - whose undertakings since *Live Aid* have included string arrangements for REM, touring with Diamanda Galas and his first solo album.

As for his and Jimmy's other 1960s session and almost-but-not-quite Led Zeppelin colleagues, Big Jim Sullivan is seldom experienced on disc anymore, though he may be heard in venues local to his home in Sussex.

The Land of Opportunity, however, beckoned Nicky Hopkins where, after tenures with Jefferson Airplane, The Steve Miller Band and Quicksilver Messenger Service, he released a solo album, *The Tin Man Was A Dreamer*, featuring George Harrison, Mick Taylor and other of his famous friends. He died in 1994 following a stomach operation in a Nashville hospital.

Five years earlier, Clem Cattini broke cover too as leader of a Tornados, reborn to work a 1960s nostalgia circuit which is no longer the netherworld it used to be - as demonstrated by brisk sales in theatre foyers of three new albums, and huge attendances at what is as much a celebration of the distinguished professional life of Clem Cattini as that of the group with whom his name will always be associated.

I wasn't really expecting him to harbour bitterness about missing the millions by not eating lunch with Peter Grant. Nevertheless, Clem was attractive in his phelegmatic candour during a conversation in his house in north London that might be described in estate agent parlance as 'ideally situated', reflecting that if he'd accepted the job with Led Zeppelin, he might have ended up like John Bonham in the legion of the lost.

At this point, I could indulge in some silly hypothetical exercise by crossing to a parallel dimension in which Cattini rather than Bonham joined Led Zeppelin after all. It would be fun to do so and might also utilise your time interestingly. Similarly, just as the Bible can prove any religious or moral theory, so the millions of words - to which I am adding - chronicling and analysing Bonham, Jones, Page and Plant's careers, together and apart, can warp the saga of Led Zeppelin to any purpose. With a certain mental athleticism, it is even possible to deny that they were ever anything special.

Following a few years as comparatively nondescript Midlands beat merchants, London session players or, in Jimmy Page's case, as a member of a once chart-topping group dying on its feet, they pooled resources and seized upon a current preference that they felt was the easiest option. After working the British club and college circuit, they landed some support spots in the States, where with one eye on the *Hot 100* and another on the mob they were paid to entertain, they gave 'em the same sort of rehashed heavy blues that a myriad of other outfits did.

This acute awareness of contemporary trends pervaded when Led Zeppelin became world famous and, to those in the know, notorious for absorbing ideas of rivals as well as those of aged bluesmen and olde tyme rock 'n' rollers, some dead, some still lurching from gig to gig just to maintain a tolerable standard of living in the evening of their life. Craftier borrowing - but borrowing all the same - from other less specific sources would emerge as rare breaths of fresh air on albums that, succeeding the initial breakthrough, lent the group greater resources and studio time than less bankable acts.

If they hadn't thus got very lucky, Led Zeppelin might have been shut down by other guitar-bass-drums-vocals groups ploughing the same furrow as Grand Funk Railroad, Man, Black Sabbath, Budgie, The Climax Blues Band or any one of countless other 'heavy' ensembles at roughly the same level of blues-plagiarised brutality, who appealed to mostly male consumers recently grown to man's estate. Then Led Zeppelin might have fizzled out by the mid-1970s with no-one in the so-called 'adult-orientated rock' forum going particularly wild over them, while still paying sufficient attention to hurl urine-filled beer cans stagewards if the band didn't boogie.

Struggling like the latter-day Yardbirds had been, Led Zeppelin would find themselves in the same endless highway dilemma as the back dated rockers and the black musicians from Chicago and Mississippi whose works they'd plundered. Now and then, John, Robert, Jimmy and John Paul, piling angrily into the same numbers that had been in the set in 1968, would make the more popular outfit topping the bill seem tame, but generally, they'd been too tired, indolent or out of touch to do much about it by 1974, one of pop's slow moments when there was no overt focus for adoration - particularly in all-important North

America - nothing hysterical or outrageous. As a result, Led Zeppelin might have been as forgotten as last season's grandad vest in an apocryphal year when cheap spirits, Mandrax and 'streaking' were among depressing diversions.

Of course, all these obtuse speculations are unfair as they could be applied to virtually any group of the late 1960s that also experienced wary ventures from post-Merseybeat pop to heavy metal, emulation of US idols, scuffling for a recording contract and countless punishing hours before the footlights. Many close shaves and remarkable coincidences helped, but it was no happy accident that the wheels of the universe came together in four interlocking musical personalities and their manager, and Led Zeppelin found themselves on top of the pile. Rather, it was a genuine natural aptitude, plus unconscious forces within their common background.

Moreover, however much filling stadiums meant that imposition of anything that needed much thinking about on the customers was like feeding a pig strawberries, they explored stylistic areas far removed from a blues core, covering all kinds of unlikely waterfronts. In the context of this discussion, they embraced a far wider artistic perspective than that indicated on a debut album that was less a new beginning than a culmination of what had gone on before. As such, Led Zeppelin was both the blueprint and the flowering of a crucial strain of post-Woodstock pop, its figurehead and its *grey eminence*. Developing and expanding on frequently opposing tendencies from the short history of 'rock' - as opposed to rock 'n' rock - Led Zeppelin dictated the aspirations of the entire movement.

NOTES

In addition to my own correspondence and interviews, I have used the following sources and items of additional information:

1. *Led Zeppelin In Their Own Words* ed. P. Kendall (Omnibus, 1981)
2. *Melody Maker*, 29 March 1958
3. *New Musical Express*, 24 February 1956
4. *Call Up The Groups!* by A. Clayson (Blandford, 1985)
5. This had replaced Page's first electric guitar, a second-hand Gibson Les Paul.
6. Sleeve notes to *Neil Christian And The Crusaders 1962–1973* (See For Miles SEECD 342, 1992)
7. *Beat Merchants* by A. Clayson (Blandford, 1995). Page was to record an arrangement of Buddy Holly-via-The Rolling Stones' 'Not Fade Away' as well as three instrumentals, 'Chuckles', 'Piano Shuffle' and 'Steelin', with personnel from the late Cyril's All-Stars (which included Jeff Beck and Nicky Hopkins).
8. *Led Zeppelin: Heaven And Hell* by C. R. Cross and E. Flannigan (Sidgwick and Jackson, 1991)
9. *Led Zeppelin* by R. Yorke (Sphere, 1974)
10. Not the singing organist with The Dave Clark Five nor the saxophonist in Amen Corner, also of the same name.
11. *Blues In Britain* by B. Brunning (Blandford, 1995)
12. *Jeff Beck: Crazy Fingers* by A. Carson (Carson, 1998)
13. *Don't Let Me Be Misunderstood* by E. Burdon and J. Marshall Craig (Thunder's Mouth Press, 2001)
14. Though Scottish author and musician Jim Wilkie would argue later that it owed much to the Gaels who colonised the southern states during the late eighteenth century. See his *Blue Suede Brogans* (Mainstream, 1991).
15. Quoted in *The Story Of The Blues* by P. Oliver (Penguin, 1969)

16. *Best Of Guitar Player*, Rolling Stones special, December 1993
17. Early examples of its use can be heard on Status Quo's 'Pictures of Matchstick Men' and Cream's 'Tales Of Brave Ulysses'. Though generally applied by guitarists (with Frank Zappa and Jimi Hendrix, perhaps, the prime exponents) other musicians have experimented with wah-wah too - among them the drummer on Love's *False Start* and jazz saxophonist Wayne Shorter - while Hendrix fed his voice through one on 1967's 'Burning Of The Midnight Lamp'.
18. Not the Brian Howard and the Silhouettes number
19. Formerly Dave Dee and the Bostons
20. *Hamburg: The Cradle Of British Rock* by A. Clayson (Sanctuary, 1997)
21. Who was to join Dave Berry's Cruisers in the mid-1960s
22. Once lead guitarist with Bournemouth's Tony Blackburn and the Rovers. By coincidence, Blackburn too covered a track that, like 'Turn Into Earth', was from 1966's *Yardbirds* LP.
23. For example, the fuzz-toned guitar on her 'Je M'Attends Plus Personne'
24. Who was also guitarist on a revival of 'Your Momma's Out Of Town' the following year by Chad and Jeremy - 'as English as a cup of tea', beamed their agent - who were big in the States, but couldn't get arrested at home
25. *Van Morrison: No Surrender* by J. Rogan (Secker and Warburg, 2005)
26. *Small Faces: The Darlings Of Wapping Wharf Launderette E1*, No. 24, November 2003 (fanzine)
27. Plant seemed rueful about this during a backstage conversation with Marriott after the latter had quit The Small Faces in 1969 to form Humble Pie with Peter Frampton of The Herd. They acquired both a solitary UK Top Twenty entry and a reputation for boorish behaviour on BBC's *Top Of The Pops* before building on The Small Faces' small beginnings in North America. Stripped of both the latter outfit's mixed piquancies of R&B, experiment and humour

and The Herd's doomy flair, Humble Pie accrued a sub-Led Zeppelin-esque megastardom over twenty-two US tour of fearfully loud amplification and heavy business.

28. Some of these were sung by Bert Ambrose's moist-lipped featured singer, Kathy Kirby - on whose 1960s hits John (and Jimmy Page) would play.

29. Among local guitarists with whom Baldwin played during this period was Pete Gage, later mainstay of Vinegar Joe (with Elkie Brooks and Robert Palmer).

30. *The Guardian*, 30 November 2005

31. *Stoned* by A.L. Oldham (Vintage, 2000)

32. A copy of 'Number One In Your Heart' found its way onto Wigan Casino's turntable to become a much-requested 'Northern Soul'classic.

33. There were two US blues entertainers known as Sonny Boy Williamson. 'Good Morning Little Schoolgirl' was the work of John Lee 'Sonny Boy' Williamson, who was murdered in 1948. The other 'Sonny Boy Williamson' was a William 'Rice' Miller, the singing mouth-organist, who toured Britain in 1964, backed by The Yardbirds.

34. His unprecedented strain of psychedelic pop spawned another million-seller in 'Mellow Yellow', a hippy anthem that was followed by 'There Is A Mountain', 'Hurdy Gurdy Man' - and bi-lingual 'Jennifer Juniper'. After 'Atlantis' struggled in that winter's charts, the arch-flower child bounced back briefly with 'Goo Goo Barabajagal (Love Is Hot)', a studio liaison with The Jeff Beck Group. However, though an unscheduled spot on the bill of Blind Faith's free concert in Hyde Park was well-received, Donovan's interminable set at 1970's rainy Bath Festival did not prove popular with a crowd waiting for Led Zeppelin.

35. *Led Zeppelin: The Classic Interviews* CD (Chrome Dreams CIS2006)

36. *Frank Zappa In His Own Words* ed. B. Miles (Omnibus, 1993)

37. Page was, however, the guitarist hired for 1963's 'Don't Bother Me', an A-side by Gregory Phillips of George Harrison's first published solo composition.

38. His immediate replacement was John 'Mitch' Mitchell, later with The Jimi Hendrix Experience.

39. *The Session Man* by P. Harrington and B. Graham (Broom House, 2004)

40. A witty paeon to lovesick obsession, 'Daydreaming Of You' was produced by Hollywood jack-of-all-trades Kim Fowley, who also supervised sessions for another Midlands act, The 'N Betweens - featuring Noddy Holder, a friend of Robert Plant.

42. *Faithfull* by M. Faithfull and D. Dalton (Penguin, 1995)

43. 'Break-A-Way' for Thomas in 1964, climbed into the UK Top Ten nineteen years later when overhauled by Tracy Ullman.

44. *Experimental Pop* by B. Bergman and R. Horn (Blandford, 1985)

45. *À propos* nothing in particular, via mutual acquaintance George Harrison, Duane Eddy was to add a bridge passage to 'The Trembler' an opus by Ravi Shankar - therefore rendering the composing credit 'R. Shankar-D. Eddy' one of the strangest ever to be printed on a record label.

46. *You Don't Have To Say You Love Me* by S. Napier-Bell (New English Library, 1982)

47. *Midland Beat*, October 1963

48. As both a solo star and as front man of The Faces - formerly The Small Faces - who were to become the so-called Woodstock Nation's very own Brian Poole and the Tremeloes

49. *Midland Beat*, April 1964

50. *Blues Fell This Morning* by P. Oliver (Cassell, 1960)

51. *The Guardian*, 14 October 2005

52. Dweezil, Zappa's elder son, was to form a group called 'Fred Zeppelin'

53. *Scouting For Boys* by R. Baden-Powell (Boy Scouts Association, 1963)

54. *Midland Beat*, December 1963

55. *Slade* by G. Tremlett (Futura, 1975)
56. *Melody Maker*, 10 July 1967
57. And had no connection with a Wolverhampton skiffle outfit of the same name containing Dave Hill
58. And was deemed skilled enough to strum one on 1974's *Flashes From The Archives Of Oblivion*, an in-concert double-LP by Yorkshire folk-rocker Roy Harper, the subject of 'Hats Off To Harper', the finale of *Led Zeppelin III*
59. Brubeck's 'Unsquare Dance', a UK Top Twenty entry in 1962, was used in an ITV commercial for the Nationwide building society in 2004.
60. Terry Dene was a British pop star whose professional life paralleled that of Elvis Presley in that he endured National Service, except that Dene's patriotic chore was to an unhappy, career-destroying end.
61. *Charlie Watts* by A. Clayson (Sanctuary, 2004)
62. *The Complete Rock Family Trees* by P. Frame (Omnibus, 1980)
63. *Midland Beat*, October 1964
64. *Black Sabbath* by S. Rosen (Sanctuary, 1996)
65. *Beat Instrumental*, September 1966
66. *Brum Rocked On!* by L. Hornsby (TGM, 2003)
67. *Back In The High Life* by A. Clayson (Sidgwick and Jackson, 1988)
68. *Strange Sounds* by M. Brend (Backbeat, 2005)
69. Sleeve notes to *The Definitive Downliners Sect: Singles A's and B's* (See For Miles SEECD 398, 1994)
70. *Blues In Britain* by B. Brunning (Blandford, 1995)
71. Both of which were among early tracks released by Bob Dylan
72. *Daily Express*, 10 August 1964
73. Another bore the title 'The Pakistani Rent Collector'.
74. Though they made as proficient a job of The Olympics' frenetic 'Good Lovin'' as either The Dave Clark Five or Brian Poole and the Tremeloes. After the flowers wilted, The Young Rascals continued to plant lucrative feet in both

the soul and rock camps with the likes of 'People Got To Be Free' - a US Number One - and, with a falsetto that was pure Motown, 'A Ray Of Hope'

75. *Led Zeppelin* by H. Mylett (Panther, 1976)

76. *The Yardbirds* by A. Clayson (Backbeat, 2002)

77. *Communications* (German fanzine), May 1984

78. *Midland Beat*, October 1966

79. Because it travelled with The Beatles, the Ludwig became the standard group drum kit for most of the 1960s, even though Ringo Starr inflicted untold damage on home trade by buying this US make - because every other drummer from schoolchildren to chart-riding professionals started hitting a Ludwig too.

80. *Disc*, 23 March 1968

81. Not to be confused with a Birmingham unit of the same name

82. The Band Of Joy's 'Hey Joe' and 'For What It's Worth' were to be included on Plant's *Sixty-Five To Timbuktu* double-album retrospective in 2003 (which also contained his CBS releases), while 'Adriatic Sea View' appeared two years earlier on a compilation cassette, *In The Forest*, issued via Kidderminster College, where Kevyn Gammond was head of music. Gammond was in Plant's Priory Of Byron, a group formed in 1999 for stage appearances and an associated album.

83. *Alexis Korner* by H. Shapiro (Bloomsbury, 1996)

84. Quoted in sleeve notes to *Band Of Joy* (Cherry Red Records, CDM RED 281, 2005). *A* Band Of Joy was to re-group in the late 1970s for an eponymous studio album and an intended benefit concert for another local outfit whose personnel - including Vernon Perara - were involved in a fatal road accident. Plant was keen to be involved, but, shortly before rehearsals, he cried off because his son, Karac, had died suddenly too. Paul Lockey assumed lead vocals.

85. *Who's Crazee Now* by N. Holder and L. Verrico (Ebury Press, 1999)

86. *The Rolling Stone Interviews Volume One* ed. J. Wenner (Straight Arrow, 1971)

87. A reunion concert was, supposedly, pencilled in (but not undertaken) at London's Roundhouse auditorium on 13 December 1970 with Hawkwind and The Pink Fairies in support.

88. *Aspects Of Elvis* eds. A. Clayson and S. Leigh (Sidgwick and Jackson, 1994)

89. Cordell and Secunda died within days of each other in February 1995.

90. Quoted in *Black Vinyl, White Powder* by S. Napier-Bell' (Ebury Press, 2002)

91. *The Independent*, 25 November 2005

92. *Brum Rocked On!* by L. Hornsby (TGM, 2003). Hobbstweadle's keyboard player, Billy Bonham (no relation) was to join Terry Reid's backing combo.

93. In 1981, Farlowe sang on Jimmy Page's soundtrack to the horror film sequel, *Death Wish 2* - and on the guitarist's solo album, 1988's *Outrider*.

94. Tim Rose's group also included Steve Dolan, a former Sundowner on bass.

95. Formerly The Paramounts, who, on Jimmy Page's recommendation, recorded the Jackie de Shannon composition, 'Blue Ribbons'96. Nevertheless, Cattini had been involved in another so-called 'supergroup' drawn from London session circles in 1969. 'Rumplestiltskin was Shel Talmy's idea,' he disclosed, 'with Alan Parker on guitar, Peter Lee Sterling as singer, Herbie Flowers on bass, Alan Hawkshaw on keyboards and myself.' Behind US counters a year earlier, an eponymous 1970 album was issued by Bell. Its highlights included an overhaul of 'Wimoweh' and an original by Cattini. In vague keeping with a band called after the fairy-tale dwarf whose name no-one knew, 'we had to use pseudonyms,' confided Clem, 'Mine was "Rupert Bear". This was because of a BBC rule at the time of not playing a

record if it was thought that it was by sessionmen - because of all that business with Love Affair. They still found out, and Rumplestiltskin was no more.'

97. *Behind The Mask*, BBC Radio One series, 1985

98. *Melody Maker*, 7 December 1968

99. 'Then Ginger Baker came to my house one night and asked me to join a big band he was putting together called Airforce,' recounted Denny Laine, 'It was a shambles - too many players all trying to out do one another, not enough discipline.' Airforce was particularly overloaded with under-employed Brummies - Trevor Burton and Traffic's Steve Winwood and Chris Wood as well as Denny - and Birmingham Town Hall was a fitting debut performance. Most stuck it out for just one more engagement - at the Royal Albert Hall - where a rambling and unrepentantly loud set was captured on tape. From this was salvaged a single, Bob Dylan's 'Man Of Constant Sorrow' sung in Denny Laine's fully-developed 'hurt' style.

100. See *Jack: The Biography Of Jack Bruce* by S. Myatt (Aureus, 2005)

101. *Brian Jones* by A. Clayson (Sanctuary, 2003)

102. Page was, reportedly, in the congregation at David Sutch's funeral at St. Paul's in South Harrow on 28 June 1999.

103. *Melody Maker*, 9 March 1963

104. *Ugly Things*, No.18, Summer 2000

105. *New Musical Express*, 4 February 1967

106. However, during the making of contingency plans when Keith Richards was facing a possible seven years in jail for a 1978 drug offence, Jimmy Page was, according to media hearsay, a prime candidate to understudy him, his Led Zeppelin duties permitting.

107. *Go*, June 1968

108. *International Times*, May 1968. The Fudge had enjoyed only one big hit - a rude 1967 awakening of The Supremes' 'You Keep Me Hanging On' - but had abided for a further three years with releases in much the same vein: all weighty 'holy'

organ, deliberated drum rolls and pseudo-Oriental guitar riffs rolling like treacle over cinematic scorings of 'Eleanor Rigby', Donovan's 'Season Of The Witch' and the late Curtis Mayfield's quasi-gospel 'People Get Ready' - which Robert Plant had sung with The Band Of Joy. It was also on a 1965 A-side by Keith Powell and the Valets. In the early 1970s, Jeff Beck was to amalgamate briefly with two former members of The Vanilla Fudge as Beck, Bogart and Appice.

109. *Mojo*, October 2005

110. *Melody Maker*, 24 October 1968

111. They truncated to just 'Velvet Opera' to cast a second album, 1969's *Ride A Hustler's Dream*, adrift on the vinyl oceans. When they petered out in the early 70s, Gantry (David Terry) fronted, allegedly, a combo which, until checked by litigation, accepted illicit bookings as 'Fleetwood Mac'.

112. I must add the raw information that, recorded for the first Led Zeppelin LP, the composition of 'Dazed And Confused' was credited to Jimmy Page.

113. *Rod Stewart* by T. Ewbank and S. Hildred (Headline, 1991)

DISCOGRAPHY

This tabulation contains details of solo releases and discs by groups in which John Bonham, John Paul Jones, Jimmy Page and Robert Plant were visible members prior to the formation of Led Zeppelin. Except where specifically stated, all recordings were vinyl and issued in Britain.

JOHN BONHAM

Singles

The Senators
She's A Mod / Lot About You
Dial DSP 7001 (June 1964)

Albums

Various Artists
Brum Beat (includes 'She's A Mod')
Dial DLP1 (August 1964)

JOHN PAUL JONES

Singles

The Tony Meehan Combo
Song Of Mexico / Kings Go Fifth
Decca F 11801 (January 1964)

John Paul Jones
Baja / A Foggy Day In Vietnam
Pye 7N 15637 (April 1964)

Albums

Various Artists
Hitmakers (includes 'A Foggy Day In Vietnam')
Marble Arch MAL 1259 (1969)

JIMMY PAGE

UK singles

Neil Christian and the Crusaders
The Road To Love / Big Beat Drum
Columbia DB 4938 (December 1962)

Carter-Lewis and the Southerners
Your Momma's Out Of Town / Somebody Told My Girl
Oriole CB 1868 (October 1963)

Jimmy Page
She Just Satisfies / Keep Movin'
Fontana TF 533 (March 1965)

The Yardbirds
Happenings Ten Years Time Ago / Psycho Daisies
Columbia DB 8024 (October 1966)

Little Games / Puzzles
Columbia DB 8165 (April 1967)

Goodnight Sweet Josephine / Think About It
Columbia DB 8368 (cancelled)

US singles

Happenings Ten Years Time Ago / non-Page track
Epic 5-10094 (July 1966)

Little Games / Puzzles
Epic 5-10156 (March 1967)

Ha Ha Said The Clown / Tinker Tailor
Epic 5-10204 (July 1967)

Ten Little Indians / Drinking Muddy Water
Epic 5-10248 (October 1967)

Goodnight Sweet Josephine / Think About It
Epic 5-10303 (January 1968)

Albums

Various Artists
Blues Anytime
Immediate IMSP 014 (1966)

Blues Anytime: Volume Two
Immediate IMLP 015 (1967)

Blues Anytime: Volume Three
Immediate IMLP 019 (1967)

US Albums

Greatest Hits (includes 'Happenings Ten Years Time Ago')
Epic LN 24246/BN 24246 (April 1967)

Blow Up: The Original Soundtrack (includes 'Stroll On')
MGM C/CS 8039 (October 1967)

Little Games
Epic LN 24313/BN 26313 (July 1967)

ROBERT PLANT

<u>Singles</u>

Listen
You'd Better Run / Everybody's Gotta Say
CBS 202456 (November 1966)

Robert Plant
Our Song / Laughin' Cryin' Laughin'
CBS 202656 (March 1967)

Long Time Comin' / I've Got A Secret
CBS 2858 (July 1967)

<u>Albums</u>

Alexis Korner
Bootleg Him! (includes 'Operator')
RAK SRAK 51 (May 1972)

<u>Cassette Albums</u>

Various Artists
In The Forest (includes 'Seaview' by The Band Of Joy)
MAS ATTACK 3 (1999)

<u>CD Albums</u>

Robert Plant
Sixty-Six To Timbuktu (includes Listen, Robert Plant CBS
singles and The Band Of Joy demos)
Mercury 9813199 (October 2003)

INDEX